SCOTTISH
HISTORY
A Complete Introduction

Teach® Yourself

SCOTTISH HISTORY
A Complete Introduction

Dr David Allan

First published in Great Britain in 2015 by Hodder & Stoughton. An Hachette UK company.

First published in US in 2015 by The McGraw-Hill Companies, Inc.

British Library Cataloguing in Publication Data: a catalogue record for this title is available from the British Library.

Library of Congress Catalog Card Number: on file

Paperback ISBN 978 1 47360 872 6

eBook ISBN 978 1 47360 873 3

1

The publisher has used its best endeavours to ensure that any website addresses referred to in this book are correct and active at the time of going to press. However, the publisher and the author have no responsibility for the websites and can make no guarantee that a site will remain live or that the content will remain relevant, decent or appropriate.

The publisher has made every effort to mark as such all words which it believes to be trademarks. The publisher should also like to make it clear that the presence of a word in the book, whether marked or unmarked, in no way affects its legal status as a trademark.

Every reasonable effort has been made by the publisher to trace the copyright holders of material in this book. Any errors or omissions should be notified in writing to the publisher, who will endeavour to rectify the situation for any reprints and future editions.

Typeset by Cenveo® Publisher Services.

Printed and bound in Great Britain by CPI Group (UK) Ltd., Croydon CR0 4YY.

John Murray Learning policy is to use papers that are natural, renewable and recyclable products and made from wood grown in sustainable forests. The logging and manufacturing processes are expected to conform to the environmental regulations of the country of origin.

Hodder & Stoughton Ltd
338 Euston Road
London NW1 3BH
www.hodder.co.uk

Also available in ebook

Contents

About the Author ix

Maps xi

Introduction xiii

How to use this book xvii

1 The land of the Scots 1
Contours and contrasts
Highland heartland
Lowland low-down
A climate or just weather?

2 Scotland before the Scots 9
First footprints
Old stones, new stones
The arrival of metal
They came, they saw, they conquered
Painted people?
The Angles' angle
Celtic connections
The coming of the cross

3 The Scots and the birth of Scotland 25
Migrants or natives?
Father of the nation?
Men from the north
Putting down roots
Contested cultures

4 Building a kingdom 39
A union of peoples?
Kingship and kin
Constantín II and the consolidation of power
Successful successors
Thanes, murders, witches?

5 Norman Scotland 51
Canmore and kingship
St Margaret and the soul of Scotland
Duncan, Donald and Edgar
The first Alexander
David I

6 The golden age   65
Looking forwards and backwards
The last of the Malcolms
A lion or a lamb?
Another Alexander
The happiest of times?
Scotland's ruin

7 A nation compromised   77
The fair Maid
Candidates for kingship
The trouble with John
Wallace's glory

8 The wars of independence   91
Edward's interventions
Destiny calls
Bruce's moment
Tightening the grip
The boy David
The staying power of the Bruces
A king incarcerated

9 The late medieval kingdom   111
The House of Stewart
Family strife
In name only
Another prisoner
The fiery king
Like father, like son
Pride before a fall
The waning of the Middle Ages?

10 Reformation and rebellion   131
Two queens and two regencies
A revolution of faith
The queen of hearts
Two kings in one?
The last king in Scotland

11 Two crowns united   151
The accidental inheritance
Good King James
The church militant
The native who was a stranger

12 The conflict of the Covenant   161
Clumsy beginnings
Let us pray
Joining with God
Allies against the king
Covenanted kings
A strangely constructive dictatorship

13 A restoration and a further revolution   177
A merry monarch has the last laugh
'Killing Time'
A king much misunderstood?
The not-so-glorious revolution
When William met Mary

14 Union and Jacobitism   197
The national crisis
An arranged marriage
Flogging a dead horse?
Rising ... then falling
The last best chance
The Butcher and some bills
Adjusting to new realities
Radicalism and protest

15 Industry and Enlightenment   223
The shock of the new
The fruitful soil
Filthy lucre
Dark satanic mills
A society in motion
Politeness and the life of the mind

16 The long Victorian age   245
Change and stability
The birth of democracy
The workshop of the world
Labouring and living
Revivalism
Recreation, culture, nationhood

17 Triumph and disaster   271
The Scottish empire
Armageddon
A flawed peace
The thistle blooms

18 Retreat and resurgence   287

Finest hour
Building Jerusalem
Winds of change?
Devaluation and devolution
The empire strikes back
'Selling off the family silver'
Not-so-New Labour
Paradise postponed?
The son of the manse
Unfinished business

Fact-check answers   319

Index   321

About the Author

David Allan is Reader in Scottish History at the University of St Andrews. He was educated at the universities of Edinburgh and Cambridge and previously taught at Lancaster as well as holding visiting fellowships in the United States at Harvard, Yale and Brown. He is the author of eight books, including *Virtue, Learning and the Scottish Enlightenment* (1993), *Scotland in the Eighteenth Century* (2001), *Adam Ferguson* (2007) and *Making British Culture: English Readers and the Scottish Enlightenment* (2008) and has published nearly 50 other articles and essays. His interests lie in many areas of modern Scottish and British history.

Maps

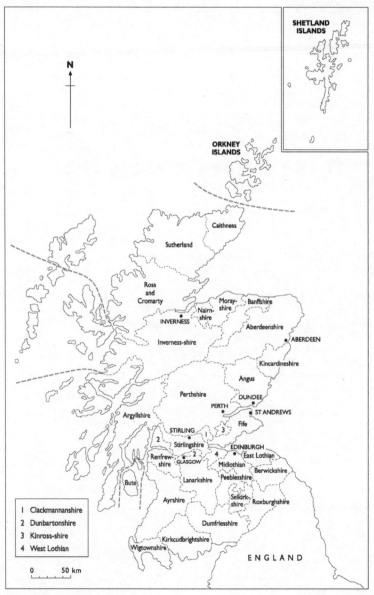

SHETLAND
ISLANDS

N

ORKNEY
ISLANDS

Caithness

Sutherland

Ross
and
Cromarty

Moray-
shire   Banffshire

Nairn-
shire

INVERNESS

Aberdeenshire

ABERDEEN

Inverness-shire

Kincardineshire

Angus

Perthshire

DUNDEE

PERTH

ST ANDREWS

STIRLING   3

Fife

2

Stirlingshire

EDINBURGH

Renfrew-   2   4   East Lothian
shire   GLASGOW

Midlothian

Berwickshire

Lanarkshire   Peeblesshire

Bute

Selkirk-
shire   Roxburghshire

Ayrshire

Dumfriesshire

Kirkcudbrightshire

Wigtownshire

ENGLAND

Argyllshire

1 Clackmannanshire
2 Dunbartonshire
3 Kinross-shire
4 West Lothian

0   50 km

Scotland: major towns and pre-1975 counties.

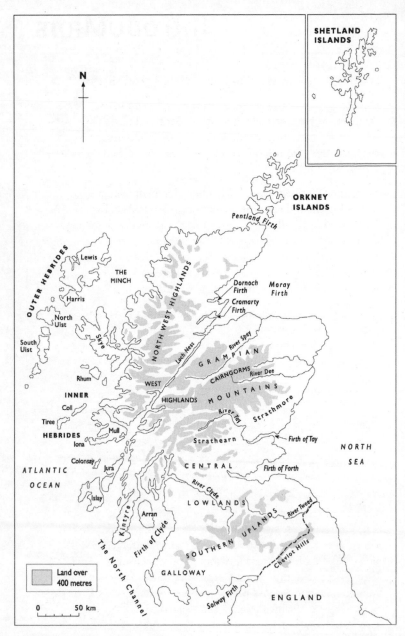

Scotland: physical map.

Introduction

Scottish geography is key to understanding Scottish history.

Occupying the northern third of mainland Britain, itself just 20 miles off the European land mass, Scotland has always been very far from cut off. Indeed it has mostly stood at a crossroads, regularly exposed to powerful influences from different directions.

From the Continent came early migrating people as well as technological and cultural revolutions – Stone Age, Bronze Age, Iron Age. Eventually there also came the Romans, who, after comprehensively colonizing southern Britain, also had a major impact further north. Although they never absorbed it into their empire, their presence had lasting military, political and economic consequences for Scotland's future.

Off the west coast, meanwhile, the Hebrides, a chain of islands stretching most of the way to Ireland, provides another potentially vital link: this proved especially crucial to Scottish Christianity, with initial Roman influences transformed by Irish connections, and also to the early Kingdom of the Scots, the political precursor to Scotland, whose roots lay on the west coast in communities with extensive Irish ties. Equally important were the isles, inlets and beaches of the north and west, which proved so inviting to seaborne peoples in the Dark Ages, most notably the Norwegian Vikings who came in numbers in the 9th and 10th centuries – and often stayed.

The Anglo-Norman lords who came from England and France from the 11th century onwards again re-oriented Scotland in a new direction. A kingdom and a Church first established on Gaelic foundations began to lose its Celtic character. Feudal power based on land and lordship became crucial, as did a Church increasingly run on Continental lines. Most significantly, however, family ties and political connections across the Anglo-Scottish border, which might have seemed to be bringing the two kingdoms' elites gradually together, eventually caused a disastrous rupture.

From the end of the 13th century onwards English kings ruthlessly exploited Scotland's internal divisions and the untimely deaths of a succession of its rulers. For 200 years the Scots, led by heroes like Sir William Wallace and new royal dynasties like the Bruces and the Stewarts, were thus preoccupied with fighting English invaders and occupiers. What emerged in Scotland during the later Middle Ages was a reputation, not always deserved, for extreme violence, political instability and bitter factionalism. But the independent kingdom of the Scots survived nonetheless, eventually being touched by the European Renaissance, which saw Scottish kings to the fore in making their country widely known for its literature and architecture.

As elsewhere in Europe, the modern age in Scotland begins with the Reformation. This not only split the Continent into ideologically opposed camps but also divided many nations in two. For the Scots the divisiveness – encouraged by the strong ties of different groups to England, France, the Low Countries, Switzerland and Germany – was particularly disruptive. It cost Scotland another ruler in Mary, Queen of Scots, who tried to maintain Catholicism. It also handed power to the Protestant nobles and Protestant clergy in a dramatic internal revolution. When her Protestant son James VI also inherited the English throne in 1603, the situation became even more precarious: Anglo-Scottish relations, though both countries shared one ruler and had officially embraced the Reformation, were badly affected because the two kingdoms had actually adopted two different and mutually incompatible forms of Protestantism.

The result was a savage and unstable 17th century throughout Britain in general and for Scotland in particular. Conditions had deteriorated under James's son Charles I, as his religious policies first provoked a rebellion among the Covenanters – radical Scottish Protestants – and then a civil war led by England's Puritans. Charles literally lost his head as well as its crown to Puritan revolutionaries and Scotland lost its independence as their leader, Oliver Cromwell, invaded. The collapse of Cromwell's republican regime and the Restoration of Charles II hardly helped mend fences inside Scotland. Indeed the old schisms remained. They quickly widened once more as the king tried to impose religious uniformity, culminating in the Killing Time of the 1680s during which the Scottish government and the Covenanters were effectively at war. The outcome was the deposition of James VII (James II of England), Charles II's Catholic successor and brother, and his replacement across Britain in 1689 by the Protestant William of Orange.

By the 1690s other hard choices increasingly needed to be confronted. Across Britain a new system of parliamentary monarchy was emerging under William and then Queen Anne. England, for its part, was now a major commercial, colonial and military power. But Scotland manifestly was not. Famines, political disasters and a sense of national crisis increasingly gripped the Scottish elites, resulting, after much anxiety and frustration, in the Treaty of Union of 1707: in an epochal decision that was controversial at the time and remains so to this day, Scotland united with England to form the new state of Great Britain, trading sovereign independence for enhanced status, wealth and power.

This was not necessarily a bad deal, as things transpired, despite attempts by the old Catholic dynasty and its Jacobite supporters to foment rebellion in the first half of the 18th century. By 1800 Scotland was transformed. Agriculture, commerce and industry all flourished and a new-found political stability and religious toleration became established. The Scots were soon famed for their success in the British Empire, as entrepreneurs, explorers, administrators and soldiers, but also, in growing numbers, as settlers. They even acquired a formidable reputation for education, science and the arts: what later came to be called the Scottish Enlightenment made Edinburgh in particular an international centre of learning, literature and intellectual life.

The 19th century saw further developments in the same vein. Scots played a disproportionate role in Britain's global dominance as both conquerors and colonizers. Scottish industry, especially in heavy engineering, also attained world leadership. But everything was clearly not well. Some felt that Scotland was losing its identity. Many worried justly about the social conditions generated in urban Scotland by rapid industrialization as well as about the effects of economic change in the Highlands. Radical politics and the rise of trade unionism were one response. Religious revivals, which produced the Free Church of Scotland, were another.

The country was particularly exposed to the international crises of the early 20th century. Scotland's casualties in the Great War were disproportionately heavy and its economic position was quickly weakened by changing global conditions: social discontent and the rise of the Labour Party resulted. By the 1960s the decline of empire was also having a significant effect. As the Scots' role in the UK was changing, a new form of political Nationalism slowly emerged, bent on restoring the country's independence.

The late 20th century was a very difficult period indeed for the Scots. De-industrialization proved acutely painful, and, while Nationalism continued to grow and the influence of religion waned, the country diverged even more from the rest of Britain in its political behaviour. England was the powerbase of the Conservative governments of the 1980s and 1990s, but the Scots voted heavily against them and resentment inevitably grew to bursting point: Margaret Thatcher, rightly or wrongly, became the most vilified mainstream politician in modern Scottish history.

The Blair government's election in 1997 led to 'devolution' – the restoration of a Scots Parliament in 1999 to determine internal Scottish affairs within the UK. Yet whether this had really resolved people's deeper anxieties was uncertain. In particular, economic vulnerability and intractable social problems remained. By 2007 a Nationalist administration was in charge in Scotland and seven years later it demanded and was granted a public referendum on creating an independent Scottish state. This produced a clear outcome after a desperately divisive campaign, but not the one the Nationalists had wanted: Scotland would remain in the Union, though with further internal devolution promised.

The longer-term results of this decision – for Nationalism, for the UK and for the Scots' place within it – were impossible to forecast in the immediate aftermath. The only certainty appeared to be that Scottish history would continue to be as unpredictable as ever.

How to use this book

This Complete Introduction from *Teach Yourself*® includes a number of special boxed features, which have been developed to help you understand the subject more quickly and remember it more effectively. Throughout the book, you will find these indicated by the following icons.

 The book includes concise **quotes** from other key sources. These will be useful for helping you understand different viewpoints on the subject, and they are fully referenced so that you can include them in essays if you are unable to get your hands on the source.

 The **case study** is a more in-depth introduction to a particular example. There is at least one in most chapters, and they will provide good material for essays and class discussions.

 The **key ideas** are highlighted throughout the book. If you only have half an hour to go before your exam, scanning through these would be a very good way of spending your time.

 The **spotlight/nugget** boxes give you some light-hearted additional information that will liven up your learning.

 The **fact-check** questions at the end of each chapter are designed to help you ensure that you have taken in the most important concepts from the chapter. If you find you are consistently getting several answers wrong, it may be worth trying to read more slowly, or taking notes as you go.

 The **dig deeper** boxes give you ways to explore topics in greater depth than we are able to go to in this introductory-level book.

1

The land of the Scots

Contours and contrasts

Scotland is a very small country – 'wee', as its inhabitants would say. And despite much local variation, there are really just two topographical zones in this, the northern third of the British mainland.

One, the Lowlands, roughly half by area, comprises the southern and eastern parts of Scotland. The Highlands, often called 'the Highlands and Islands' to reflect the substantial off-shore contribution, lie to the north and west of the Highland Boundary Fault, a geological feature which cuts Scotland in two between Arran on the west coast and Stonehaven on the east.

The stark contrast this produces, with a jagged landscape dominated by mountains and water beyond the Fault and a less dramatic mixture of rolling hills and low-lying coastal plains below it, has exercised a profound influence throughout history over the peoples of northern Britain.

In many ways we shall see, they still determine some of the most basic patterns of Scottish life today.

Highland heartland

In the far north and west, the Scottish Highlands possess the oldest landscapes anywhere in the British Isles.

Around 3,000 million years ago, the hard grey rocks that provide the beautiful but largely barren wildernesses of Wester Ross, Sutherland and the Isle of Lewis were first formed volcanically and then plunged deep into the planet's crust. There they re-crystallized before finally being thrust upwards to form imposing mountain ranges.

So far back in time did this chain of events occur that Scotland, Britain and Europe were not yet even formed. Instead the Lewisian gneisses were uplifted in a part of the earth's early surface that would subsequently be torn asunder, through the actions of plate tectonics, eventually arriving on opposite sides of a newly created Atlantic Ocean. Eroded over aeons of time, they formed a dramatic but unyielding surface which, with its endlessly varied rock formations and profusion of water features, is wonderful to look at but hard to tame. The generally thin and poor-quality soils that result, tilled only with difficulty, are shared with places now as distant from modern Scotland as Greenland and the eastern seaboard of Canada. But when emigrants from the North-West Highlands arrived on the North American coast after 1750, it was no accident that in Labrador and Nova Scotia the demanding landscape greeting them looked strangely like home and they decided to settle where they landed.

The historical consequences of other somewhat later geological processes are also still felt in Scotland. In certain northern and western districts, the gneisses were overlain with sandstone. A softer sedimentary rock produced by gradual compression of materials deposited by ancient rivers, its faster erosion created majestic outcrops, standing proud of the surrounding landscapes. The weirdly shaped mountains of Assynt and Torridon, a favourite playground of the climbers and hill-walkers who first became vital to the Highland economy in the late 19th century and remain crucial today, are the outstanding evidence of this process.

The remainder of the Highlands comprises either metamorphic rocks, chiefly schists and slates, created around 500 million years ago when the American and European plates closed, or granites, produced by subsequent vulcanism. As elsewhere in Europe, erosion, and in particular glaciation, has cost these formations most of their original height. But, reaching typically to 3,000-4,000 feet, they still lend the Highlands a ruggedly mountainous character – visually spectacular to 21st-century eyes, certainly, but historically difficult to traverse and in most places also economically challenging because resistant to arable cultivation and with few useful minerals to extract.

All along the west coast, the Inner and Outer Hebrides comprise offshore islands created by rising sea levels. On the adjacent mainland, deep clefts contain a mixture of tidal and freshwater 'lochs' (lakes), cut mainly by the scouring actions of immense, mile-deep glaciers in the Ice Ages. A crucial result is an abundance of welcoming beaches and easily accessible islands and bays and thus a historical receptiveness to ship-borne travellers. The Scots themselves, the founders of Scotland as a political entity, were an important early instance of a sea-going people exploiting this feature. Later it proved equally alluring to Viking raiders and colonists from Norway.

Lowland low-down

The Lowlands, despite the name, are not homogenous, their landscapes actually varying from mid-sized hills to coastal cliffs and sand dunes.

Scots on the Rocks

Exceptionally diverse geology in an unusually compact geographical area eventually made Scotland central to the emergence of modern earth science. In the 1780s Edinburgh-born James Hutton, based on evidence like the local igneous formations, the granite Cairngorms and the uplifted and warped sedimentary folding exposed in the sea cliffs of Berwickshire, concluded that the earth's surface must be the unimaginably ancient product of on-going natural processes. John Playfair and Sir Charles Lyell, both from Angus, made this interpretation the basis of 19th-century views of the planet. Sir Roderick Murchison from Ross-shire (a lunar crater is now named after him) identified and labelled several of the major geological periods in the earth's history.

In practice they divide into two broad areas. On the one hand there is a wide central valley – running from the Firths of Tay and Forth in the east to the Firth of Clyde in the west – sometimes called the Central Lowlands or just the Central Belt. On the other there are the southernmost parts of the Lowlands, from Galloway in the far south-west to Berwickshire in the far south-east, usually, from their proximity to England, known as the Borders, or else, because they are generally hilly, described as the Southern Uplands.

Even the Central Lowlands are remarkably diverse, however,
and not completely flat. Mostly they are reasonably low-lying
and dominated overall by three 'firths' (wide tidal river mouths),
today home to three of the country's four largest cities, each
with significant ports – Glasgow, Edinburgh and Dundee. But
there are numerous exceptions. These include the evidence of
long-ago volcanic eruptions that give Edinburgh one of the
world's more visually arresting skylines and Stirling Castle the
imposing rock from which historically it controlled access to
northern Scotland. They also include the igneous rocks out of
which Aberdeen ('the granite city'), just beyond the Highland
Boundary Fault, is substantially constructed.

Mainly lying on sedimentary materials, the Central Lowlands
were reasonably open to human development. Not just
continuous deforestation, drainage and arable farming but also
widespread settlement and significant urbanization started in
medieval times. The large quantities of accessible rock on or
very near the surface explain the historical Scottish preference
for building in natural stone not manufactured brick. Workable
coal seams and iron ore deposits were also close by. It was
upon these that world leadership in heavy engineering, and the
emergence of Glasgow as the country's largest city, would be
based in the Victorian age. Later still, in the 1970s, Aberdeen
would also boom as Europe's oil capital on the back of huge
offshore finds.

South of a line running approximately from Ballantrae on the
west coast to Dunbar on the east – along the country's second
major geological fault – the Southern Uplands ensure another
region of scant population, scattered towns and largely pastoral
agriculture. Because it includes one of the narrowest points in
mainland Britain, from the Solway Firth to the Berwickshire
coast, this region also turned out to be convenient for the two

kingdoms' negotiators in the 13th century to fix the long-contested boundary between Scotland and England close to where it still lies today.

A climate or just weather?

Despite its exceptionally varied landscape, Scotland, again because of its limited size, enjoys little climatic range. Everywhere, despite a proverbial day-to-day unpredictability, it is generally mild and intermittently wet – albeit with more rainfall to the west and north, more sunshine in the east and more winter snow at altitude.

A ubiquitous feature, produced by moist Atlantic airflows encountering rising ground in proximity to water, is mist – whether the dense coastal fogs on the east coast in summer (known locally as 'haar') or the hillside vapours all year round, different forms of 'Scotch mist' help explain why this particular phrase has become metaphorical in the wider English language.

Scotland's absence of meteorological extremes also explains the excellent joke that it really has 'only two seasons': 'winter and July'. But this only makes it all the more intriguing that the Scots, like the English, talk so animatedly about something that lacks the real dramatic interest often found elsewhere in the world.

Over longer periods, however, climatic variations have been far greater. Tropical forests 300 million years ago laid down the rich coal deposits below the Central Lowlands that powered Scotland's industrialization and the oil below the North Sea that is so important to the country today. Glaciation, most recently just 10,000 years ago, shaped the mountains and 'glens' (valleys) for which the Highlands in particular are famous. Along with the dense woodland of the Caledonian Forest that once covered much of post-glacial northern Britain, this topography, which long hindered travel and communication, increased the chances that the Highlands in particular would evolve a self-contained society and culture, distinct from the populations further south.

The historical consequences of much more recent climatic fluctuations have also been far-reaching, as historians have only recently begun to appreciate. The so-called 'Medieval Warm Period', when average annual temperatures peaked around 1 degree Celsius higher than in the 20th century, probably assisted the Viking incursions that transformed northern Britain. It has even been suggested that it made wine-production feasible in 12th-century Scotland and it certainly permitted the cultivation of crops 1,000 feet up in the Border hills – improbable nowadays. Conversely the 'Little Ice Age' that followed – its depths captured forever in paintings of winter fairs on the frozen Thames and in Holland as average 17th-century temperatures plunged to at least 2 degrees lower than now – played a major role in the disastrous Scottish harvests and famines of the period that finally helped bring about political and economic union with England.

Whatever else has shaped Scotland's unique history, the combined effects of landscape and climate have certainly been very much to the fore.

Fact check

1 What divides Scotland from Arran to Stonehaven?
   a   River Clyde
   b   River Forth
   c   The Solway Firth
   d   The Highland Boundary fault

2 Which part of Scotland is geologically oldest?
   a   The south-east
   b   The south-west
   c   The north-west
   d   The north-east

3 Name 'the granite city'
   a   Glasgow
   b   Aberdeen
   c   Dundee
   d   Edinburgh

4 When did the 'Little Ice Age' bottom out?
   a   17th century
   b   14th century
   c   12th century
   d   8th century

Dig Deeper

Richard Fortey, *The Hidden Landscape* (London, 1993).
G. Y. Craig, *The Geology of Scotland* (London, 1991).

Scotland before the Scots

First footprints

Early human history in Scotland is shrouded in uncertainty. But about one crucial thing we can be sure: the first people there were certainly not the Scots.

The initial signs of mankind's presence are actually the faint traces left by the migratory people who moved constantly across the landscape after the last Ice Age. One which dates to the Mesolithic era (the Middle Stone Age) was an encampment near modern Biggar which, significantly, lies close by both the Tweed and the Clyde, the major rivers of the Southern Uplands: digs in 2009 revealed a cache of flint tools for killing and butchering wild animals from around 8500 BC. Another structure, comprising hearths and a series of holes for timber wall-supports and dated to around 8400 BC, came to light in 2012 on the south bank of the Firth of Forth during preparatory excavations for the new Queensferry Crossing bridge.

A more extensive habitation from around 8500 BC, again indicated by post-holes as well as by some stone implements and discarded and carbonized hazelnut shells, was found in 2008 at Cramond, yet another well-connected waterside site, where the Almond enters the Forth. A mixture of animal bones, redundant seashells and tools found at Sand in Wester Ross and apparently from around 7500 BC also hints tantalizingly at Mesolithic hunter-gatherers fleetingly setting up camp in a prime coastal location.

Such small and mobile groups, however, whose physical impact on any location was necessarily both brief and comparatively slight, will always remain a fascinatingly elusive quarry for archaeologists.

Old stones, new stones

The advent of the Neolithic (the New Stone Age), which started around 4000 BC when a warming climate first encouraged the cultivation of crops in the previously inhospitable northern parts of Britain, is more easily traceable because of the more substantial structures for settled living that people now began to construct.

Early pottery items and other signs of an inhabited artificial island (known as a 'crannog') from around 3500 BC, for example, have been found at Eilean Dòmhnuill on the Hebridean island of North Uist. The cross-shaped standing stones (or 'megaliths') at Callanish on the Isle of Lewis, too, seem to date from this era, perhaps 2900 BC. But Neolithic culture, with its shift towards permanent living accommodation, is most brilliantly illuminated by the remarkable concentration of stone dwellings and other buildings in Orkney.

Two spectacular constructions stand out and now form the core of a UNESCO World Heritage Site. At Skara Brae on Mainland, the largest Orkney island, is the best-preserved group of Neolithic stone houses anywhere in northern Europe: built around 3100 BC, it comprises ten large buildings made of local flagstones. Nearby Maeshowe has a massive chambered stone cairn from around 2800 BC and a passage grave beneath a 24-foot high grass mound.

Archaeological evidence confirms that the people responsible for these complexes lived in farming communities, used grooved-ware pottery, kept domesticated sheep and cattle and grew cereals with success.

The arrival of metal

The Bronze Age, starting around 2000 BC in Scotland, saw the introduction of the mining, smelting and metalworking techniques that lends it its familiar archaeological label. As a result, while the large-scale physical evidence looks not dissimilar, the much smaller artefacts are quite different from the Neolithic.

These speak eloquently of greater wealth and a more sophisticated material culture. Nothing previously seen in northern Britain compares with the rich and varied artefacts in the Migdale Hoard – ranging from a bronze axe-head to jet buttons – found in 1900 near Bonar Bridge in Sutherland.

By about 700 BC the Iron Age had reached northern Britain, further extending the range and quality of metalware available in everyday life as well as for ceremonial use. But this did not simply mean iron: indeed, the unearthing in 2009 of four gold torcs (neck-rings) in a field at Blair Drummond in Stirlingshire, with a mixture of Scottish, Irish and southern French origins, was another reminder of the widening cultural networks and greater material sophistication this period brought.

More typically, however, the Iron Age was associated with increasingly elaborate social and economic arrangements in everyday life. There is also more evidence of fortified settlements and dry-stone 'brochs'.

This perhaps implies the emergence of better-defined Celtic tribal identities like the Votadini, whose ramparted fortress at Traprain Law to the east of Edinburgh is the period's outstanding large-scale structure. Less attractively it probably also indicates the emergence of powerful political forces and wider scope for conflict.

They came, they saw, they conquered

The Romans' earliest contacts with Scotland, bringing down the curtain on the Iron Age, were a decisive phase, not least because they generated the first written accounts of Scotland and its Celtic peoples. In this sense Scottish history only really begins once Latin authors start to write about a country which, referring especially to the dense forests beyond the Tay, they gave its oldest surviving name: it was the naturalist Pliny the Elder who around AD 77 first described what he called *silva Caledonia* ('the woods of Caledonia').

The first identifiable individual from Scotland had also only just emerged from the very edge of the world as known to Rome, an unnamed Orkney ruler who joined other British leaders in submitting to the Emperor's overlordship at Colchester in AD 43. It is probably best to think of this man as representing the increasingly well-developed tribal power structures through which Iron Age society in northern Britain organized itself. It also suggests that even in the far north some people knew about – and could participate in – transformational developments at the other end of their island.

Not until the campaigns beginning in AD 71, however, did the Romans themselves venture properly into Scotland itself. But in that year Quintus Petillius Cerialis, provincial governor of Britannia, sent the legions northwards. Quickly establishing relations with the Votadini, who became reliable allies, and subduing the neighbouring Selgovae on the Solway coast, the Romans soon encountered those whom they now knew as Caledonii.

It was 30,000 Caledonian warriors, led by one Calgacus, whom Roman forces, under the new governor Agricola, are said to have routed in the famous Battle of Mons Graupius in AD 83 or 84.

Mons Graupius

Much fun has been had in the fruitless attempt to find Mons Graupius. In the absence of archaeological finds suggesting a lost ancient battlefield, the arguments are based on the likely routes for an invading expeditionary force moving into the Caledonii's territory from the south, the pattern of known Roman army encampments across central and north-eastern Scotland and the proximity of appropriately mountainous landscapes of the sort described by Tacitus, whose account provides us with our only information about the battle. A complicating factor is Tacitus's claim that Agricola sent a naval force in advance to harry his opponents before engaging them with his legionaries, a detail which implies a site not far from salt water. Plausible contenders include Bennachie in Aberdeenshire, Hill of Megray in Kincardineshire, the Gask Ridge in Perthshire, and as far away as Sutherland and/or Caithness. Troublingly, it has even been proposed that this great triumph of Roman arms never happened and was simply invented by Tacitus in order to burnish the military reputation of Agricola, his politically ambitious father-in-law.

The Romans' subsequent grip on northern Britain, however, despite Mons Graupius, was neither continuous nor comprehensive. Moreover, given the costly infrastructure and manpower required for full colonization and the obvious harshness and limited economic potential of much of the landscape, with its extensive mountains and forests, it may well be that not even attempting to incorporate it permanently into the Empire was simply a sensible practical judgement.

'He [Agricola] sent his fleet ahead to plunder at various points and thus spread uncertainty and terror, and, with an army marching light, which he had reinforced with the bravest of the Britons and those whose loyalty had been proved during a long peace, reached the Graupian Mountain, which he found occupied by the enemy.'

Tacitus, *Agricola* (c. AD 98)

Yet under successive dynasties, notably the Antonine emperors in the early 2nd century and again under Septimus Severus early in the 3rd, Scotland was still subjected to repeated Roman incursions, re-garrisoning and at least partial occupation. This is why, although modern Scots pride themselves on their country never having been formally colonized by Rome, the familiar signs of Roman military power are nonetheless highly visible in the landscape.

Most strikingly, there are the walls – not just Hadrian's, mainly in stone, built after AD 122, that runs from the Solway to near Newcastle and delineates what was then the northern frontier of Britannia, but also the less well-known Antonine Wall, from around AD 139, comprising a ditch and embankment that marks, defends and controls a more ambitious boundary at Scotland's narrowest point, between the Firths of Clyde and Forth. There are in addition the characteristic roads, especially Dere Street, running from York to near Falkirk, and several others in the Borders and Central Lowlands.

Imperial authority was also expressed through the building of at least 150 marching camps like the example at Thomshill in Moray or the group of 6 at Ardoch in Perthshire as well as more than 50 full-scale legionary fortresses such as Trimontium near Melrose and Cawdor in Inverness-shire. Excavations have shown that Roman engineers often modified these facilities at different times – hinting at repeated use over longer periods.

The Romans, however, clearly brought more than imposing infrastructure. Many of their coins have been found in Scotland. So have a vast array of other artefacts, ranging from elaborate brooches to scrap metal hoards. Archaeological evidence from locations with a nearby Roman presence, like East Coldoch in Stirlingshire, also indicates that bread made from locally-produced wheat had become a staple food in native communities while elsewhere the Romans began the cultivation of walnuts and sweet chestnuts and introduced the consumption of figs (whose seeds have been found in excavations along the Antonine Wall), dates, olives, almonds, ginger, cinnamon and pine nuts to northern Britain.

All of this suggests that when they were present the incomers actually co-existed productively and peacefully most of the time with the indigenous Celtic peoples.

Painted people?

A further consequence of extensive contact with Roman power was probably the forging of certain native communities into more substantial and coherent political entities.

This may have been especially important after the last major occupation in the 3rd century. For Severus's army left behind a land whose southernmost regions remained in the hands of familiar Celtic tribes like the Votadini but the rest of which was dominated by a confederation of peoples probably brought together in part by the long-term pressure exerted by Rome. Intriguingly, the Romans themselves also began describing this larger grouping in a new way – as the Picts.

Key idea: Picts

The Picts are one of the great mysteries of Scottish history. The name, from the Latin *pingere* 'to paint', which first crops up with the Roman writer Eumenius in AD 297, was seemingly a nickname given by the legionaries to northern Britons who often decorated themselves with tattoos or dyes. What the Picts actually called themselves is unknown. Nor can we even be sure when or how they began to see themselves as a single people.

There are several things we can say with confidence about the Picts. One is that they too were Celts, almost certainly those previously labelled Caledonii, who lived beyond the Forth and the Clyde and who were therefore less well known to the Romans. Another is that, like all other native Britons, and although Pictish itself is now largely lost, they clearly spoke a Brythonic tongue (sometimes called a P-Celtic language) not dissimilar to that of the Votadini and the Selgovae.

Most importantly, it is obvious that the Picts had evolved a sophisticated artistic culture, albeit one that operated within relatively narrow confines. For they have left us some marvellous standing stones decorated with complex Celtic symbols and evocative pictures of people and animals, such as the Dupplin cross from Perthshire and the Aberlemno cross-slab from Angus, as well as gold and silver jewellery, like that found at Norrie's Law in Fife in the early 19th century. Surprisingly, however, for a population whose military prowess fires the imaginations of some modern Scots, not a single complete Pictish sword, helmet or shield is currently known. Nor, even more interestingly for a settled farming people, are there many ordinary domestic artefacts.

The easiest way of confirming the Picts' one-time presence is simply to look for modern placenames beginning with 'Pit-' (probably Pictish for something like 'piece of land') such as Pitlochry, Pitsligo and Pitlessie, particularly densely congregated in north-eastern Scotland. In search of the Picts' detailed history, however, we have only the contemporary observations of Irish, Welsh and English writers, above all Bede in the early 8th-century *Ecclesiastical History of the English People*, as well as certain much later Scottish material, usually written by people whose own cultures had challenged and then eventually obliterated Pictish civilization.

Nevertheless, these sources do confirm that by the 5th century the most powerful Pictish political structure was a kingdom known as Fortriu. Almost certainly focused on Moray and Easter Ross (though it was long believed to centre on Strathearn in Perthshire and on Angus), it also extended its influence as far south as the Forth. While there has been a convention of regarding Fortriu as synonymous with what some historians now call Pictland (or Pictavia), there were clearly also some other smaller Pictish kingdoms in a dependent relationship with Fortriu, among them Fib in modern Fife, Cait in Caithness and Circinn in Angus.

The Angles' angle

Although the Picts were undoubtedly the leading political presence across most of the immediate post-Roman Dark Ages in northern Britain, other peoples also exercised an influence that would extend far into the future.

One were the English, or, to give them their early name, the Angles, who invaded mainland Britain from the Continent in the 5th century. By the mid-7th their territories included all those parts of modern south-east Scotland up to the Forth – the former territory of the Votadini, now transformed into the Anglian kingdom of Bernicia – as well as modern England as far south as the Humber.

Edinburgh itself, then a small fortified settlement close to the Forth, was very much part of this emerging English domain: its original name, inherited from its previous Celtic rulers, was Din Eidyn (probably Brythonic for 'the hill fort of the sloping ridge').

Key idea: English in Scotland

The Anglian advance to the Forth in the 5th and 6th centuries was profoundly important for Scotland's future character. Above all the Bernician period ensured the early and permanent use of a form of the English language (called 'Inglis' before 1500 but eventually, and confusingly, re-named 'Scots') in Berwickshire and the Lothians and therefore in the districts where the Scottish kingdom's political and cultural centre of gravity later became fixed.

This English encroachment, however, did not go unchecked. Indeed there was intermittent conflict between the Angles and the different Celtic groups whom their expansionism threatened. One such encounter forms the dramatic subject of *Y Gododdin*, a poem about a battle fought at 'Catraeth' (probably Catterick in Yorkshire) around AD 600. This work, whose title is believed to preserve the Brythonic name by which the people called the Votadini by the Romans were actually known to themselves, is today recognized as a major early work of Welsh literature – the modern inhabitants of Wales being the principal inheritors of the largely lost native Brythonic-speaking culture that once dominated mainland Britain.

A larger-scale Anglo-Celtic confrontation, of more far-reaching significance for Britain's future, is described in some detail by Bede and confirmed by Irish and Welsh sources. This time dateable with extraordinary precision to Saturday 20 May 685, it took place at somewhere afterwards known in English as Nechtansmere ('Nechtan's lake'), perhaps near modern Dunachton (originally 'Dun Nechtan' or 'Nechtan's hill-fort') in Moray. Here, the Picts, led by King Bruide, inflicted a crushing defeat on the previously all-conquering Ecgfrith, king of the powerful Anglo-Saxon kingdom of Northumbria, of which Bernicia had come to form one part. Ecgfrith himself fell in the battle.

> '... rashly leading his army to ravage the province of the Picts, much against the advice of his friends, ... the enemy made show as if they fled, and the king [Ecgfrith] was drawn into the straits of inaccessible mountains, and slain with the greatest part of his forces, on the 20th of May, in the fortieth year of his age, and the fifteenth of his reign.'
>
> Bede, *Ecclesiastical History of the English People* (731)

This decisive Dark Age Armageddon seems effectively to have freed the Picts from the threat of subservience to the Northumbrians. It allowed them to reinforce their own influence at least as far south as the Tay. At the same time it dealt a severe blow to English hopes north of the Forth. If Scotland as we know it had not one but several moments of birth – or at least identifiable points when the eventual emergence of a distinct kingdom and national identity in northern Britain became likely – then Nechtansmere has to be numbered among them.

Celtic connections

A further important Celtic people clearly operating independently of the Pictish hegemony were those who developed the kingdom of Alt Clut, later known as Strathclyde.

Speaking Cumbric, another now-extinct Brythonic language, the people of Alt Clut, like their neighbours the Votadini, had been much affected by a long and probably overwhelmingly fruitful relationship with the Romans. Indeed it is likely that many of them were simply the people previously described by Latin sources as the Selgovae.

Alt Clut's political authority extended down into what is now Cumbria in modern northern England. Yet its core territory stretched from Galloway in the far south-west of Scotland up towards the Firth of Clyde in the north. On the northern shore of the latter a fortress at Dumbarton, built on another of the Central Lowlands' imposing volcanic plugs, emerged as its main stronghold – hence the kingdom's name (*Alt Clut* being Cumbric for 'rock of the Clyde').

Arthur – Scottish national hero?

By the 13th century King Arthur was a potent English icon, used by the Kings of England, his self-declared successors, to claim sovereignty over all of mainland Britain. Yet if Arthur's story has any genuine historical roots they lie among the Brythonic-speakers fighting the relentless Anglo-Saxon expansion of the 5th and early 6th centuries. This is why the earliest references to Arthur and his many battles are not English at all but come from Celtic sources (*Y Gododdin* mentions Arthur at the turn of the 7th century, with more details coming from the Welsh monk and historian Nennius in the early 9th). Intriguingly, a number of sites with evocative Arthurian connections dot southern Scotland's landscape, once defended from Northumbrian invasion by Alt Clut and the Votadini – notably Merlin's grave at Drumelzier in Berwickshire, Arthur's Seat in Edinburgh and Arthur's reputed resting place in the Eildon Hills in Roxburghshire. Just conceivably, then, this eventual symbol of aggressive English imperialism across Britain began as one of its die-hard Celtic opponents in Scotland.

Crucially it was in Alt Clut that something else of immense long-term significance probably happened. This was the building of the first church in Scotland.

The coming of the cross

The best-known story of how Christianity arrived in Scotland remains present – and still important to many – in the public imagination. This gives pride of place to St Columba, an Irish missionary of royal stock who after 563, working from the Hebridean island of Iona, today the principal pilgrimage destination for Scottish Christians, ministered to the pagan inhabitants of Pictland.

In a nation that has for centuries defined itself mostly by not being part of England, and which in more recent times has become increasingly proud of its affinities with other Celtic peoples, particularly the Irish, the significance accorded to this determined and visionary figure from Donegal is understandable. Yet Christianity in Scotland almost certainly pre-dates Columba.

To start with, the far west had longstanding cultural ties with Ireland, which had known Christianity even before the missions of Palladius and St Patrick in the early 430s. Roman cultural influence in northern Britain must also have been a factor: there were Christians in southern Britain in the mid-2nd century and bishops at London and York by 314. Meanwhile, tradition has always maintained that it was at Whithorn in Galloway that the *Candida Casa* (Latin for 'white house', constructed of light-coloured stone), the very first Christian building in what later became Scotland, was erected in 397.

This was reputedly the creation of St Ninian, a British-born bishop about whom no fact is certain but who is said to have been inspired, like Patrick, by experiencing Christianity in France and then studying at Rome. Whithorn duly became a pilgrimage destination, revered by medieval Scots as a place of special sacred significance. And even nearly a millennium and a half later, when Pope Benedict XVI came to Scotland in 2010 for only the second-ever visit by an incumbent pontiff, it was, significantly, on 16 September, the Feast Day of St Ninian, that he chose to arrive in the country.

The survival of Alt Clut, like the Pictish society to the north,
despite the power and ambitions of the Angles, had confirmed
at least one thing: these Celtic peoples' futures did not lie simply
as an integral part of an English-dominated confederation
across mainland Britain. But which of the competing groups
occupying the diverse terrain between the Southern Uplands and
the Pentland Firth would eventually place their own stamp on
this landscape as a whole?

As things turned out, the answer lay in the far west, among
the islands and along the jagged coastline. Here there existed
yet another culturally distinct population, chiefly notably for
the fact that, though they too were Celts, they did not speak
a Brythonic, or P-Celtic, tongue. Instead they used Gaelic, a
Goidelic or Q-Celtic language like that which dominated in
Ireland. Obscure and peripheral though these people might
have appeared at the time to Pictish or to Anglo-Saxon eyes,
they would eventually lend their name to the whole of northern
Britain: they were the Scots.

Fact check

1 When did Scotland's first traceable inhabitants emerge?
   a The Bronze Age
   b The Iron Age
   c The Mesolithic era
   d The Roman period

2 What was a 'broch'?
   a a precious item
   b an Iron Age fort
   c a tribal gathering
   d a battle

3 Which Roman author identified the 'woods of Caledonia'?
   a Pliny the Elder
   b Cicero
   c Julius Caesar
   d Tacitus

4 When was the battle of Mons Graupius?
   a AD 43
   b AD 71
   c AD 83 or 84
   d AD 122

5 What does the name 'Pict' mean?
   a Northerner
   b Warrior
   c Town-dweller
   d Painted person

6 Name the Anglo-Saxon kingdom in what is now south-east Scotland
   a Wessex
   b Mercia
   c Bernicia
   d East Anglia

7 Who brought Christianity to southern Scotland?
  a St Andrew
  b St Ninian
  c St Patrick
  d St Martin

Dig Deeper

Patrick Ashmore, *Neolithic and Bronze Age Scotland* (London, 1996).
Caroline Wickham, *Scotland's First Settlers* (London, 1994).
David Breeze, *Roman Scotland* (London, 1996).
Sally Foster, *Picts, Gaels and Scots* (London, 1996).
Chris Lowe, *Angels, Fools and Tyrants: The Britons and Anglo-Saxons in Southern Scotland* (Edinburgh, 1999).

The Scots and the birth of Scotland

Migrants or natives?

The Scots first began to attract attention and specific comment from other people around the end of the Roman period. Why they did so, however, and in what circumstances, remains unclear.

If the traditional story of the Scots' original 5th-century arrival as emigrants from Ireland is to be believed, they would at first perhaps have been more interested in raiding and exploring this potential new country than in settling and exploiting it. But, finding their initial experiences agreeable and profitable, they would soon have realized the benefit of coming in greater numbers and putting down roots. Mass exodus from northern Ireland to the Scottish coast would then presumably have followed in reasonably short order.

> 'In process of time, Britain, besides the Britons and the Picts, received a third nation, the Scots, who, migrating from Ireland under their leader Reuda, either by fair means or by force of arms, secured to themselves those settlements among the Picts which they still possess.'
>
> Bede, *Ecclesiastical History of the English People* (731)

Yet there are excellent reasons for doubting this conjectural tale of large-scale seaborne migration.

Most importantly, many other ancient and medieval peoples – including the Romans and the English – created elaborate migration myths to explain their own origins. That Scotland's version, when it finally appears in the 11th century, has most of the usual elements, such as an ancient Mediterranean ancestor with an appropriate-sounding name (in this case Scota, an otherwise-unknown Egyptian princess from the time of Moses) and intervening periods spent in a series of symbolically significant locations (the Scottish tale employs Galicia in Spain, probably because it chimes with 'Gael'), overwhelmingly suggests deliberate borrowing from well-known literary models rather than an accurate record of historical events two millennia before.

At the same time, archaeology confirms that there had been constant traffic between the northernmost parts of Ireland and western Scotland from far back in pre-history, in effect creating a single cultural and economic zone. Accordingly, a recent invasion by an alien race is an unnecessary as well as a deeply implausible explanation for the existence of a Gaelic-speaking population on the west coast of northern Britain in the late 5th century.

What is beyond doubt is that, at some point shortly before that time, the *Scoti*, as the Romans had latterly described them (perhaps borrowing from the Old Irish word *scuit*, meaning 'wanderer'), began to acquire an enhanced profile in outside observers' eyes. This is because the Scots were clearly emerging as a significant political force in what is now Argyll (from the Gaelic *Earra Ghàidheal* or 'coast of the Gaels') as well as in Bute and the western districts of Inverness-shire. And the name that the Scots themselves gave to this new power, in their own Gaelic tongue, was Dálriata (or Dálriada).

Dálriata

Dálriata's capital lay at Dunadd (meaning 'fort on the river Add') near modern Kilmartin in Argyllshire. But there were other centres of power, reflecting the common Gaelic practice of recognizing subordinate kings and multiple tribal kindreds. Dunaverty in Kintyre, for example, was home to a dependent dynasty while Dunseverick in Antrim was a key early power base, at least before attention finally shifted decisively to mainland Britain. Most intriguingly, that Dálriata eventually came to be focused inside what was to become Scotland was probably a result of failure as much as of success. At Degsastan around 603, for example, somewhere in northern England, the raiding Scots under Áedán Mac Gabráin were defeated by Aethelfrith's Northumbrians. Under Domnall Brecc they also fought a number of unsuccessful battles in Ulster, including at Mag Rath (near Moira in modern County Down) in 637. These checks helped ensure that it was in what became Scotland and not in either England or Ireland that Dálriata's interests would increasingly be concentrated.

At the risk of reading history backwards, by far the most interesting question to ask about Dálriata's evolution following its first appearance in the 5th century, because it sheds valuable light on what came afterwards, is: what can we say about the Scots' dealings with the Picts? After all, this was a relationship out of which in time a unified kingdom, the crucible of Scotland itself, would emerge.

From an early stage there was clearly conflict between these two Celtic peoples, a reality that helps explain the conventional historical narrative in which Scotland was supposedly created by the defeat of the native Picts and their subjection by the immigrant Scots. Yet the Picts most certainly did not succumb quickly. In 558 a certain Bruide of the Picts emphatically defeated the Scots under Gabran. Nearly two centuries later Dálriata again tasted bitter humiliation when Óengus, King of Fortriu, occupied Dunadd in the 730s.

There are also tantalizing hints that, for all the underlying tensions and regular confrontations, the Scots and Picts were on occasion able to identify common interests as Celts threatened by English expansionism. At Nechtansmere, for instance, when Northumbrian hopes of extending their influence throughout northern Britain were dashed, Scots from Dálriata as well as men from Alt Clut fought alongside the triumphant Picts.

Even more significant is the evidence for what anthropologists call acculturation – which is to say, the steady seepage of one group's culture into another's over time, gradually eroding differences and encouraging greater homogeneity. As a result, we need to be extremely careful before accepting the conventional wisdom that something called Scotland – or as it was initially known, the Kingdom of Alba (the name is Gaelic and pronounced 'Al-a-pa') – was the result simply of the Scots subjugating the Picts in some epochal Dark Age battle.

Father of the nation?

Steadily increasing cultural and social intimacy between Scots and Picts, then, was almost certainly vital to Scotland's eventual emergence. But short-term political and strategic circumstances must also have played an important part.

No figure is more important in this process than Kenneth Mac Alpin (or Cinéad Mac Ailpín, in his Gaelic manifestation), who was crowned King of the Picts at Scone (pronounced 'Scoon') in Perthshire, long an important Pictish ceremonial site, in 843.

Traditionally viewed as the last King of Dálriata, who either secured the Pictish throne by right of conquest (the orthodox interpretation between the 13th and the 19th centuries) or else, benefiting from close family ties, succeeded by inheritance in the female line (an explanation favoured for much of the 20th), scholars now emphasize Kenneth's essential Pictishness. This seems sensible because when he died on 13 February 858, according to contemporaries Kenneth clearly did so as 'King of the Picts' and not as king of Alba, much less as the ruler of anything yet recognized as Scotland.

> 'And so Kenneth, the son of Alpín, the foremost of the Scots, ruled Pictavia successfully for 16 years. However Pictavia was named after the Picts; whom, as we said, Kenneth destroyed... Indeed, two years before he came to Pictavia, he took over the kingdom of Dálriata.'
>
> Chronicle of the Kings of Alba (early 11th century)

The two peoples and two kingdoms, then, were probably converging. But despite being accelerated by important figures like Kenneth, who embodied the increasing cultural and familial connections between Picts and Scots, especially at elite level, this was evidently a slow, fitful and as yet incomplete process.

That is why we now need to turn to what may have been the most important catalyst in the final disappearance of both Pictavia and Dálriata and their absorption into something called the Kingdom of Alba. This was the arrival of a potent new force: the Vikings.

Men from the north

Few historical groups are as recognizable as the Vikings – the name conjuring up unmistakable images of flowing blond locks, shaggy beards, horned helmets, fearsome weaponry and high-prowed longships.

Key idea: Vikings

The Vikings (from the Norse *víking* or 'seaborne adventurer') were Scandinavians who harried, harassed, occupied and ruled many of the islands and coastal regions of north-western Europe between the late 8th and mid-11th centuries. Explanations for this sudden explosion of activity have included climate change melting the Baltic and Norwegian pack ice to open up seaborne trade and travel, internal population growth and consequent pressure on food and land in Scandinavia which propelled emigration and colonization, and the invention of the shallow-draughted but sturdy longship suited to both river navigation and ocean-going exploration.

The first arrival of the Vikings in Britain is conventionally dated, thanks to the writings of terrified chroniclers, to the year 793, when they violated the monastic calm of Lindisfarne off the Northumbrian coast. The same culprits soon also sacked Iona, Scotland's holiest island. Here, in a pattern of devastation that recurred twice more in the next dozen years, the Vikings, with a ready eye for rich pickings and easy targets, attacked the monastery and plundered its treasures. In 825 they returned yet again, murdering the abbot and all his companions when they tried to defend their precious relics. Another abbot fell victim as late as 986 during an attack on Iona by Scandinavians who had established a forward base at Dublin.

Yet colonization and settlement were from an early stage an integral part of the Scandinavians' interest in the British Isles. And Shetland and Orkney, nearest to Norway and accessible by sea, were probably the first parts of Scotland to be occupied.

> 'Year 793. Here were dreadful forewarnings come over the land of Northumbria, and woefully terrified the people: these were amazing sheets of lightning and whirlwinds, and fiery dragons were seen flying in the sky. A great famine soon followed these signs, and shortly after in the same year, on the sixth day before the ides of January, the woeful inroads of heathen men destroyed god's church in Lindisfarne island by fierce robbery and slaughter.'
>
> The Anglo-Saxon Chronicle

What happened to the existing Pictish populations is unclear. Some historians follow later Viking sources, which either recall the eradication of the natives or else imply the islands were uninhabited before the Norse arrived: the overwhelmingly Scandinavian placenames in modern Shetland and Orkney leave open the grim possibility of near-genocide by bloodthirsty invaders. Other scholars, however, favour less melodramatic explanations. For peaceful co-existence, intermarriage and steady integration may have been the mundane norm, albeit with a dominant Scandinavian overlay steadily displacing the Picts' Celtic culture. The simple truth, however, is that we do not know.

> 'In the days of Harold Fairhair, King of Norway, certain pirates, of the family of the most vigorous prince Ronald, set out with a great fleet, and crossed the Solundic sea; and stripped these races of their ancient settlements, destroyed them wholly, and subdued the islands to themselves.'
>
> The History of Norway (late 12th century)

Putting down roots

Since the Vikings were initially illiterate and produced no contemporary written histories of their own, archaeological evidence – which by its nature tells us more about their way of dying than about their way of life – is our main source for the Scandinavian settlement of the 9th and 10th centuries.

For very obvious reasons those districts most readily accessible by sea were especially exposed to Viking colonization. Their cemeteries, for example, characterized by pagan grave-goods, occur from an early stage not only in Shetland and Orkney but also across the Western Isles and in the far north and west. Ship burials beneath earthen or sandy mounds, the most atmospheric of ends to a significant Viking career, are also found from the 9th century onwards, notably one on Colonsay – a warrior buried with his horse and a formidable collection of weaponry – and three on nearby Sanday, all in the southern Hebrides.

Hoards fill out more details. Most with clear Viking origins occur across the same arc of coastal regions from Argyllshire to Caithness. Particularly fine examples were found at Skaill on Orkney (including fabulous silver brooches, necklets and armlets) and on the Hebridean islands of Tiree and Islay – the latter two, each containing silver ingots as well as coins, dateable with reasonable accuracy to around 975. Most spectacular are, however, the 78 walrus ivory chess pieces and 14 round 'table men' found in a sandbank at Uig on the Isle of Lewis in 1831. They originated in 12th-century western Norway around Trondheim.

Scandinavian buildings have also been excavated, sometimes in significant groupings. At Brough of Birsay, a small island off the Orkney mainland with earlier Pictish settlement, a number of Viking structures were erected from the 9th century, comprising a mixture of residential, agricultural and communal facilities, and eventually, once the inhabitants converted to Christianity, even a Norse church. At Jarlshof in Shetland, too, on a Bronze Age site, settlers constructed what is today the best-preserved such complex in Britain, an elaborate community including a smithy, a bath-house and a large hall.

The fact that the smaller materials found at Jarlshof include just a single spearhead but a range of domestic artefacts such as dress-pins, combs and loom-weights nicely emphasizes that those who lived there had become long-term occupants organized into a stable and reasonably prosperous community.

Certainly there is no hint that these people still lived as their Vikings forefathers had done – as seaborne warriors bent on a life of fleet-footed raiding.

Contested cultures

Clearly the Viking communities gradually became permanent in many districts. Probably they intermarried with the natives while evolving distinctive Norse-speaking populations who observed the peculiar customs of their Scandinavian ancestors. As a result, there remained ample scope for antagonism between the newcomers, with their Nordic culture and social organization, and the country's pre-existing Celtic power structures – notably the Picts of Pictavia and the Scots of Dálriata.

In the first place the Scandinavians' political identity, backed by serious military capability, long remained a critical factor. Most obviously, a powerful earldom of Orkney and Shetland (initially the domain of a Norse *jarl* or lord) dominated not just the Northern Isles but also Caithness and Sutherland in the far north of the mainland. Indeed, this whole area remained apart from the rest of Scotland, for a time falling under the auspices of the kingdom of Norway, until the Northern Isles' final re-absorption, by agreement between the two monarchs, as late as the 15th century.

Similar autonomy was established by the 10th century in the Western Isles and adjacent parts of the mainland – whose rulers at times extended their grip as far as Ulster and the Isle of Man. Originally these were strong-willed Norse leaders like Ketil Flatnose, the first to call himself King of the Isles. But as elite intermarriage with the natives slowly Gaelicized them, this line of independent regional rulers soon became known as the Lords of the Isles, resulting eventually in Celto-Scandinavian figures like the famous Somerled in the 12th century, whose own sons were in later times claimed as the common Scottish ancestors of Clans MacDougall and the MacDonalds.

Scotland's internal development was also affected by the simultaneous Scandinavian penetration of England and Ireland. Dumbarton, for example, Alt Clut's capital, was captured in 870 after a long siege by Ivarr the Boneless and Olaf the White, the magnificently named joint kings of Dublin. This old British fortress became a Scandinavian strongpoint. It was later said, implausibly but dramatically, that 200 ships carried off the captives into Irish slavery. What remained of Alt Clut became known as Strathclyde, centred on Govan on the south side of the firth.

Even in the 11th century the kings of Scots would still have to deal with the uncomfortable reality of Scandinavian power elsewhere in the British Isles. In particular, the English reign of King Cnut (or Canute), along with the brute force available to his Scandinavian earls of Northumbria, limited Scotland's ability, even once it finally swallowed Bernicia and the formerly Anglian districts of Edinburgh and the Lothians, to extend its own territory further south.

The interaction between the Vikings, the Scots and the Picts, was, however, the most important process for Scotland's future, with the Scandinavian presence often shaping native developments. For example, it was they who eliminated Kenneth Mac Alpin's rivals to the Pictish throne in a great battle fought somewhere north of the Tay in 839. Other kings, like Constantín I, Kenneth's son, beheaded in Fife in 877, similarly paid a grisly price for crossing the fearsome Scandinavians.

Yet the Vikings' impact was not purely destructive. Ultimately it was the stresses imposed by their activities, and the existential threat they posed to the older Celtic societies, that galvanized the emergent Kingdom of Alba. They presented the Scots and the Picts, hitherto locked in a troubled embrace, with a make-or-break situation. That Scotland first came into existence during the 9th century, and that it still exists today, might therefore in some measure be an unintentional by-product of the arrival of those terrifying blond-haired raiders whose mighty longships first crunched into the sandy beaches of Iona in the 790s.

Fact check

1 Name the first Scottish kingdom
   a Alt Clut
   b Bernicia
   c Pictavia
   d Dálriata

2 Who was Kenneth Mac Alpin?
   a King of the Picts
   b King of the Scots
   c King of Fortriu
   d a Viking ruler

3 When did the Vikings first raid Britain?
   a 825
   b 998
   c 793
   d 1066

4 What was a 'clan'?
   a People with a shared surname
   b a family
   c a township
   d a tribe

5 What was a 'jarl'?
   a Viking ship
   b Viking house
   c Viking lord
   d Viking sword

6 Which two main groups formed the Kingdom of Alba?
   a Angles and Picts
   b Picts and Scots
   c Picts and Vikings
   d Scots and Vikings

Dig Deeper

James Fraser, *From Caledonia to Pictland* (Edinburgh, 2009).
Alex Woolf, *From Pictland to Alba 789–1070* (Edinburgh, 2007).
Ewan Campbell, *Saints and Sea-Kings: The First Kingdom of the Scots* (Edinburgh, 1999).
Anna Ritchie, *Viking Scotland* (London, 1993).

Building a kingdom

A union of peoples?

The formation of Alba was clearly a slow and uneven process. Certainly it was by no means inevitable. But nor, though, was it inexplicable.

Above all it was the outcome of an evolving relationship between the Scots and the Picts. This in turn was accelerated by the pressure exerted by the Scandinavians who between 800 and 1050 represented the primary threat to the two leading rival Celtic kingdoms in northern Britain.

To reconstruct even the basic outlines of this process, we are again at the mercy of inadequate, sparse and often also potentially misleading sources. Most are external, from Ireland, England, Wales or Scandinavia, and frequently were written at a significantly later date, by people with only indirect knowledge of earlier events inside Scotland. Yet about some of the most important features of Alba's emergence – including several of its rulers, now among the best-known names in all of Scottish history – we can be slightly more confident.

Kingship and kin

All the evidence confirms that kingship in Alba was a perilously hard-edged business. Success or failure was not only of wider political significance. It was personally a matter of life and death for those who wore the crown.

Key idea: Kingship

Although invested with all sorts of religious and mythological symbolism, kingship in early Scotland was fundamentally about taking, keeping and using supreme authority for as long as possible in a specific geographical area. Because Alba was itself only just becoming defined as a cultural and political unit and also suffered from chronic internal disunity as well as grave external threats, its rulers faced particular challenges in asserting their sovereignty. Many if not most early Scottish reigns ended violently as a result.

Donald II, the son of Constantín I, reigned from 889 to 900. Although little is known about it, this may have marked a decisive moment in the monarchy's development, since Donald was the first who, when he died, was described by the Irish chroniclers as 'King of Alba'. Donald's immediate predecessor Giric, later (and inaccurately) known as Gregory the Great and credited (equally inaccurately) with conquering Ireland and England, also seems to have played an important role. Some historians have even argued that it was in fact Giric who helped bring about the fusion of Scots and Pictish rulership.

> 'Doniualdus son of Constantini held the kingdom for 11 years. The Northmen wasted Pictland at this time. In his reign a battle occurred between Danes and Scots at Innisibsolian where the Scots had victory. He was killed at [Dunnottar] by the Gentiles.'
> Chronicle of the Kings of Alba (early 11th century)

Either way, by the end of the 9th century Alba was acquiring recognizable coherence. Donald II, ultimately another victim of the Vikings, was succeeded by a second Constantín, another Mac Alpin and probably Donald's cousin. The most striking fact about Constantín II is that, in this age of constant warfare and ever-present danger for kings, he enjoyed the longest and most secure reign of any early Scottish monarch.

Constantín II and the consolidation of power

Partly because of his longevity but also because Alba's growing prominence attracted increasing comment outside Scotland, we know more about Constantín II than about any of his often shadowy predecessors.

Above all, it is clear that attempts to create a single Scottish identity as a focus for loyalty towards the kings and Kingdom of Alba were the dominant theme of his reign. In particular, Constantín's strategy for unifying Alba involved making it more uniformly Gaelic in culture and ethos as well as in its political leadership.

Constantín, Gaelic Christianity and the Culdees

The aggressive cultivation of Irish-style Columban Christianity was an especially important part of Constantín's strategy for unifying his kingdom. This was spearheaded by a group of monks known in Gaelic as the Céli Dé or 'servants of God' (later widely anglicized as Culdees), whose influence, starting first at Iona but then fanning out across the rest of Alba, became profound. The use of the Culdees as cultural and ideological agents of Mac Alpin kingship made sense. Although Kenneth had appointed a bishop at Dunkeld and Constantín probably granted oversight of the entire kingdom to a bishop at the pilgrimage shrine at St Andrews in 908, the Church in early Alba had previously lacked any real diocesan organization or coherent central control. It was into this power vacuum that the Culdees fitted. From bases like St Andrews and Loch Leven in Fife, Abernethy in Perthshire and Monymusk in Aberdeenshire they aggressively disseminated a standardized Celtic Christianity and strong allegiance to the Scottish kings, especially across the old Pictish lands.

Equally, Constantín II played a noteworthy part in wider British history as a result of his attempts to extend the authority and influence of Alba. Much of the time, like his predecessors, this meant dealing with Scandinavian incursions. In 904, for example, a Viking force sacked Dunkeld before being defeated somewhere in Strathearn. At Corbridge near Hadrian's Wall in 918 Constantín fought alongside Ealdred, the exiled English ruler of Northumbria, in the defeat of Ragnall, its dangerous new Viking lord and ally of the Dublin monarchy.

Yet the greatest external threat came from the English, and especially the West Saxon (or Wessex) dynasty – the descendants of Alfred the Great who were unifying England under their own power.

Around 921, *The Anglo-Saxon Chronicle*, England's best-known surviving source, records that, along with Constantín, the kings of Strathclyde and Viking Dublin met with Edward, Alfred's son, and accepted him as their superior. Interestingly and significantly, this is also the first occasion on which the word 'Scottas' is used in the *Chronicle* to describe Constantín's subjects: again this hints that a single political and cultural identity was now becoming visible to observers of northern British affairs.

On 12 July 927 at Eamont Bridge in northern England, Constantín, along with King Owen of Strathclyde, once more met with an English monarch, this time Athelstan, Edward's son, and formally acknowledged West Saxon overlordship.

Key idea: Overlordship

Overlordship, meaning the fact or claim of one ruler's sovereign authority over another, was a major feature of early medieval European politics. It was a particular issue where kingdoms were in their infancy or faced powerful neighbours reluctant to accept their independent status. Alba, where both problems arose, was long troubled by the issue of how far its own ruler owed some sort of allegiance to the King of England or alternatively was genuinely his royal equal. The question was not finally settled until the 16th century, only shortly before a King of Scots actually inherited the English throne and united the two crowns in one person.

Clearly caught, like other British rulers, in some sort of subordinate relationship to England, Constantín even appeared periodically at Athelstan's court, including at Buckingham in 934, where a document revealingly described him in Latin simply as *subregulus* (i.e. an under-king). By this time Athelstan had successfully expanded his authority throughout Northumbria, and perhaps as far as the Forth, sweeping all before him: Alba, for all its growing coherence and relative internal stability, faced domination from without.

It was in 937 that, along with the Viking ruler Olaf Guthfrithson of Dublin and in association once more with Owen of Strathclyde, Constantín finally rebelled and invaded Athelstan's territory. The aim was surely simple: to limit once and for all the expansionary power of the kings of England. Unfortunately for this uniquely broadly based Celto-Scandinavian coalition, it was an utterly disastrous decision. At the bloody and decisive Battle of Brunanburh, whose precise location, like so many military engagements in this early period, is now lost to history, but which probably took place either near Bromborough in modern Cheshire or near the River Humber in Yorkshire, Constantín and his miscellaneous allies were crushed by Athelstan's army.

> 'Never was there more slaughter on this island, never yet as many people killed before this with sword's edge: never according to those who tell us from books, old wise men, since from the east Angles and Saxons came up over the broad sea.'
>
> The Anglo-Saxon Chronicle (mid-10th century)

Unlike so many kings in this era, Constantín II's power in Alba nonetheless endured. And even more unusually, he ended his days peacefully, retiring to the Culdee monastery at St Andrews in 943 where he died nine years later.

Successful successors

Constantín II's reign, marked by steady and deliberate Gaelicization in language and in other aspects of life, was followed by several others that, while certainly shorter and less eventful, helped further consolidate the Kingdom of Alba.

Key idea: Gaelicization

With Norse gradually retreating to the northern and western fringes and Pictish, once pervasive in the east, starting its long march towards extinction, by the 10th century most of Alba's population, especially north of the Forth and Clyde, were probably making everyday use of the same Gaelic language – the secure basis of a common culture and a vital building block for a Gaelicized Scottish identity.

Greater unity was forged by a tendency to adopt Gaelic cultural norms. Not just the kings of Alba, still eventually buried on Iona, but also the kingdom's elites increasingly cultivated a strongly

Gaelic self-image, often adopting complicated Dálriatan pedigrees tying them into the distant mythological origins of the Scots. Distinctively Gaelic socio-political organization spread too: the first references to a *mormaer* (a Gaelic title for a regional leader answerable to the king) occur in the early 10th century, in relation to an unnamed man who fought at Corbridge and then to another named Dubacan, apparently responsible for Angus, killed at Brunanburh.

The Church likewise built confidently on its specifically Gaelic heritage. This in turn gradually eroded the older traditions not only of Ninian among the Picts but also of Northumbrian Christianity in the south-east. Instead there emerged a new and more organized Irish-influenced structure that exploited St Columba's charismatic legacy within a framework of greater ecclesiastical jurisdiction. Continuing to expand the status and power of the Culdees, the great culture carriers of Gaelic Christianity, was probably also a key priority for the later Mac Alpins as it had been for Constantín II.

Yet there remained obstacles to Alba's consolidation. Internal threats continued to come from rival members of the Mac Alpin family, to whom Celtic traditions of alternating successors from different branches of the wider bloodline provided obvious encouragement. Other challenges were posed by regional powerbases offering concentrations of support for those wishing to reject the monarch's authority: the fact that Alba was itself in the process of emerging from out of several contrasting parts ensured that there were always viable examples. Of course, where both threats came together, the consequences for the monarchy were even more worrying.

One who was successful in dealing with them was Malcolm I, seemingly Constantín II's immediate successor. Malcolm was forced to lead his army into Moray where he killed Cellach, a rebellious local leader, who may well have been taking advantage of the strong regional identity in the north-east dating from its times as the original heartland of Pictish Fortriu.

Malcolm II, the last of the Mac Alpins, whose lengthy reign lasted from 1005 to 1034, faced similar tests. His rule was marked by intermittent conflict with Northumbria, now under Scandinavian control, including a major victory alongside his Strathclyde allies at Carham in 1018, the most important consequence of which was Lothian down to the Tweed – essentially the eastern part of the modern Anglo-Scottish border – being ceded to Scotland. By marrying his daughter to the Norwegian Earl of Orkney, he also managed briefly to acquire control over the Northern Isles through his grandson Thorfinn Sigurdsson.

It was probably also under Malcolm that Strathclyde was finally absorbed by Alba. Virtually nothing is known about this important process but by the mid-11th century it was all but complete: even Cumbric, its distinctive Brythonic language, eventually died out, leaving just a peculiar fading echo in local placenames, and was replaced in daily use initially by Gaelic and later by Scots.

Moray, however, was, as so often, different. With its deep Pictish roots it remained a troublesome rival centre within Alba. Today few people remember the *mormaer* Findláech and his ambitions for the Scottish throne. But those of his son will never be forgotten: this was Mac Bethad – better known as Macbeth.

Thanes, murders, witches?

On Malcolm II's death in 1034, the throne passed from the direct Mac Alpin male line to those whose claims rested initially on female descent. In the first instance this meant Duncan I, the son of Malcolm's daughter, whose claim was underpinned by his having been designated as Malcolm's *tànaiste* (Gaelic for 'chosen heir') from among the eligible candidates.

Duncan's reign was brief and unhappy. It was scarred by a reckless invasion of England in 1039 in retaliation for a Northumbrian attack on Strathclyde, culminating in an unsuccessful siege of Durham and a humiliating retreat. Mac Bethad, described in Latin as *dux* or leader, had come to the fore following Duncan's accession and may have been the power behind the young king's throne. The disastrous English expedition may even have been masterminded by the more experienced Mac Bethad.

What we do know is that Duncan next invaded Moray in an apparent attempt to curtail Mac Bethad's over-mighty influence. This too proved a mistake – fatally so for Duncan. At Pitgaveny near Elgin on 14 August 1040 he was killed in battle. Mac Bethad, his claim resting on his mother or grandmother having been Malcolm II's daughter, became king.

Mac Bethad's reign was in fact as successful as many in this period. Not the least of his achievements was surviving for 17 years the perennial threats offered by both internal and external enemies.

> '...after slaughter of Gaels, after slaughter of Vikings, the generous king of Fortriu will take sovereignty. The red, tall, golden-haired one, he will be pleasant to me among them; Scotland will be brimful west and east during the reign of the furious red one.'
>
> The Prophecy of Berchán (early 12th century)

Mac Bethad, often known as the 'red king' (he was perhaps ginger-haired), faced down all of the customary challenges, including an uprising by Duncan's father Crinan, whom he killed at Dunkeld in 1045. He was even sufficiently secure that he allegedly risked leaving the country, making a pilgrimage to Rome in 1050. But the persistent problem of regional resistance remained. Mac Bethad struggled with Orkney in particular: Thorfinn Sigurdsson defeated Mac Bethad both at sea and on land in asserting his independence from a King of Alba whose sovereignty he refused to recognize.

Even greater dangers came from elsewhere. In 1052 the court of Alba provided sanctuary for political exiles from England. Two years later the Northumbrians, perhaps retaliating, invaded Scotland, inflicting major losses on Mac Bethad's army. Unconnected with this, there was also a rising by Duncan's son Malcolm, a plausible claimant to the throne, who had been brought up safely either in England or in Orkney.

This was what finally brought about Mac Bethad's death in battle on 15 August 1057 at Lumphanan in Aberdeenshire. The next year his son Lulach was also killed in Strathbogie, the crown passing into Malcolm's hands.

The Scottish Play

Shakespeare's *Macbeth*, first performed in London in 1611 but probably composed somewhat earlier, revolves around the ambitions, crimes and eventual downfall of a usurper, made all the more tragic because of the terrifying clarity with which the brooding anti-hero foresees but is unable to prevent his own ultimate fate. It has become all but impossible to approach the historical Mac Bethad without viewing him through the prism created by Shakespeare. Yet, as the compelling figment of a brilliantly original poetic imagination, the play's dastardly but painfully human protagonist is only very loosely based on the real Scottish king. *Macbeth* is in fact best understood simply as the playwright's attempt to dramatize the contrast between good and bad kingship and to offer a wider warning against plots and intrigue while also entertaining England's new Scottish ruler James VI and I (a descendant of the victorious Malcolm as well as Shakespeare's patron) with a flattering tale drawn from the history of his native country.

The death of Mac Bethad and Malcolm's accession actually marked the end of a chapter in the history of Scotland and in particular of Scottish kingship. The new one would be written by different hands, leading the country as a whole in a strikingly different direction.

1 Who were the Culdees?
   a   Gaelic missionary monks
   b   Scottish warriors
   c   Pictish nobles
   d   Viking settlers

2 What was the unifying cultural identity of the Kingdom of Alba?
   a   Anglo-Saxon
   b   Pictish
   c   Scandinavian
   d   Gaelic

3 Name the ruling dynasty of early Alba
   a   Canmore
   b   Stewart
   c   Bruce
   d   Mac Alpin

4 When was the battle of Brunanburh fought?
   a   793
   b   878
   c   937
   d   1018

5 What was a 'mormaer'?
   a   a Pictish war-leader
   b   a Viking raider
   c   an Irish priest
   d   a Gaelic regional ruler

6 Where was the real Mac Bethad from?
   a   Ireland
   b   Norway
   c   Moray
   d   Galloway

7 Who actually killed Mac Bethad?
   a   Malcolm III
   b   Macduff
   c   Lulach
   d   Thorfinn Sigurdsson

Dig Deeper

Alex Woolf, *From Pictland to Alba, 789–1070* (Edinburgh, 2007).

G. W. S. Barrow, *The Kingdom of the Scots* (Edinburgh, 2003).

J. L. Roberts, *Lost Kingdoms: Celtic Scotland and the Middle Ages* (Edinburgh, 1997).

Edward Cowan, 'The Historical Macbeth' in W. D. H. Sellar (ed.) *Moray: Province and People* (Edinburgh, 1993).

5

Norman Scotland

Canmore and kingship

The beneficiary of Mac Bethad's elimination, Malcolm Canmore or simply Malcolm III, is not always well understood. Yet it is beyond dispute that Canmore, whose dynasty became known as the House of Dunkeld, was of considerable importance to Scotland's evolution.

Above all, Canmore engineered a shift in Alba's cultural and political orientation. The earlier phase of Gaelicization had united its inhabitants by making them look west to their Scottish heritage rather than south to England and Europe. But this process largely came to an end by the mid-11th century and Canmore was the most important figure responsible for this fundamental change of direction.

Norman knights had first sought refuge in Scotland under Mac Bethad. But under Canmore the trickle became a flood, helped by the Norman conquest of England and by Canmore's own southern connections. These early Norman arrivals included heavyweight landed dynasties like the Sinclairs (from St-Clair-sur-Epte in Normandy) and the Flemings (as the name implies, originally from Flanders). Such families also took the lead in importing feudalism to Scotland under Canmore and his successors.

Key idea: Feudalism

Developed on the Continent and then imposed on England by the Conqueror, feudalism involved the granting of landed property by lords (the king and major magnates) to their vassals (lesser landowners) in return for their obedience and service – most importantly as loyal knights and providers of military muscle. It therefore ultimately transformed social relations, elite culture, warfare and political power across much of Scotland too.

The same decisive reorientation of Scotland towards mainland Europe and England was seen also in Canmore's second marriage in 1070 to Margaret, who began life as the Hungarian-born sister of an uncrowned Anglo-Saxon prince in exile. This was crucial, for it meant that Scotland's monarchs were afterwards related not only to the old English royal house but also, once Henry I had married Edith (known in England as Maud or Matilda), Canmore's daughter with Margaret, in 1100, to the Norman and Plantagenet kings of medieval England. Through the veins of Malcolm III's successors therefore coursed the blood of the West Saxons as well as the Mac Alpins.

Canmore's own relations with the English monarchy were cagey, not least because the implications of William's victory in England took time to become clear across the rest of Britain. Canmore met him at Abernethy in 1072, prudently repeating the submission made by Constantín II – acknowledging William as overlord and even handing over a son of his first marriage, Duncan, another future ruler, as a hostage. Canmore formally agreed peace with William again in 1080. But punctuating these periods of edgy mutual toleration between ambitious monarchs with widely differing resources were periodic eruptions of violence. Scottish forces, for example, harried Northumbria on several occasions while the English more than once raided deep into Strathclyde.

St Margaret and the soul of Scotland

Margaret's influence on her adoptive country was profound. Certainly it is no coincidence that she was soon canonized – becoming Scotland's only royal saint and for centuries second only to St Andrew (an apostle but with extremely tenuous genuine ties with Scotland) in popular esteem.

Margaret's reputation for piety and devotion, beginning with a youthful interest in becoming a nun and continuing with extensive charitable donations and personal care for the poor, was deserved. But she was also determined to clarify and purify Scottish Christianity, hitherto the unwieldy and confusing product of disparate Irish, Pictish, Northumbrian and Roman influences.

A key reform under Margaret's direction was the widespread celebration of Easter communion. She also emphasized observing the Sabbath by abstaining from work and attending mass. Both measures tied ordinary worshippers into the routine liturgical life of the national Church.

Her piety also had tangible consequences. One was St Margaret's Chapel, the first Norman building in Scotland, today at the heart of Edinburgh Castle. Another was her encouragement of the cult of Scotland's patron saint at St Andrews, instituting free passage for pilgrims crossing the Forth at what thereafter became North and South Queensferry.

Simultaneously Margaret tried to resolve the cultural ambiguities that were the accidental legacy of the Scottish Church's complicated history. Latin replaced local Celtic dialects as the universal medium for mass. As a result, while the everyday use of Gaelic continued to spread, especially north of the Forth and Clyde, and while French and English increasingly prevailed among the elites, a visitor from anywhere in western Europe would have understood the key Christian ritual as performed in any Scottish church.

Margaret also promoted the Continental forms of monasticism. This too moved Scotland's religious life away from its traditional ties to Iona and Ireland and towards France and England. And it represented – though there is evidence Margaret herself admired them – a long-term challenge to the Culdees. Fittingly, since it was already a major royal centre and where she herself would be buried, the first Benedictine community was established at Dunfermline in Fife in the 1070s, with monks secured by Margaret with the help of the Archbishop of Canterbury.

Even more important, perhaps, Margaret's passion for the new monasticism was transmitted to her sons. This in turn would permanently alter the character and organization of the Scottish Church.

Duncan, Donald and Edgar

Canmore's sons provided four of the next five kings, their names signifying the cultural and political shifts their father had begun. Duncan II, reigning for several months in 1094 and whose mother was Thorfinn's widow, Canmore's first wife, had a Celtic name recalling earlier kings of Alba. Later came Margaret's offspring, all with names declaring affinity with English and European traditions of rulership – Edgar (1097–1107), Alexander I (1107–24) and David I (1124–53).

When Canmore was killed in 1093, along with his chosen successor, Edward, Duncan's half-brother, during yet another invasion of England, the crown was seized by Canmore's brother Donald Bane, who became Donald III after expelling Margaret's children and her English allies from Edinburgh.

> 'Year 1093... Mael Coluim son of Donnchad, over-king of Scotland, and Edward his son, were killed by the Normans in Inber Alda in England. His queen, Margaret, moreover, died of sorrow for him within nine days.'
> Annals of Ulster (late 11th century)

Donald, however, rapidly faced an invasion from Duncan. Having been in England as a hostage, having been knighted by the Conqueror's successor William Rufus and having also acquired an English wife, Duncan's takeover was strongly supported by Norman knights from England.

Yet Duncan's reign likewise proved fleeting. Perhaps because of his unfamiliarity with Scotland and his reliance upon English backers, he too faced almost immediate rebellion. Donald, who had survived Duncan's coup, provided a focus for what it is tempting to interpret as a Gaelic backlash against the kingdom's steady anglicization. Duncan was quickly murdered by the mormaer of Mearns and Donald reinstated late in 1094.

Donald himself, however, soon met the same fate as Duncan, when another of his Canmore nephews, Edgar, Margaret's eldest, exploited his family's connections with England, and particularly with its Norman feudal elite, to devastating effect. Aided by his English uncle and assisted by Rufus's knights, Edgar invaded Scotland in 1097. The exact circumstances receive conflicting treatment from the chroniclers but Donald, whether blinded and imprisoned or simply assassinated, was swiftly eliminated as a threat to Margaret's descendants.

Amid the familiar treachery and bloodshed, however, there were symbolic changes taking place that would be of great significance for Scotland's future. First, Donald was the last monarch to be laid to rest among his Gaelic ancestors on Iona: all later kings were interred on the mainland, usually in churches or monasteries founded on the Norman model by Margaret and her descendants. Second, Duncan II, despite the extreme brevity of his reign, was the first King of Alba to bear the Latin title *Rex Scottorum* – making him, in the subsequent English translation, the first 'King of Scots'.

Edgar's tenure, notable for confirming the Norse king Magnus Barelegs's rightful possession of Kintyre and the Western Isles, made a largely peaceful contribution to the country's growing anglicization. Certainly he was the first of a series of Scottish rulers who knew the English court and the English kings exceptionally well.

In 1098 he founded the Benedictine priory at Coldingham in Berwickshire under the auspices of Durham Cathedral. Initially staffed by English monks, this community commemorated St Ebba, one of Northumbrian Christianity's early heroines. Edgar also made Edinburgh Castle his political and administrative centre, retaining Dunfermline, where he, like his mother and most of his family, would be interred, as the monarchy's principal religious site.

The first Alexander

Unmarried and childless, Edgar was succeeded in 1107 by his brother Alexander I. But he also ensured that their younger brother David would be granted substantial authority across the south of Scotland – essentially in Lothian and the former Strathclyde.

Alexander's rule marked a continuation of the previous reign. In keeping with the pious reputation of Margaret and her sons (it should be noted in passing that he had been named not after the ancient Greek ruler but after a recent pope), there were additional monastic foundations, this time at Scone and on Inchcolm in the Firth of Forth (an island on which in 1123 he was shipwrecked and cared for by a hermit). Run by the Augustinians, the most fashionable of the recently established European monastic traditions, the first occupants came from existing communities in England.

The Tironensians, a mainly French order, also came. The first arrived at Selkirk in 1113 under David's encouragement in his capacity as prince of the Cumbrians, before moving to Kelso once he was king. Alexander also revived the ancient see at Dunkeld, with its Columban associations. And he helped defend the Bishop of St Andrews's autonomy – recognized since at least Constantín II's time as the Scottish Church's de facto leader – from the aggressive claims of the Archbishop of York.

Alexander, however, for all his piety, justified his nickname 'the Fierce' by displaying considerable military and political authority. One potential threat, neutralized peacefully, came from David, with whom a dispute over the latter's claim, backed by their brother-in-law Henry I of England, to additional lands in Upper Tweeddale, was settled by negotiation. But elsewhere Alexander's soldierly prowess was fully tested.

> 'Now the king [Alexander I] was a lettered and godly man; very humble and amiable towards the clerics and regulars, but terrible beyond measure to the rest of his subjects; a man of large heart, exerting himself in all things beyond his strength...'
> John of Fordun, *Chronicle of the Scottish Nation* (late 14th century)

He was particularly relentless in subduing the wayward rulers of outlying regions, especially the mormaers of Mearns and Moray – the latter, of course, the family of Mac Bethad and Lulach and therefore descendants of Alba's old ruling house. Attacked when holding court at Invergowrie near Dundee, Alexander pursued them beyond the Grampians, finally defeating them near Beauly.

Like his recent predecessors, Alexander enjoyed a close and generally cordial relationship with England's Norman kings. Indeed, following Edith's union with Henry I and also his own happy marriage to Henry's illegitimate and intensely religious daughter Sybilla (who sadly died young and childless), Alexander was also close family. In cementing these English ties, however, he had in fact set Scotland on a course that would in succeeding centuries have the most explosive consequences.

David I

Alexander having died without legitimate sons, it was David, Margaret's youngest – whose name recalled both a recent Hungarian ruler and the greatest of biblical kings – who succeeded in 1124.

David's time as prince of the Cumbrians had given him a powerbase across Lothian and Strathclyde as well as further strengthening his English connections. The latter influenced how he ruled. In particular, David bolstered Scotland's emerging feudal elite with yet more Norman imports.

These included the Bruces, from Brus in Normandy, whom he established in Annandale; the Comyns, who left northern France for Durham and then Roxburghshire; the Douglases, transplanted from Flanders to Lanarkshire; and the Lindsays, who moved from Lincolnshire to Lanarkshire. Most important, though no one knew it at the time, were the Fitzalans, who came from Brittany via England, to whom David granted a lordship in Strathclyde: they later became royal stewards – and thus, it turned out, the progenitors of Scotland's royal House of Stewart.

David's strong English links also brought marriage, encouraged by Henry I, to the hugely eligible Matilda, the Earl of Northumbria's daughter. This was how David inherited the Huntingdon earldom and estates in England – which in turn further reinforced his personal contacts within a cross-border network of Norman knights and landowners.

In his immediate claim to the throne, David faced difficulties from Alexander's illegitimate son Malcolm. Only with Henry I's help and with his own Norman knights to the fore was he able to march into central Scotland, defeat his nephew and have himself formally crowned at Scone in 1124.

David was also confronted by the familiar threat of hostile subordinates in the peripheral regions. The mormaers of Moray in particular were recalcitrant opponents, and it was with them that the defeated Malcolm took sanctuary. For his part David initially had to accept limits to his authority. North of the Forth was effectively loyal to Malcolm, around whom resistance to the new monarch, associated with the

French-speaking court of Henry I rather than with the Gaelic-speaking heartlands of his own kingdom, gathered. Indeed, David's early reign was marked by regular visits to his English estates and a continuing closeness to Henry that probably did nothing to win over Scottish doubters.

In 1130, however, David's army, again backed by Henry and Norman mailed knights, crushed Malcolm's forces at Stracathro near Brechin, killing Óengus, Lulach's grandson and mormaer of Moray, in the process. Malcolm himself was captured in the far west by Henry's fleet. Four years later this dangerous rival was imprisoned in Roxburgh Castle. From here Malcolm disappears from the historical record, the silence inviting us to reach sinister conclusions about his fate.

Malcolm's elimination and the subduing of Moray confirmed David's kingship. But it had also underlined his dependence on an Anglo-French elite of warrior landowners who needed to be imported and rewarded. This in turn increased Scotland's entanglement in English politics, especially in the conflicts following Henry I's death in 1135. David found himself involved partly because of personal loyalty to Henry's daughter and intended heir, his own niece Matilda, against her usurping cousin Stephen. But David was clearly also interested in the opportunities it brought to extend the Scottish crown's territories into northern England, particularly Northumberland.

Within days of Stephen's coronation in December 1135, a Scottish army had entered England. This occupied Carlisle and Newcastle before the first Treaty of Durham was signed: Carlisle was ceded to David, as was confirmation of his son's rights to the earldom of Huntingdon which Stephen had previously annulled. Poor relations continued, however, leading to re-invasion and David's demand that Stephen concede the earldom of Northumbria. After a victory at Clitheroe in Lancashire the Scots were defeated in the Battle of the Standard, fought near Northallerton in Yorkshire in 1138. But David's demands were largely met. His rights to the two English earldoms were acknowledged and Scotland continued in possession of Cumberland and Northumberland.

This might be why on David's death at Carlisle in 1153 he was described in Irish chronicles as 'King of Scotland and England' – an exaggeration, surely, but an indication of his success in pushing his influence southwards. Another terminological innovation captures something else significant: for the first time a Scottish king's official Latin title alternates between the older *Rex Scottorum* (King of Scots) and the new *Rex Scotiae* (King of Scotland) – emphasizing sovereignty over a defined territory rather than leadership of a people, and perhaps hinting also at a Norman-style king sitting atop a feudal pyramid of property owners.

At home, David's mature kingship saw a broader programme of consolidation designed to integrate the most truculent districts. This was especially obvious in the north. Burghs – chartered towns with a legal right to internal self-government and to hold markets – were founded at Elgin and Forres, providing new centres of administrative control and hopefully diverting local energies from plotting into trading. We also first hear of something like a Parliament in David's reign: the earliest-known organized meeting of Scotland's lay and ecclesiastical leaders with their king probably took place at Edinburgh Castle around 1140.

Monasticism was unsurprisingly crucial to David's campaign to increase his kingdom's cohesion. A new Benedictine priory was founded at Urquhart in Moray, initially using monks from Dunfermline. Kinloss, a Cistercian house, formed part of the same programme. In the far north, where the Scandinavian legacy made integration more difficult, David formed a bishopric of Caithness in the 1140s and appointed a Scottish incumbent. He also married a lord's son from Atholl with the daughter of the Earl of Orkney in an attempt to extend royal power over the Northern Isles.

David's programme for the Scottish Church, like the importation of French-speaking families, can be thought of as essentially a process of continuing Normanization. Episcopal power, long weak, was key. As prince of the Cumbrians he had appointed a new Bishop of Glasgow, turning the diocese into the kingdom's second most important ecclesiastical jurisdiction after St Andrews. As king he also gave regular diocesan powers to old Gaelic bishoprics like Dunblane, Dunkeld and Brechin.

He even pushed this progressive territorialization of church authority to its logical conclusion by extending the parish system in the localities.

> '[David] was plainly beloved by God; for at the very outset of his reign, he diligently practised the things of God, in building churches and founding monasteries, to which, also, he gave increase of property and wealth, as each had need'
>
> John of Fordun, *Chronicle of the Scottish Nation* (late 14th century)

Monasteries, with their substantial wealth, wide local influence and imposing architecture based on foreign designs and often built with the help of immigrant craftsmen, physically embodied David's approach. His strategic foundations in outlying regions like Moray and Ross were accompanied by an even greater number in the kingdom's core areas. Among those founded either by David himself or by his feudal allies and associates were Kelso (a transfer from Selkirk), Jedburgh, Holyrood, Lesmahagow, Newbattle, Dryburgh and, above all, Melrose, established by English Cistercians in 1137.

David and the historians

No Scottish ruler had a more mixed reception from posterity than David I. He was long praised for his piety and for developing the country's political and religious institutions. But in the 16th century his reign was reinterpreted by some historians as a disastrous wrong turning. In particular, his passion for monasteries, bishoprics and doctrinal orthodoxy, Protestant scholars believed, had destroyed Scotland's distinctive earlier traditions of Celtic Christianity. David, they argued, had actually enslaved the Scots to a rigid and idolatrous form of Continental Catholicism from which only the Reformation had finally managed to rescue them. In more modern times David's acceleration of the Canmore dynasty's building of closer ties with England and abandonment of the kingdom's older Gaelic identity has again made him a much more equivocal figure for those concerned to trace the historical processes by which not only Scotland's independence but also its separate culture were steadily eroded.

Yet despite the ways in which Normanization clearly also entailed anglicization, David defended the autonomy of the Scottish Church. This was crucial, since despite St Andrews's long-standing primacy inside Scotland, ultimate legal supremacy was claimed by the Archbishop of York from 1125 – not only over the southernmost dioceses of Glasgow and Galloway, once Northumbrian-influenced, but even over the whole Scottish Church, which notably lacked its own archbishopric. The disagreement, which the papacy failed to settle, rumbled on for years. It was also further complicated by David's occupation of much of northern England and his own ambitions to control both the York archdiocese and the powerful Durham bishopric.

Such ambiguities in Anglo-Scottish affairs were, of course, greatly exacerbated by the cultural and political reorientation of Scotland that had taken place in the period of almost a century between Canmore's accession and David's death. As things turned out, they also pointed the way to the considerable difficulties between the two kingdoms that would scar succeeding centuries.

Fact check

1 Name the dynasty founded by Malcolm III
  a Mac Alpin
  b Dunkeld
  c Stewart
  d Pictavian

2 What was Queen Margaret's background?
  a Anglo-Saxon/Hungarian
  b Irish
  c French
  d Scandinavian

3 Where did the Sinclairs and the Bruces originate?
  a Ireland
  b Norway
  c Scotland
  d Normandy

4 Who was the first ruler called (in Latin) 'King of Scots'?
  a Malcolm III
  b Edgar
  c Duncan II
  d Alexander I

5 Where was David I prince before becoming king?
  a Moray
  b Galloway
  c Argyll
  d Cumbria

6 What were 'burghs'?
  a self-governing market towns
  b royal palaces
  c ports
  d cathedral cities

🔑 Dig Deeper

A. A. M. Duncan, *The Kingship of the Scots 842–1292* (Edinburgh, 2002).

Eileen Dunlop, *Queen Margaret of Scotland* (Edinburgh, 2005).

Richard Oram, *The Canmores* (Stroud, 2002).

Richard Oram, *David I* (Stroud, 2004).

6

The golden age

Looking forwards and backwards

David's four immediate successors ruled for nearly a century and a half during which a crucial watershed in Scotland's development was passed. Above all, the existence of a unified realm under these mainly long-lived and well-regarded kings had at last been settled. Ultimately neither Malcolm IV (1153–65), nor William I (1165–1214), nor Alexander II (1214–49), nor Alexander III (1249–86) could doubt that they ruled over a widely recognized and functioning political entity called the kingdom of the Scots.

It is not hard to see why this era, and in particular the final part, would later be regarded as a time when Scotland had been peculiarly blessed. Certainly what came afterwards strongly encouraged nostalgia for the relative calm and stability of Alexander III's reign.

Clearly, though, while such a rose-tinted view is psychologically understandable given subsequent events, we also need to ask whether it is actually justified.

The last of the Malcolms

Malcolm IV, David's grandson, was in some ways lucky to have become king at all. His father Henry, Earl of Huntingdon, was the expected successor, but the latter's death in 1152 left Malcolm as the heir. Crowned Malcolm IV at Scone on 27 May 1153, he was in questionable health and just 12 years old.

Malcolm lived up to his Canmore inheritance. Conspicuously godly, he founded the Cistercian monastery at Coupar Angus. Government was also further consolidated. Sheriffs – judicial and administrative officers exercising royal power across England since Anglo-Saxon times – now appeared in Scotland in places like Linlithgow, Forfar and Dunfermline, initiating the county system of local government.

Malcolm also faced the usual threats. His youth (he acquired the unwelcome nickname 'the Maiden') hardly helped. Nor did his continuing encouragement of influential immigrants whose prominence affronted traditional interest groups: the Hay family, yet another Norman dynasty with a great Scottish future ahead, first appeared at Malcolm's court and quickly married into the Celtic aristocracy. Together with rival claimants to the throne with plausible blood connections and viable regional power bases, these factors brought serious challenges to Malcolm's kingship.

In the first year of the reign the famous Somerled, independent ruler of the Celto-Scandinavian lands of Argyll and the Hebrides, attempted to extend his own authority eastwards, in league with some of Malcolm's distant Gaelic relations. Somerled's diversion by other disputes initially helped Malcolm, before the royal army, marshalled by Walter Fitzalan ('the Steward') and the Bishop of Glasgow, defeated and killed Somerled and many of his invading force at Renfrew in 1164. There were also risings in Galloway and Moray and a rebellion by the mormaer of Strathearn in 1160. Each time Malcolm exploited the military power and political authority accumulated by his predecessors to see off the challenge.

His most intractable problem, however, and one which damaged his posthumous reputation, was the predictable one. For Henry II unsurprisingly resented Scottish occupation of the territories taken by David and was able to manipulate Malcolm's dual status as a neighbouring monarch and as the holder of lands and titles in England.

Malcolm was duly forced to do homage to Henry at Chester in 1157. Although allowed to retain the earldom of Huntingdon, he surrendered Cumbria and Northumberland, including the city of Carlisle and the earldom of Northumbria, which thereafter remained English. Malcolm even served in Henry's French campaigns, being knighted for his loyalty in 1159. Such an honour, of course, appeared less flattering to many Scottish observers, suggesting that their own ruler, already stripped of hard-won lands and titles, had accepted subordination to the King of England.

> 'King Malcolm came to King Henry at Chester – at whose
> instigation I know not – and did homage to him, without
> prejudice, however, to all his dignities, in the same way as
> his grandfather, King David, had been the old King Henry's
> man; hoping, some suppose, by so doing, to be left in peaceful
> possession of his property. At that place, however, accursed
> covetousness gained over some of his councillors, who were
> bribed, it is said, by English money ; and the king was soon
> so far misled by their clever trickery as, in that same year, to
> surrender Northumberland and Cumberland to the king of
> England, after having consulted with only a few of his lords'
>
> John of Fordun, *Chronicle of the Scottish Nation* (late 14th century)

A lion or a lamb?

Malcolm IV died unmarried at Jedburgh of natural causes in
1165, aged just 24, a diminished figure, having ceded territory
and status to a powerful rival king. His brother and successor
William, however, one of Scotland's longest-reigning sovereigns,
would be remembered quite differently.

William I

Long after his death, and probably not before 1300, William I became
known, as he still is today, as 'the Lion'. Yet this was probably
because he placed a lion on the Scottish royal standard rather than
a particularly ferocious temperament or military prowess. Indeed,
William's success, such as it was, lay in his longevity rather than
in any great or lasting victories. Most features of his reign followed
the familiar Canmore pattern. There were attempts to extend
government's reach – for example, conferring royal burgh status
on Dumfries (chartered in 1186), Ayr (1205) and Perth (1210). Highly
visible acts of piety were also undertaken – including the foundation
of the great Tironensian abbey at Arbroath in 1178 that would play
such an important part in Scotland's later struggles against English
domination and where William himself was buried. Again, too, there
were continuing problems with rebellions in Galloway and Ross,
which William regularly needed to tackle.

William's principal aim as king was the recovery of what Malcolm IV lost – particularly the earldom of Northumbria, previously in his personal possession. But in this he was thwarted. Captured on 12 July 1174 in Northumberland in an ill-advised skirmish during a wider revolt against Henry II in which the Scots participated opportunistically, William was imprisoned at Newcastle and then Northampton before ending up in one of Henry's castles in Normandy.

Humiliated even more than Malcolm, some of the key southern Scottish strongpoints, including the castles at Edinburgh, Stirling and Berwick, came into Henry's uncontested possession. William was even obliged to raise funds to pay for the English occupation and his own ransom.

Few Scottish monarchs have been so comprehensively humbled as William was by that year's Treaty of Falaise, acknowledging English overlordship and placing the Scottish Church firmly under the Archbishop of York. By the next year William had himself sworn fealty to the English sovereign and as late as 1186 married an aristocratic English wife, a granddaughter of Henry I, specifically chosen by Henry II: reinforcing William's submission, Henry ensured that the bride's dowry, a gift rather than recognition of an entitlement, was none other than Edinburgh Castle.

The long-term implications of William's embarrassment were fortunately limited. Henry's successor Richard, desperate to fund the Third Crusade, permitted annulment of the Treaty of Falaise through the Quitclaim of Canterbury in 1189. A payment of 10,000 silver marks ended the English occupation and released Scotland formally from subordination. The Pope, lobbied by William's bishops, also underlined the Scottish Church's independence.

In truth, William the Lion's reign ought to have taught some sobering lessons about the power and ambitions of the kings of England and the growing difficulties their Scottish counterparts would face in rebuffing them.

Another Alexander

Alexander II's reign looks mostly like those of his predecessors back to Canmore – a mixture of trials and tribulations inside and outside Scotland, some noteworthy royal strengths offset by significant weaknesses, and, taking the long-term view, a number of promising developments.

On the one hand Alexander faced continuing difficulties with those regions that most resented Normanization. Ross and Moray, under their mormaers, as well as Galloway, with its powerful Gaelic lordship and closeness to England and Ireland, all attempted resistance. The most dramatic incident was the savage murder of a baby girl, the last representative of the MacWilliams, descendants of Canmore who claimed both Moray and the Scottish crown: on Alexander's orders her brains were smashed out against the market cross at Forfar in 1230.

Less easily fixed was Alexander's relationship with the King of England, hardly helped by the still-simmering disputes over Cumberland and Northumberland. Initially Alexander followed his father's example in exploiting King John's weakness. He sided with the rebel English barons and the French, even sending an army into England that reached Dover unopposed before John signed Magna Carta in 1215.

After Henry III's accession, however, and the return of more settled conditions in England, Alexander's approach mirrored that of his pragmatic uncle Malcolm IV. His response to Henry, whose ten-year-old sister Joan he married in 1221 (she died childless in 1238), was to avoid undue antagonism, instead offering tactical concessions with good grace. A key result was the Treaty of York in 1237. This drew a boundary between the two kingdoms, never again substantially altered, which followed the natural barriers of the Solway in the west and the Tweed in the east.

'Afterwards, in the year 1220, Alexander, king of Scotland, went, with some of the chief men of the kingdom, under a safe-conduct, to meet Henry, king of England, at York, about the Feast of the Holy Trinity. There negotiations were busily carried on between them. The king of Scotland bound himself to wed the eldest sister of the king of England...'

John of Fordun, *Chronicle of the Scottish Nation* (late 14th century)

Alexander's long reign also extended other familiar trends. New royal burghs were chartered at the old Strathclydian capital of Dumbarton (1222) and at Dingwall in Ross (1226). The first Parliament of Scotland for which records of the proceedings survive also occurred at Kirkliston near Edinburgh in 1235.

Alexander again encouraged Anglo-Norman immigration. The Umfraville family, originally from Normandy and lately settled in Northumberland, took possession of the earldom of Angus. The Balliols, with deep roots in Picardy but more recently in County Durham, married into the Celto-Scottish aristocracy of Galloway, acquiring great power and influence in the south and west.

Least surprising of all, another descendant of St Margaret enthusiastically established monastic houses. In Alexander's case this meant the Cistercian abbey at Balmerino in Fife (1227), the Dominican friaries in Edinburgh and at Berwick (both 1230) and the priory at Pluscarden in Moray (again 1230). When Alexander died in 1249 he was buried, appropriately, in Melrose Abbey, and was succeeded by his son Alexander, the late-born child of his second marriage to the French noblewoman Marie de Coucy.

The happiest of times?

Ascending the throne at just eight and married at ten to Henry III's daughter Margaret, Alexander III's reign began auspiciously. He resisted Henry's attempt to have him do homage for the Scottish kingdom and, as he grew to adulthood, the achievements of his father appeared likely to endure.

Alexander made significant strides towards loosening the Scandinavian grip on the north and west. In 1262 he demanded that King Haakon of Norway cede the Western Isles to Scotland. And when Haakon responded, not surprisingly, with a seaborne attack, Alexander's army fought him in the indecisive Battle of Largs in Ayrshire in 1263, a reversal for the previously confident Norwegians which effectively demonstrated the impossibility of successfully maintaining their claims off Scotland's west coast. Accordingly under the Treaty of Perth of 1266 they agreed that Alexander, in return for a cash payment, should acquire the Hebrides. Two decades later he bestowed the Lordship of the Isles upon the MacDonald chieftain, in whose family it thereafter descended. Alexander, then, was a determined and successful political operator who, through good judgement and the astute deployment of power, made a conspicuously effective King of Scots.

His personal life, however, was less fortunate. Margaret died in 1274, having provided him with two sons who predeceased him and a daughter Margaret, who married Erik, Haakon's successor as King of Norway. She too predeceased Alexander, leaving just her own half-Norwegian daughter, again Margaret, whom in 1284 he was forced to take the precaution of having recognized by Parliament as heir-presumptive.

Alexander's second wife, Yolande of Dreux, actually fell pregnant immediately following their marriage in 1285. But tragically this child was stillborn. As a result Alexander's granddaughter Margaret, in Norway and some way short of her third birthday, was in early 1286 his most likely hypothetical successor. It was therefore lucky that the King of Scots was just 44 years of age and in rude health.

Scotland's ruin

The night of 19 March 1286 was dark and stormy, with snow and rain on a strong northerly wind. Alexander III spent the day in Edinburgh but he was now riding on horseback, against well-meant advice, as he neared Kinghorn on Fife's southern coast. What happened next had allegedly been predicted a day earlier by Thomas of Ercildoune – also known as Thomas the Rhymer – who had foreseen Alexander's fatal fall down steep ground onto the beach below.

> 'Alas for the morrow, day of misery and calamity! Before the hour of noon there will assuredly be felt such a mighty storm in Scotland that its like has not been known for long ages past. The blast of it will cause nations to tremble, will make those who hear it dumb, and will humble the high, and lay the strong level with the ground'
>
> Thomas of Ercildoune (1286)

Over the edge, in a national as well as a personal calamity, tumbled not only Scotland's king but also its best chance of peace and stability. The next 200 years would instead be marked by chronic upheaval and warfare as rival claimants to the throne struggled for dominance and opportunistic English interventions regularly threatened the kingdom's very existence.

Fact check

1 What was a 'sheriff'?
   a a Celtic warlord
   b a county official
   c a courtier
   d a churchman

2 Who was Somerled?
   a a border landowner
   b a bishop
   c a King of Scots
   d a Celto-Scandinavian ruler

3 When was the Treaty of Falaise signed?
   a 1174
   b 1189
   c 1205
   d 1286

4 When was the first Scots Parliament whose proceedings are documented?
   a 1226
   b 1235
   c 1286
   d 1320

5 When did the King of Scots secure sovereignty over the Western Isles?
   a 1189
   b 1205
   c 1266
   d 1286

6 Where was Alexander III killed?
   a Edinburgh
   b St Andrews
   c Stirling
   d Kinghorn

7 Who was Alexander III's heir?
   a Margaret
   b Yolande
   c Erik of Norway
   d Edward I of England

Dig Deeper

Grace Windsor, *Scottish Monarchs: The House of Dunkeld* (Charleston, 2011).

Richard Oram, *Alexander II* (Edinburgh, 2012).

Marion Campbell, *Alexander III, King of Scots* (Colonsay, 1999).

Norman H. Reid, *Scotland in the Reign of Alexander III* (Edinburgh, 1990).

7

A nation compromised

The fair Maid

If the decades before 1286 were indeed Scotland's lost golden age, the centuries that followed were more like an age of steel.

Not that violence and political instability were new. Kings of Scots in particular were no strangers to vindicating their authority on the battlefield, sword in hand. Most faced a combination of challenges from inside the country – from ambitious kinsmen and over-mighty subjects – and from outside, especially from English monarchs eager to assert sovereignty over all of Britain. What was new after 1286 was that English power on an unprecedented scale, applied so as to increase political uncertainty and exploit deep divisions within Scotland, now placed the kingdom's independence in jeopardy.

Alexander III's accidental death, an unmitigated disaster that left his granddaughter Margaret, the so-called 'Maid of Norway', in formal possession of the crown, illustrates this vulnerability vividly. Given Margaret's infancy and location overseas, royal power was delegated by Parliament to four barons and the bishops of St Andrews and Glasgow – collectively designated the Guardians.

Had Margaret's claim been unchallenged, this cumbersome arrangement would still have been difficult to sustain. But there were actually several other potential successors. And not all of them could resist the opportunity that Margaret's age, gender and physical absence presented.

Late 1286, for example, saw a rising in the south-west, led by two Robert Bruces, father and son, respectively 5th Lord of Annandale and Earl of Carrick. The father was David I's great-great-grandson. A regent during Alexander III's own minority, he had been named the king's preferred successor before Margaret's birth. Annandale, then, was a credible claimant.

Yet the Bruces' revolt was quelled. Other contenders, some with equally powerful claims, were also kept at bay by the Guardians. Uneasily but successfully, the kingdom was governed in this way for three more years, deferring some of the most serious issues about how, when and with what consequences Margaret might eventually rule.

One thorny question, however, affecting all young elite females, did need to be grappled with. This was the sensitive matter of pre-determining her future marriage. Margaret's father, the King of Norway, wanted her engaged to Edward, infant son and heir of Edward I, King of England.

Eventually in 1290 the Scots Parliament and the English ruler agreed the Treaty of Birgham. It decreed that Margaret, whose claim to the Scottish crown the English acknowledged, would reign in her own right as Queen of Scots. It also stipulated that, while any offspring with Edward would inherit both thrones, Scotland would remain a distinct kingdom, governed separately.

What no one could have anticipated, however, was what happened next. Margaret, travelling by ship to Scotland, died at Orkney, aged just seven, apparently of natural causes, in the autumn of 1290.

With the leading candidate suddenly removed from the game, the field of play was dramatically levelled. This completely unexpected development had only one predictable outcome. It encouraged a host of other competitors to enter the fray.

Candidates for kingship

In some ways the extent of the political uncertainty created by these personal tragedies can be gauged from the fact that no fewer than 14 contenders now stepped forward. Each staked a claim in what became the Great Cause – 'cause' being the Scots law term for a 'case' – with competing parties exchanging legal arguments in court.

Who wants to be king?

Some candidates possessed flimsy justifications and must privately have doubted their own chances. Robert de Pinkeney, great-great-great-grandson of David I, was undermined by being reliant upon an allegedly illegitimate great-grandmother. Not a man to allow implausibility to thwart ambition, even King Erik of Norway advanced a claim based on being Margaret's father and the previous king's son-in-law. Stronger arguments also existed. One was for John Comyn (known as the 'Black Comyn'), the great-great-great-great-grandson of Donald III, himself a Guardian and, as Lord of Badenoch, head of Scotland's pre-eminent baronial family with extensive landholdings in the north-east. In the event, however, Comyn threw his considerable weight behind an even stronger claimant, his brother-in-law John Balliol. Comyn's decision was characteristically shrewd for Balliol's claim was actually superior to the Bruce's because the latter, with ancestry back to David I through one fewer generations, was dependent upon his mother Isabel who had been the younger sister of Balliol's grandmother Margaret. According to the law of primogeniture whereby elder children have precedence – a system of inheritance common among the Scottish feudal elite following Normanization – the undeniable fact that Margaret had been born before Isabel rendered Balliol's case more persuasive than that of Bruce.

One peculiar aspect of the way the Great Cause was conducted requires special comment. This was the pivotal role of Edward I of England. For the threat of civil war between the supporters of the two leading Scottish contenders convinced the Guardians that having the final judgement endorsed by a powerful and authoritative external judge would help contain the threat of internal instability.

Before assisting, Edward demanded that the Guardians acknowledge his overlordship. This they did. Edward was even allowed temporarily to occupy the principal royal fortresses, another sign both of his aspirations for Scotland and of the weakness of the kingless kingdom. A court comprising 104 'auditors' or judges was then appointed, 24 by Edward and 40 each by Balliol and Bruce. Edward himself presided as the arguments unfolded in the Great Hall of Berwick Castle.

On 17 November 1292 Balliol, clearly in possession of the stronger legal claim, was declared victorious. Importantly, this enjoyed the support not only of Edward but of most Scottish nobles, including even some of the Bruce auditors. To all intents and purposes with the consent and good wishes of those who really mattered, Balliol became King John and was crowned at Scone on St Andrew's Day.

The trouble with John

It is hard to approach John's reign with an open mind, given the distaste in which he came to be held. Even before his death he was being mocked as 'Toom Tabard' ('empty jacket') – an embarrassing nickname perhaps referring to the Scottish royal insignia that Edward later had stripped from John's knightly apparel.

It was John's misfortune to be from the outset the King of England's man. Yet this was largely unavoidable in the circumstances. Most Scottish leaders, the Bruces as well as the Guardians, had formally submitted to Edward as a condition of his role in the Great Cause. It therefore seems unlikely that anyone chosen would have been able just to ignore this affiliation.

Edward, no shrinking violet in exercising his sovereign rights, hardly helped. His treatment of John, emphasizing his inferior status, made it more likely that the Scottish elites, accustomed to being big fish in a small pond, would react against the King of England's attempts to transform them into comparatively minor players on a much larger stage.

Insults to John and to Scottish pride came thick and fast. In the first month he was required to do homage to Edward as King of Scots at Newcastle. He was also informed that Edward, his feudal lord, would adjudicate any internal Scottish disputes. Military burdens followed in 1294, including support for the English campaign in France. Even the Treaty of Birgham was repudiated, with John forced to accept both the theory and the practice of English suzerainty.

These accumulating slights led to a decisive event at Stirling in July 1295. A group of Scots nobles and clergy, comprising four earls, four bishops and four barons, constituted a council of advisors to guide John and protect the kingdom's threatened autonomy. They won a treaty of mutual aid from King Philip IV of France, to be sealed by marrying John's son and heir to Philip's niece – the formal beginning of the famous 'Auld Alliance' (or 'old alliance') and a flagrant breach of what Edward understood as his Scots subjects' obligation of loyalty.

John's council also took direct action against those closely associated with English domination. Ironically, given the role that the Bruces would soon take in Scotland's battle for independence, the Earl of Carrick, son of the competitor in the Great Cause, was immediately caught out. At this stage he was a vital ally of Edward, who in 1295 even entrusted him with command of strategically sensitive Carlisle Castle. Accordingly his Annandale properties were confiscated by John and handed to his Comyn backers after Carrick ignored a general Scottish call to arms.

That the loyalties of Scotland's elite were divided ought not to shock us. Partly this happened because feudal noblemen instinctively prioritized their own families' interests, which frequently differed from those of the monarch. Partly too the varied responses reflected the effects of Normanization as well as the extensive recent intermarriage between the English and Scottish elites. The fact that Patrick, Earl of March and previously another contender for the crown, aligned himself with Edward, while his wife, Marjorie, a Comyn, garrisoned March's own castle at Dunbar for John, illustrates in extreme form the acute conflicts of allegiance that resulted.

Edward's response to these developments was considered, direct and brutal – in other words, entirely in character.

An English army crossed the border, sacked Berwick and on 27 April 1296, led by the Earl of Surrey and with Carrick prominent on Edward's side, defeated John's army near March's castle. The death toll was quite limited on the field of battle in what appears to have been largely a cavalry engagement. But several Scottish earls, including numerous Comyns, were captured and taken to England as prisoners. Facing overwhelming odds, James the Steward surrendered Roxburgh Castle, the last great Scottish fortress in the Borders. Edward then occupied Edinburgh, quickly taking the castle. Stirling, which the Scots made no attempt to defend, was next, followed by Perth.

At Montrose on 8 July the inevitable conclusion was reached. King John of Scotland abdicated in person before King Edward of England. This is where the Scottish royal arms were ripped from John's jacket by the Bishop of Durham in a humiliating gesture symbolizing his loss of monarchical status.

Flushed with victory, Edward had the Stone of Destiny, the oblong of red sandstone on which Scottish kings had been crowned from early times, removed from Scone to Westminster Abbey, where it would spend the next seven centuries. He also convened a Parliament at Berwick in August 1296 where he received homage from much of the Scottish nobility, including Carrick and his son, another Robert Bruce. Surrey as governor and Sir Hugh de Cressingham as treasurer were put in charge of running this annoyingly insubordinate part of Edward's realm.

Scotland seemed to have been bent successfully to the King of England's ferocious will. Having earned for himself the name *Malleus Scottorum* (Hammer of the Scots), Edward's triumph over those whom he saw not as foreign enemies but as rebellious subjects appeared complete.

Wallace's glory

This was not, however, the case. For this first part of the Wars of Independence would finish not with meek acceptance of Edward's rule but rather with a bold uprising, ultimately unsuccessful but utterly inspirational for later generations, that etched itself forever into the Scottish consciousness.

One leader was Andrew Moray, from a respected knightly family with Flemish origins which had arrived in the north-east in David I's time. His ancestors' successful assimilation into the peculiar culture and society of the part of Scotland from which they soon took their name ensured that he sympathized with its tradition of resistance towards centralizing Scottish regimes – whether run by a Canmore monarch or an ambitious King of England.

Moray's principal colleague was from a different social background. A minor landowner, he was sufficiently obscure that we can only guess whether his family originated in England or in Wales and whether his birthplace was in Ayrshire or in Renfrewshire (some sources say Ellerslie, others Elderslie): this was the indomitable William Wallace.

The man from the shadows

The legend has it that Wallace's dramatic arrival on the national stage was preceded in May 1297 by his slaying of William Heselrig, sheriff of Selkirk – allegedly because, according to Blind Harry, who wrote a sympathetic poetic biography two centuries later, the Englishman had murdered Wallace's wife, Marion. There are numerous other tales, none well documented, of Wallace's early taste for extreme violence, including the purported killing of the son of an English aristocrat in a quarrel at Dundee and a yearning for vengeance for the death of his father and brother at the hands of English soldiers. Yet another story, partly supported by one slightly ambiguous contemporary legal record and perhaps helping to explain the repeated English accusation that Scotland's national hero was in fact little more than a common thief, even has Wallace involved in a robbery at Perth as late as June 1296. Whatever the truth, Wallace was certainly not a man to turn the other cheek, and when he finally emerges into the light of recorded history in the summer of 1297 he does so as the leader of resistance to Edward across central and southern Scotland.

How far this rebellion was planned in detail we do not know. Some historians have seen evidence of a co-ordinated national rising. Others have portrayed an unpopular regime, its authority successfully flouted by charismatic opponents, experiencing successive waves of spontaneous resistance by unconnected groups eager to mount their own challenges.

What we do know is that Wallace's military capabilities first shone brightly when defeating English forces in small-scale engagements, such as one at Scone, where he fought alongside Sir William Douglas, in the process taking much treasure with which to fund subsequent adventures. Edward's army managed a bloodless victory in July 1297 at Irvine in Ayrshire, where a large Scottish force, riven by dissension, ultimately saw its leaders, including the young Robert Bruce of Carrick, re-affirm their loyalty to the English ruler – the 'capitulation of Irvine' as it was called. But the momentum overall remained with the rebels.

Moray had simultaneously waged war in the north. He brazenly attacked Castle Urquhart on Loch Ness in May 1297: it fell that summer. Other English strongholds in the north-east were soon in Moray's hands and Edward's supporters forced to flee. In one particularly courageous move, which Blind Harry typically credits to Wallace but for which Moray, who controlled operations in the area, seems almost certain to have been responsible, English ships at anchor at Aberdeen were burned.

The response of Edward, busy campaigning in Flanders, was to order the Comyns and the Bishop of Aberdeen to defeat Moray. They seem not to have been especially enthusiastic. A brief and inconclusive encounter at Enzie in late August 1297 hints strongly at a reluctance by fellow Scots to engage in serious hostilities against each other.

Edward was left with little choice but to seek to re-impose control in Scotland with a substantial English force. Commanded by Surrey and Cressingham, it was this army that took the fateful decision to march towards Stirling, site of the strategic bridge across the Forth giving access to central and north-eastern Scotland. Here Moray and Wallace, previously besieging Edward's castle at Dundee, waited patiently on the north bank.

The battle on 11 September 1297 brought them a stunning victory. First allowing just enough of the English cavalry and foot soldiers to cross, the Scots infantry, an experienced and confident force by now, attacked ferociously. The normal medieval military assumption that well-trained armoured horsemen would defeat soldiers on foot was undermined by the skilful ways in which Wallace and Moray deployed the forces available to them.

Surrounded by a determined enemy and with a narrow bridge behind them, the English army on the north bank was cut to pieces. Cressingham himself died, the chroniclers recording that

Wallace subsequently had his skin flayed and a strip turned into a baldrick for his sword. Observing the carnage from the south bank, Surrey, later much criticized, retreated to Berwick rather than hold his own position against the onrushing Scots.

> 'We come here with no peaceful intent, but ready for battle, determined to avenge our wrongs and set our country free. Let your masters come and attack us: we are ready to meet them beard to beard'
>
> Sir William Wallace at Stirling (1297)

Stirling Bridge has always been regarded as a glorious high point in Scotland's medieval history. It certainly encouraged successive generations to believe in the real possibility of national independence despite England's far greater military resources. And yet its aftermath was in reality somewhat mixed.

To start with, Moray disappears hereafter from national affairs: it is usually assumed that he must have died later in the year from wounds received at Stirling. Wallace, for his part, was able to complete the business of throwing off Edward's grip on Scotland by such actions as the capture of the Dundee garrison and slaughtering the occupants of the castle at nearby Cupar in Fife.

He was rewarded for his astonishing achievements by being knighted by a group of admiring Scottish noblemen, possibly including young Bruce. He was also appointed Guardian, the first to hold this office on his own – nominally acting still to defend Balliol's kingship but arguably increasingly representing much of the wider kingdom and its population.

Less productively, Wallace followed his victory with an unfocused foray into Northumberland and Cumberland which, lacking siege equipment, achieved little. Possibly it was designed to show that the Scots' military power reached further than Edward had ever imagined. It certainly encouraged other Scots to rebel: Bruce in particular abandoned his previous oaths to Edward and burned the castle at Ayr to deny it to the English. The raid south also, however, confirmed for Edward the need to take personal charge of bringing the Scots to heel.

On 1 April 1298 Edward crossed the border with 15,000 men. Harrying the country around Edinburgh, the aim was to bring Wallace to battle. The initial response of the resistance was sensibly to avoid a set-piece encounter on unfavourable terms against an experienced and well-equipped adversary. Instead Wallace tried to make life difficult for the English army by destroying potential food supplies and tempting it to move deeper and deeper into hostile territory. Of course, some kind of confrontation would in the end still be required if Wallace wanted Edward's invasion to be defeated.

This eventually took place at Falkirk, on the road from Edinburgh just a few miles short of Stirling, on 22 July 1298. And it was a disastrous defeat for Wallace in which his military reputation was badly tarnished.

Part of the problem was that, while Wallace no longer had Moray, Edward was an infinitely superior battlefield commander and tactician to Surrey and Cressingham. Wallace also faced an opponent with many powerful Scottish allies. The late-14th-century Scottish chronicler John of Fordun even places Bruce himself back by Edward's side, although most historians doubt its accuracy.

The earls of Angus and Dunbar, however, definitely assisted Edward, providing vital intelligence on Wallace's intentions. He also had a contingent of Welsh archers and Italian crossbowmen. The medieval equivalent of mobile heavy artillery, they offered the destructive firepower with which to pulverize the Scots' densely packed formations from a safe distance before the remnants were put to the sword by his armoured knights, battle-hardened veterans of Edward's French wars. In the slaughter at Falkirk, several of Wallace's closest allies fell, including second-in-command Sir John de Graham and Macduff, the Earl of Fife's son.

In the short term Edward's crushing victory was even less successfully exploited than Wallace's at Stirling Bridge. Lacking supplies and with some allies deserting him, Edward had no option but to retreat to Carlisle. Wallace, meanwhile, resigned as Guardian and was replaced by Robert Bruce and John Comyn, a pairing capable at least in theory of uniting the kingdom's major factions in the struggle against English overlordship.

Wallace's story after Falkirk is less happy. In 1299 he was in France seeking Philip IV's support. He also tried to secure the Pope's backing: some believe Wallace visited Rome in person. But, returning home in 1303 to conduct guerrilla operations in the Borders, he was eventually betrayed on 5 August 1305 by John de Menteith at Robroyston near Glasgow and handed over to his enemies. Conveyed to London he was immediately put on trial for treason in Westminster Hall. The outcome, though Wallace boldly rejected the English ruler's jurisdiction over him, was a foregone conclusion.

> 'I cannot be a traitor, for I owe him no allegiance. He is not my Sovereign; he never received my homage; and whilst life is in this persecuted body, he never shall receive it. To the other points whereof I am accused, I freely confess them all. As Governor of my country I have been an enemy to its enemies; I have slain the English; I have mortally opposed the English King; I have stormed and taken the towns and castles which he unjustly claimed as his own. If I or my soldiers have plundered or done injury to the houses or ministers of religion, I repent me of my sin; but it is not of Edward of England I shall ask pardon'
>
> Sir William Wallace on trial (1305)

On 23 August Wallace was dragged naked through the streets of London tied to a hurdle and then at Smithfield, the traditional place of execution, subjected to a traitor's death: he was first partially hanged; then, cut down alive, his entrails were drawn from his body and burned; and finally he was beheaded and his body quartered, with the parts despatched for public display in different parts of Edward's kingdom.

Fact check

1 Whom did the Treaty of Birgham arrange for Margaret to marry?
- **a** The Bishop of St Andrews
- **b** Robert Bruce
- **c** Erik of Norway
- **d** Prince Edward of England

2 What was contested in the 'Great Cause'?
- **a** England's overlordship
- **b** The Scottish crown
- **c** Norwegian sovereignty
- **d** Highland power

3 Who won the 'Great Cause'?
- **a** John Balliol
- **b** Robert Bruce
- **c** Sir William Wallace
- **d** John Comyn

4 When did the 'Auld Alliance' begin?
- **a** 1286
- **b** 1292
- **c** 1295
- **d** 1302

5 Which of the following Scots was loyal to King Edward of England in 1295-6?
- **a** Marjorie Comyn
- **b** James the Steward
- **c** King John of Scotland
- **d** Robert Bruce

6 Where did Wallace achieve victory in 1297?
- **a** Edinburgh
- **b** Stirling
- **c** Aberdeen
- **d** Dunbar

7 Where did Edward defeat Wallace in 1298?
- **a** Stirling
- **b** Falkirk
- **c** Ayr
- **d** Castle Urquhart

8 Where did Wallace die?
- **a** Smithfield
- **b** Rome
- **c** Ayrshire
- **d** Edinburgh

Dig Deeper

G. W. S. Barrow, 'A Kingdom in Crisis: Scotland and the Maid of Norway', *Scottish Historical Review* (1990).
Edward J. Cowan, (ed.) *The Wallace Book* (Edinburgh, 2007).
Andrew Fisher, *William Wallace* (Edinburgh, 2002).
Fiona Watson, *Under the Hammer: Edward I and Scotland 1286–1307* (East Linton, 1998).

8

The wars of
independence

Edward's interventions

The years after Falkirk were hard for those defending Scotland's independence.

After Wallace's resignation, the country's fortunes were initially in the hands of men whose difficult personal relationship symbolized Scotland's internal divisions: the younger John Comyn (the 'Red Comyn', son of the 'Black Comyn') and Robert Bruce.

Their selection as Guardians was therefore not a plausible recipe for consensus so much as an attempt to minimize instability by balancing the two major factions. This point was underlined with the addition of a supposedly neutral third figure, William de Lamberton, appointed Bishop of St Andrews under Wallace's influence because of his strong support for national independence.

This awkward compromise was sorely tested by Edward's continued aggression. Caerlaverock Castle, for example, the Maxwell family's fortress in Dumfriesshire, was attacked in July 1300. Edward's army, which successfully captured this vital Border stronghold, included 87 of his leading barons, and was equipped with Warwolf, a large trebuchet (or catapult) reputedly capable of hurling 200-lb missiles against the walls.

In August that year Pope Boniface VIII wrote asking for an end to his assaults on Scotland but Edward only accepted a truce with the Scots at the end of the campaigning season. One result of the tensions created by Edward's interventions, and by the unsatisfactory nature of a shared Guardianship, was the resignation first of Bruce late in 1300, replaced by Sir Ingram de Umfraville, and then of Comyn and Lamberton as well as Umfraville in May 1301. They were replaced by Sir John de Soules, who like Wallace before him became sole Guardian. His selection as a neutral figure was merely a different answer to the same question of how to deal with a bitterly divided elite.

The summer of 1301 brought no respite, the English capturing Bothwell in Lanarkshire despite the close attentions of Soules' forces. Edward advanced on Linlithgow to the west of

Edinburgh, previously his forward base in the Falkirk campaign. Building a substantial fortification, he spent Christmas there with his son, the future Edward II.

In January 1302 he again signed a truce and many Scots now took the opportunity to make their peace with him. The details are sketchy but Bruce in particular appears once more to have renewed his oaths to Edward. The best explanation is that with Soules and many other leading figures still seeking Balliol's reinstatement and the latter released from his English prison by Papal intercession and actively seeking French military support for a victorious return, Bruce's own claim to the throne looked in growing jeopardy. It may also have mattered that Bruce's father was dying and feared for the family's prospects if his son persisted in defying a powerful monarch who seemed likely to dominate Scottish politics for the foreseeable future.

It was at this time, with much of Scotland's elite prudently backing Edward (who in 1302 was confident enough to hold a Round Table tournament at Falkirk, deliberately echoing King Arthur's claim to rule all of Britain), that the French king also undermined the cause of independence. Facing domestic revolt and needing peace with England, Philip IV decided to cut the Scots loose and, without his influence, the Papacy also withdrew diplomatic support. So critical was this that Soules travelled to Paris to plead with Philip.

In his absence and with Bruce evidently unreliable, Comyn was re-appointed to assist him as Guardian. But in May 1303 Philip and Edward signed a formal peace treaty nonetheless. Scotland, in short, stood alone.

In this encouraging situation Edward continued to seek collective submission. In the summer of 1303 he marched via Edinburgh, Perth and Dundee to Aberdeen, which he reached in August, and moved on into Moray and Badenoch before over-wintering at Dunfermline. Edward's easy and unmolested movement through the country's heartlands was a clear indication of his forbidding military strength. Yet in the final analysis, of course, this impressive feat was still not quite the same as permanently occupying and successfully pacifying Scotland.

By February 1304 every significant figure except Soules (still in France) and Wallace (in his final act as a guerrilla leader) had formally made peace with Edward and accepted his overlordship.

The outlines of a permanent settlement were also visible, with Comyn in particular submitting to Edward in return for agreement that certain laws and privileges traditionally enjoyed by the Scottish elite would be protected. This also explains Wallace's hounding, capture and execution the next year: the special hatred reserved for him by Edward was because he was the last person of consequence to reject an arrangement that would finally allow the King of England to impose his will on Scotland.

With Wallace dead by August 1305, it appeared that Scotland was at last adjusting to life under Edward. A Scots Parliament had confirmed his sovereignty in May and appointed representatives to negotiate the complete assimilation of Scotland into his kingdom's political system. With the Guardianship in abeyance, Edward's nephew the Earl of Richmond was placed in charge and given oversight of key Scottish military sites. He was to be assisted by a council of leading noblemen and bishops including Lamberton, Comyn and Bruce, all sworn to be Edward's men. Edward, to all intents and purposes, had won.

Destiny calls

One reason why the situation was not quite as desperate as at first sight it appeared was that Bruce in particular, encouraged by the increasing certainty that Balliol would not return, had actually not abandoned his own claim to the throne. As a result, Edward continued to treat Bruce, clearly the most devious and unpredictable of Scottish leaders, with suspicion: in 1305 he required him not to maintain his castles in an offensive posture and took back some lands he had earlier been given. Edward's doubts about Bruce's sincerity were shrewd. For since June 1304 he and Lamberton had been in a secret pact.

This linked Bruce's claim to the crown of an independent Scotland with the leading bishops' determination to maintain an independent Scottish Church. Yet the trigger for Bruce's decision to lead the fight against Edward's occupation was seemingly trivial and may not even have been premeditated. At a meeting inside the Greyfriars Church at Dumfries on 10 February 1306, Bruce, in a fit of temper following a verbal altercation, stabbed John Comyn in front of the high altar. Comyn was then finished off by a Bruce retainer, Roger de Kirkpatrick.

This single episode transformed everything. It was the most spectacular act of sacrilege imaginable and in religious terms required the immediate help of Lamberton and other leading bishops with whom Bruce was already allied. The murder obviously also ended any prospect of the rival Scottish dynasties living together peacefully under Edward. Bruce now either had to surrender himself to Edward and face the consequences or do whatever was necessary to become king in his own kingdom.

> 'Ah! Freedom is ane nobil thing!
> Freedom makis man to have liking,
> Freedom all solace to man givis:
> He livis at ease that freely livis!'
> John Barbour, The Brus (1375)

More immediately, however, the murder made Bruce an outlaw. Three nights sleeping rough while Comyn's men hunted him through the Border hills were a foretaste. Absolution came from Robert Wishart, Bishop of Glasgow, before whom Bruce knelt to confess his mortal sin. Rather than seeking his excommunication, Wishart, in consort with Lamberton, instead encouraged other Scots to regard Bruce as their rightful king. Wishart also hurriedly led him to Perth to be crowned at Scone on 25 March 1306, in the presence of several bishops and leading earls.

In another fascinating illustration of the split loyalties dividing the Scottish elite, the coronation was re-enacted two days later because an important participant had been delayed. This was Isabella MacDuff, who, with her brother in English captivity, exercised her family's traditional prerogative as earls of Fife to place the crown on the new ruler's head. It was therefore a woman who literally transformed mere Robert Bruce into Robert I, King of Scots.

Brave as well as independent minded, Isabella was the wife of Comyn's cousin the Earl of Buchan, from whom she clearly differed violently in matters of high politics. Her husband John pursued his family's revenge for the murder at Dumfries and became a natural leader among Edward's allies. Isabella, however, inspired the Scots' resistance to English rule by crowning the rival claimant and defiantly overturning the original judgement in the Great Cause.

Robert's early experiences as king, for all that he must have longed for the moment, must have fallen short of his expectations. Mainly this was because the vengeance of Edward and the Comyns was so swift. There followed a prolonged period during which Robert and his entourage were in fear of their lives – as, for example, after their defeat by Aymer de Valence, future Earl of Pembroke and brother-in-law of the Red Comyn, at Methven in Strathearn on 19 June 1306.

First Robert escaped to Strathfillan in the southern Highlands. But here he and his small army were again defeated at a place afterwards known as Dalrigh (Gaelic for 'field of the king'), this time by the powerful MacDougall clan, associates of the Comyns and relations of Balliol. Next he hid in the Atholl mountains, taking the precaution of sending his wife, Elizabeth, and some of his other supporters to Kildrummy Castle in Aberdeenshire. Finally Robert himself fled to the greater safety of Ireland's northern coast along with a few hand-picked men, to plot a guerrilla campaign against overwhelming odds.

The year 1307 was another unhappy one for Scotland's new king. Edward marched north, having also had Robert excommunicated for his sins. The fugitive's estates were given to more supportive families. Worse, Edward's forces captured Kildrummy: some of the male defenders, including Robert's brother Nigel, were hanged, drawn and quartered; the women, who initially escaped to Tain and were captured there, were transported to prisons and publicly displayed in wooden cages, open to the elements, for the next four years – Mary Bruce, Robert's sister, at Roxburgh and Isabella MacDuff at Berwick. For her part, Elizabeth Bruce, probably because she was the daughter of Edward's ally the Earl of Ulster, was treated more gently, being taken to England and placed under house arrest. Even so, she did not meet her husband again for eight years.

Military events were more encouraging for the new monarch. From Rathlin Island the Bruces returned to Scotland in two separate parties. Robert and his brother Edward conducted hit-and-run operations from the Carrick hills that they knew so well, before defeating Aymer de Valence at Loudoun Hill in Ayrshire on 10 May. He then moved north to attack the Comyn-held castles at Inverlochy, Urquhart, Nairn and Inverness, leaving Edward in charge in Galloway while his ally James Douglas harried Bruce's enemies in the Borders. Later that year Robert attacked the Comyns' strongholds in Ross-shire and Aberdeenshire. But Robert's other two brothers, Alexander and Thomas, were less fortunate. Landing at Loch Ryan in the far south-west, they were swiftly captured by a MacDougall ally of Balliol and executed at Carlisle by the English.

The long-term outlook for Scotland was changed significantly by an event which took place just south of the border on 7 July 1307: Edward I's death from dysentery and his replacement by his far less imposing and less able son Edward II. Yet in the short-term nothing much changed. The King of Scots continued his aggressive and highly mobile campaign against both Comyn and the English. In 1308 Robert defeated the Earl of Buchan's army decisively in a major engagement at Inverurie, attacked Buchan's estates, captured Aberdeen, routed a MacDougall force in the Pass of Brander in Argyllshire and eradicated the last important Comyn stronghold, the traditional MacDougall fortress at Dunstaffnage.

As this run of victories showed, Robert's mastery of guerrilla tactics and the flexible nature of the military resources available to him – particularly when set-piece battles were avoided and fast-moving, roving strikes were made instead – allowed him gradually to extend his influence over most of Scotland, especially north of the Tay.

By March 1309 the credibility of Robert's claim to sovereignty throughout his kingdom was underlined when his first Parliament met at St Andrews. His authority was further strengthened when the clergy, meeting in council, recognized him as King of

Scots. Over the next few years, he made steady progress towards effective domination of the country, largely untroubled by Edward II's weak rule or by the badly damaged Comyns (the Earl of Buchan himself had died in 1308).

English-held fortresses fell in succession, gradually eliminating the military basis of Edward's flimsy grip on Scotland: Linlithgow (1310), Perth (1312), Roxburgh (1314) and Edinburgh (captured that same year by Robert's nephew Thomas Randolph, later Earl of Moray). Only Stirling held out.

Defended by Sir Phillip Mowbray, the castle was besieged by Edward Bruce who reached an agreement with the occupants at Easter 1314, perhaps unwisely, that they would surrender unless relieved by 24 June. It was in this situation that Edward II, although embroiled in conflict with his English barons, ordered preparations in the late spring of 1314 for a major counter-offensive.

Bruce's moment

Edward II had clearly concluded that saving Stirling, the key to central and northern Scotland, was worthy of a full-scale expedition. Similar recognition of the castle's decisive importance explains Robert's willingness, after years of avoiding pitched battles against much larger and better-equipped opponents, to risk a conventional engagement.

On 17 June 1314 Edward's force of approaching 20,000 men, including perhaps 3,000 cavalry, set out from Berwick. The leaders of this great feudal host once more reflected the divided loyalties of the Scottish elite. At Edward's side were Robert's old enemy the Earl of Pembroke, Sir John Comyn of Badenoch (son of the Red Comyn), Henry de Beaumont (the new Earl of Buchan inheriting through a Comyn wife), several MacDougalls, the Earl of Angus (an Umfraville with a Comyn mother) and even Sir Ingram de Umfraville (former Guardian but a staunch Balliol supporter).

Inside two days they were at Edinburgh. Three further days saw them at Falkirk, approaching Stirling itself. For its part Robert's army, just 7,000 strong, had drawn up in three main formations, mainly hidden from sight in the woods near the small stream known as Bannock Burn, which flows across the boggy plain of the Forth south of Stirling. One, to the rear, was commanded by Robert. His brother Edward led the centre while Randolph was in the front. Mostly they comprised spear-wielding infantrymen, along with some archers, backed up by a small force of horsemen under Sir Robert Keith.

On 23 June the English army moved onto the plain between them and Stirling. The English cavalry in particular were already uncomfortably bunched, obliged by the obstacles in their way, including traps dug by the Scots, to approach the Bannock Burn by a single narrow road that limited their ability to deploy their full weight of numbers in a single manoeuvre. Mowbray, confident enough to leave the castle to meet Edward, actually advised against a battle, especially on such difficult terrain, but Edward ignored the warnings and pressed on. The English knights, leading from the front, therefore approached what they took to be Robert's army.

Henry de Bohun, a young Englishman, seeing a mounted Robert wearing a crown at the front of his formation, attempted to charge the king with his lance. But Bohun, too hot-headed by half, was felled with one well-aimed blow to the head from the royal battle-axe. Randolph's men also performed great work, untroubled by any enemy archers and so able effectively to repel the English cavalry.

As evening fell, a Scottish knight who had deserted Edward's cause brought word of demoralization in the English camp, news which further encouraged Robert to press home the advantage and fight once more in the morning.

On 24 June 1314 the main part of the greatest battle in Scottish history came to a brutal conclusion. Concentrating on those parts of the much larger enemy force that tried repeatedly to cross the Bannock Burn, Robert's men found that their smaller numbers on such a constricted site were no disadvantage. Edward's poorly organized army, immobile and unable to mount mass cavalry charges, found it difficult to make headway in breaking up the determined and well-drilled Scottish formations. In return, however, they were subjected to continual attack from Robert's spearmen and archers.

Several prominent supporters of Edward were killed in the increasing confusion, including the Earl of Gloucester and Sir John Comyn of Badenoch, before the English army as a whole turned and began to retreat.

Edward himself attempted to gain refuge in Stirling Castle but was denied entry by Mowbray, unwilling to break the terms of his agreement with Edward Bruce. Finally, the King of England reached Dunbar from where he took ship for London. Many in the English army died in the withdrawal, harassed by Robert's forces as well as by the wider Scottish population. Barely 5,000 of the 16,000 foot soldiers who had set out probably made it back home.

Tightening the grip

Bannockburn ushered in a period during which Robert's campaign to assert his right to the Scottish throne could be carried outside Scotland to wherever and whenever English power, the one constant threat to the Bruce cause, could be challenged.

This explains why Robert continued the age-old Scottish strategy of attacking northern England. Yorkshire and Lancashire felt the full force of his wrath: both were invaded and forced to pay tribute to him. In 1315 Robert capitalized upon his own Irish affiliations – through his de Burgh marriage and his mother's Gaelic ancestry – to extend his campaign across the North Channel, ostensibly to liberate the Irish from the English yoke but also to weaken Edward II's authority and secure Scotland's south-west flank from invasion.

This strategy was unsuccessful. Outside Ulster, with its traditional links to nearby Scotland, the invaders received only very limited encouragement from Ireland's elites, whether Celtic or Norman. Even some of the de Burghs' allies fought against Edward Bruce's army. A number of towns and monasteries, including Kells, were sacked, and there was little sign of the kind of pan-Gaelic rising against the English anticipated by Robert. In fact, the violence, disruption and famine brought by the Scots only made their intervention predictably unpopular with most natives.

The whole sorry venture reached its disappointing culmination on 14 October 1318 with the Battle of Faughart near Dundalk, where Edward was killed by Anglo-Irish forces: in a grisly touch, his head was severed, packed in salt and sent as a trophy to the King of England.

If Bruce military power outside Scotland therefore had severe limitations, Robert's diplomatic campaign produced more durable achievements. For international public opinion was energetically canvassed, and especially that presided over by the Church, with a letter in Latin to Pope John XXII, dated 6 April 1320, which sought the lifting of Robert's excommunication.

Drafted at Arbroath Abbey and signed by 51 Bruce supporters, this later came to be known as the Declaration of Arbroath, the most famous expression of independent Scottish nationhood ever composed.

> *'... from these countless evils we have been set free, by the help of Him who though He afflicts yet heals and restores, by our most tireless Prince, King and Lord, the Lord Robert. He, that his people and his heritage might be delivered out of the hands of our enemies, met toil and fatigue, hunger and peril, like another Maccabaeus or Joshua and bore them cheerfully. Him, too, divine providence, his right of succession according to our laws and customs which we shall maintain to the death, and the due consent and assent of us all have made our Prince and King. To him, as to the man by whom salvation has been wrought unto our people, we are bound both by law and by his merits that our freedom may be still maintained, and by him, come what may, we mean to stand.*
>
> *Yet if he should give up what he has begun, and agree to make us or our kingdom subject to the King of England or the English, we should exert ourselves at once to drive him out as our enemy and a subverter of his own rights and ours, and make some other man who was well able to defend us our King; for, as long as but a hundred of us remain alive, never will we on any conditions be brought under English rule. It is in truth not for glory, nor riches, nor honours that we are fighting, but for freedom – for that alone, which no honest man gives up but with life itself.'*
>
> The Declaration of Arbroath (1320)

This was an immensely powerful statement, simultaneously asserting fierce loyalty to Robert and yet also willingness to oppose him if he should cease to defend Scottish freedom from foreign domination. Its strong hint at some form of popular sovereignty has also impressed many modern observers, though it remains unclear how meaningful such a notion really was in the minds of a faction within the early 14th-century feudal elite whose grip on power it tried to advance.

The Declaration's contemporary impact is harder to assess. We know Robert's excommunication was rescinded. Peace negotiations also began with papal endorsement. But these dragged on, mainly because Robert insisted that his right to the throne be accepted, and in 1327 he renewed the French alliance and invaded northern England once more. Edward II's deposition and the regency of the young Edward III helped matters and in 1328 the Treaty of Edinburgh–Northampton was signed. This recognized both Robert's kingship and permanent Scottish independence while also fixing the border as it had been in Alexander III's time. Underpinning the deal, Edward III's six-year-old sister Joanna married Robert's son and heir David.

When on 7 June the following year Robert I died at Cardross, he left the kingdom more secure than it had been for more than four decades. Much more problematically, however, he also left it with a four-year-old successor.

Bruce in bits

As was common for many deceased kings, Bruce's mortal remains went their separate ways. The body was interred at Dunfermline but the heart was removed at Bruce's request (apparently in penance for his sacrilegious murder of Comyn) and taken on crusade against the Moors in Spain by Sir James Douglas. Although Douglas was killed the heart was retrieved and later buried at Melrose Abbey, where recent archaeological testing has confirmed it still lies.

The boy David

While his father spent many long years plotting to seize the crown, David II was fortunate to wear it from infancy and to do so for more than 40 years.

Yet his reign was not unruffled. Indeed, this was a desperately difficult period for Scotland. For through the first half of his reign David was initially a child incapable of governing in his own right; then in exile, unable to return to his own kingdom; and then finally a prisoner under Edward III's personal control.

Central to David's problems was the rapid unravelling of the Treaty of Edinburgh–Northampton, not least owing to the fact that Edward, a minor when it had been signed, considered it a shameful surrender that had unreasonably compromised his own sovereign privileges.

Other factors, however, also undermined the recent settlement. Above all there were many noble families with Scottish estates whom Robert I had disinherited after Bannockburn because their owners had demonstrated a primary allegiance to the King of England. This policy made sense to Robert, forcing a divided elite to clarify their ambiguous loyalties. These decisions had also been confirmed by the Treaty. Yet this left a body of wealthy and influential men in England with a keen interest in overturning that settlement and recovering their lost Scottish inheritances.

A further difficulty for David was the familiar one during a minority or interregnum of there being a Guardian exercising authority on the king's behalf. In the first instance this meant Thomas Randolph, Earl of Moray, but after his death in 1332 the role was taken by the Earl of Mar. The latter, however, fell victim to the first invasion of Scotland led by the supporters of Edward Balliol, the most prominent of the disinherited and son of the deposed King John (who had died in French exile in the year of Bannockburn).

Edward Balliol, whose demands for a return of his family's properties were backed by Edward III, landed on the Fife coast in July 1332. In a two-day engagement on 10 and 11 August, led by Balliol himself and by the titular Earl of Buchan, they defeated Mar's army on Dupplin Moor near Perth. The Guardian was killed, only ten days after his appointment, as was Sir Robert Keith, veteran of Bannockburn. This was a stark illustration of the continuing vulnerability of Scotland to English-backed interventions, for all the manifest military achievements of Robert I's reign.

A plague on both their houses

The worst human disaster ever to afflict Scotland hit in David's reign: the Black Death, initially called 'the foul death of England', crossed the border in 1349. Lack of contemporary records makes precise quantification impossible but between one-third and one-half of a population of only around one million may have died, many succumbing horribly within days of showing symptoms. By the 15th century, with Scotland, like other northern European countries, also suffering from falling average temperatures as the 'Medieval Warm Period' ended and agricultural conditions steadily deteriorated, the total population may have dropped to barely half a million. Shockingly, Scotland still may have got off lightly because bubonic plague, the pandemic's main component, was probably less virulent in the cool and damp climate.

The weakness of David II's position was further highlighted by Edward Balliol's coronation at Scone on 24 September as well as by the need to appoint a new Guardian, this time Sir Andrew Moray of Bothwell, the son of Wallace's celebrated colleague at Stirling Bridge who also just happened to be Robert I's brother-in-law and David's uncle. Yet even this only worked as a short-term expedient. Moray was captured at Roxburgh in April 1333 while attacking Balliol's supporters.

Captive in England, Moray was replaced as Guardian by Sir Archibald Douglas, half-brother of the Bruce's ally Sir James. Douglas, however, lasted no longer than his immediate predecessors, falling in battle at Halidon Hill near Berwick on 19 July 1333, beside other leading nobles like the Earl of Ross, when Balliol's forces, assisted by English archers, routed the Scots once more.

Understandably alarmed and with Balliol in command of much of southern Scotland, David's supporters despatched the boy-king into a protective French exile early in 1334. He would be out of the country for seven years, living at Château-Gaillard in Normandy, while Edward Balliol – King Edward in the eyes of his Scottish allies and of England – attempted to impose his will more widely on the kingdom that he had taken by force.

The staying power of the Bruces

Balliol's hold on Scotland, for all his ability to inflict decisive defeats in battle, was never either extensive or secure. He had genuine support in places like Fife, Galloway and the Borders. But much of the kingdom remained loyal to the Bruces and instinctively hostile to someone whose legitimacy as king was hotly disputed and who was in any case transparently dependent on English backing.

Worse, Balliol's actions, though surely unavoidable given the commitments and alliances on which his power rested, made it less likely that he would win over the doubters – or indeed successfully retain all of his original Scottish supporters.

A key problem, unsurprisingly, was Balliol's reliance on Edward III – just as the assumption back in 1292 that Edward's grandfather was pulling his strings had proven so disastrous for the credibility of Balliol's father. This relationship was confirmed by Balliol's explicit acceptance of the King of England as his overlord. Furthermore, Balliol conceded vital Scottish interests: great Border fortresses such as Roxburgh, strategic towns such as Dumfries and Berwick and the whole area of Lothian around Edinburgh were given to Edward III in 1334.

The precariousness of Balliol's authority was even clear in the wake of his apparently conclusive battlefield victories. For following Dupplin Moor and his coronation in 1332, he had been forced to flee half-clothed and take refuge in England, having been surprised and attacked by nobles loyal to David II at Annan in Dumfriesshire.

The 1333 campaign that culminated in his triumph at Halidon Hill was again followed by widespread flouting of his demands across Scotland. Yet another invasion by Edward III in 1335 led to the ravaging of the countryside around Glasgow and Perth but, with the Scottish resistance again avoiding pitched battles, no effective means of imposing control presented itself. In short, a strange kind of stalemate existed.

With Sir Andrew Moray released from English detention and re-appointed Guardian, the Scots, with French encouragement, attempted to negotiate peace with England. Although some were prepared to recognize Balliol if he accepted David as his heir, David himself rejected this, a chain of events that led Edward III to re-invade, now sending no fewer than three separate armies to attack towns as far distant as Elgin, Aberdeen and Glasgow.

This was an important turning point, however, for it led Philip VI of France to commit openly to supporting the Scots. Edward prudently returned to England to defend his kingdom, leaving Moray and other Bruce supporters to regain almost complete control of Scotland by 1338.

In June 1341 it was finally possible for David II, now 18 years of age, to come back to Scotland and to begin governing in his own right.

A king incarcerated

David's return, however, was by no means the end of his troubles.

His kingdom was war-torn and divided. Many nobles had sided with Balliol and some southern districts even had rival Scottish and English administrations. Royal revenues had also been decimated by conflict and by years of non-collection, while David himself was a young and inexperienced ruler needing to establish his own authority from scratch. Nor was this all. For a combination of continuing tensions with England and the consequences of the French alliance would soon lead to David's darkest hour.

This occurred in 1346 when, in support of France, David, probably not without some reluctance, mounted an ill-judged invasion of England. The brief campaign, starting with the usual harrying of the north and the sacking of Hexham Priory, culminated in the Scots' defeat at Neville's Cross near Durham on 17 October, where an English army commanded by Lord Ralph Neville and Lord Henry Percy destroyed David's force, killing the Earl of Moray and capturing the Scottish king.

Carried off to England, David spent the next 11 years in captivity, in London and at Windsor and then latterly at Odiham Castle in Hampshire. Not until October 1357, and the payment of a ransom of 100,000 marks by the Scottish nobility under the terms of a new treaty signed at Berwick, was David in a position to return to Scotland and reclaim his throne.

Yet the payment of such a large sum proved problematic. It was obviously humiliating. It was also financially beyond Scotland's means, forcing David, the son and heir of the victor of Bannockburn, into a remarkable expedient. For over the next few years David continued negotiations with Edward, which had clearly begun during his captivity, with the aim of having the ransom annulled in return for making either Edward or one of Edward's sons (other than the next King of England, so that the separateness of the two kingdoms would be preserved) his own successor as King of Scots.

It is probable that David, who was childless, knew that this scheme would be unacceptable to most of the Scottish elite – and in particular that it would be opposed by the supporters of his current heir, his powerful and well-connected nephew Robert the Steward, the son of the Bruce's daughter Marjory. And David's doubts were fully justified.

The Scots Parliament rejected the proposal in 1364. But David continued his negotiations in secret, seeking at least to reschedule the ransom. Fortunately war with France remained Edward's priority and in 1369 he conceded a reduced payment from David, a mere 56,000 marks.

David's second period in residence as King of Scots was characterized by his attempts, never quite successful, to restore royal authority over a kingdom in which absentee monarchy and the related emergence of potent rival sources of power were established political facts. Robert the Steward, his lieutenant during David's long periods out of the country and his close kinsman and likely successor, enjoyed immense prestige and influence. So too did the Douglas family, staunch allies of Bruce kingship but also an ambitious and assertive landed dynasty in their own right.

David recognized the realities of having to work with rather than against such weighty individuals when he granted the Steward the earldom of Strathearn (the previous holder of the title had fallen at Neville's Cross) and created a new earldom in the name of the Douglases. David tried to balance these unavoidably powerful influences, however, by advancing other families as his own personal allies, notably the Erskines and the Drummonds. He even took Margaret Drummond as his second wife in 1364 (divorcing her in 1370, still without having produced a direct heir).

Yet the last decade of David's reign was nonetheless marked by tensions between the king and his over-mighty magnates. Indeed, both the Steward and the Douglases were implicated in a rebellion in 1363, obscure in origin but probably arising out of their determination to protect their own families' positions from new royal favourites. But David was in no position to punish the perpetrators. That he simply accepted their submission and re-confirmed Robert's right of succession merely underlines the weakness of the King of Scots in relation to his most important subjects.

When David died suddenly at Edinburgh Castle on 22 February 1371 the crown fell straightforwardly into the lap of the Steward, David's 55-year-old nephew, as Robert II. The Bruces' kingship, for all Robert I's plotting and scheming, had lasted not 70 years. Scotland would now be ruled by a new dynasty whose name was a reminder of the hereditary stewardship their ancestors had held: the House of Stewart.

Fact check

1 Who was William de Lamberton?
   a Robert Bruce's brother
   b Bishop of Glasgow
   c Earl of Carrick
   d Bishop of St Andrews

2 What was 'Warwolf'?
   a catapult
   b siege engine
   c troop carrier
   d broadsword

3 Who was John de Soules?
   a Earl of March
   b Guardian of Scotland
   c Bishop of Glasgow
   d Wallace's cousin

4 Where did Edward I of England hold a Round Table?
   a Edinburgh
   b Stirling
   c Falkirk
   d Linlithgow

5 Where did Robert Bruce kill John Comyn?
   a Dumfries
   b Bannockburn
   c Arran
   d Menteith

6 Who crowned Bruce as King of Scots?
   a John de Soules
   b Isabella MacDuff
   c Robert Wishart
   d William de Lamberton

7 Name the English commander of Stirling Castle
   a Aymer de Valence
   b Hugh de Cressingham
   c Sir Phillip Mowbray
   d Earl of Surrey

8 When was the Declaration of Arbroath issued?
   a 1314
   b 1320
   c 1326
   d 1330

Dig Deeper

G. W. S. Barrow, *Robert Bruce and the Community of the Realm of Scotland* (Edinburgh, 1976).

Edward J. Cowan, *For Freedom Alone* (East Linton, 2003).

Fiona Watson, *Under the Hammer: Edward I and Scotland 1286–1307* (East Linton, 1998).

Colm McNamee, *The Wars of the Bruces* (East Linton, 1997).

The late medieval kingdom

The House of Stewart

It is worth pausing at this point to consider the significance of the Stewarts' dynastic triumph.

Not only is this useful because Robert II's family would eventually rule England and Great Britain too. It is also important because their rise and rise – from immigrant Breton landholders and government servants to Scottish royalty by 1371 – tells us a great deal about how politics and society had changed over recent centuries, as well as about the ways in which it had not.

Above all Robert's accession completed a process begun under the Canmores in the 11th century. In particular, like the two Bruces before him, it reflected the transformation of the kingdom's leaders. Once overwhelmingly Gaelic in heritage and culture, Scotland's elite was increasingly dominated by those with French or English origins. Inevitably this had knock-on effects for wider society, the most important being the beginning of the retreat of the Gaelic language in everyday usage and its gradual displacement outside the Highlands by the version of English we know as Scots.

This re-configured elite, however, did not bring greater peace and stability. It is, after all, unlikely that high-achieving dynasties, their members propelled onwards and upwards by exceptional levels of ambition and ruthlessness, will suddenly decide to live in harmony just because one kinsman in particular has finally reached the summit. Stewart Scotland, at least as much as any other medieval European society, demonstrates the essential truth of this observation.

Family strife

Robert II's reign began with a clear warning of the challenges to come, with William, Earl of Douglas, leading armed resistance to the coronation. Afterwards, Robert recognized the need to combine entrenching the Stewarts' new-found domination with sensitive treatment of powerful rivals. His daughter, for example, was married off to Douglas's son. The rebel earl was also given control of much of southern Scotland. Robert's own sons, meanwhile, acquired major earldoms and the command of important castles. Some of these were taken from others but, in further evidence of Robert's astute balancing act, substantial compensation was generally awarded.

Appreciation of another long-term problem, and a desire to stop a recurrence of the disastrous uncertainty following Alexander III's demise, saw Robert have the Scots Parliament pre-determine the succession. In 1373 it was agreed that precedence should be given strictly to male claimants descended through other males. Robert also sought to integrate the distant regions. A daughter married the Lord of the Isles, creating new bonds between the crown and the Gaelic Highlands, while his young son David was given the earldom of Caithness.

Robert's greatest problem, however, could not be so neatly solved. For many Scottish landowners remained loyal to the King of England and castles like Berwick and Roxburgh also remained firmly in English hands. Robert's clever response was to encourage reliable Border noblemen to harry the forces of occupation while denying official responsibility and avoiding large-scale confrontations. Incremental gains were the reward, like the recovery of Annandale in 1376 and Teviotdale in 1384.

Yet Robert also suffered greatly from his own strategy for extending the Stewarts' power. His fourth son, Alexander, Earl of Buchan, used violence and intimidation in the north-east in a campaign of outrageous insolence that peaked shortly after Robert's death in 1390 in the infamous sacking of Elgin, its cathedral and other churches. Remembered as 'the Wolf of Badenoch', this infamous prince was a complete liability, undermining Robert's policy of trusting his own family to exert Stewart authority and at the same time demonstrating the king's inability to exercise effective central control.

Robert's unwillingness to engage in open war against England also gradually undercut support. These signs of weakness were what probably lay behind the decision of the king's council in November 1384 to appoint Robert's son and heir John, Earl of Carrick, as lieutenant. Carrick's seizure of power, though, was brief. Although his closer involvement in the Anglo-French conflict delivered the famous Scottish victory at Otterburn in August 1388, the death of his ally the Earl of Douglas in the battle provoked a struggle for the Douglas estates which was won by Sir Archibald Douglas (the 'Black Douglas'), with whom Carrick's relationship was strained.

> 'It fell about the Lammas tide,
> When the muir-men win their hay,
> The doughty Earl of Douglas rode
> Into England, to catch a prey.'
> *The Battle of Otterburn* (c. 1390)

This Douglas, backed by Robert II's younger son, Robert, Earl of Fife, sidelined Carrick, triggering Fife's own elevation to the lieutenancy and bringing about Buchan's marginalization as Fife also took control in the north-east. Robert II, however, did not long outlast the dynastic strife. He died in April 1390 and was buried at Scone where Carrick was duly crowned.

In name only

Carrick's reign was again unsettled. The new king even changed his name: born John, unhelpfully recalling 'Toom Tabard', he thought it better to rule as Robert III. Yet he experienced the same challenges as his predecessors.

Like Robert II, he was marginalized by powerful magnates and undermined by disobedient family members. As a result, for much of the time he was unable to exercise full regal authority.

The most important aspect of Robert III's kingship, as of so many previous Scottish monarchs, was his continual struggle to assert himself. In some ways he was successful. He achieved control over foreign policy. He also checked the excessive influence of his brother Fife and the 'Black Douglas' by the old device of advancing a rival, in this case the Earl of Angus (the 'Red Douglas'). But Robert's rule was ultimately marred by family in-fighting. His son David, initially Earl of Carrick and then Duke of Rothesay, was as ambitious as Fife, who had now become Duke of Albany. Accordingly, it was no surprise when in January 1399 the king's council handed power to Rothesay as lieutenant for three years.

Conflict resolution 1396-style

Few episodes better illustrate the normalization of extreme violence within and between Scottish kinship groupings than the Battle of the North Inch, fought at Perth in September 1396. The combatants were Clan Chattan (a federation led by MacKintoshes) and 'Clan Kay' (unidentified but probably Camerons). Unwilling to end a now-obscure feud by negotiation, 30 men from each side were instead told to fight to the death in front of King Robert III and a crowd of eager spectators. In this combination of trial by combat and large-scale sporting event, 19 of the victorious Chattans were killed before their sole surviving opponent swam to safety across the Tay.

Rivalry between Rothesay and Albany dominated what remained of Robert III's unhappy reign. As lieutenant Rothesay inevitably challenged his uncle's powerbase in central Scotland. Once his term of office ended, however, he was incarcerated by Albany at Falkland Castle in Fife, where he allegedly died of starvation – foul play by Albany and the 'Black Douglas' is virtually certain – in March 1402.

Appointed lieutenant in Rothesay's place, Albany now controlled affairs. It was in this desperate situation that Robert's 11-year-old heir James was first sent as a figurehead to challenge Albany's authority in the Douglas-dominated Borders and then, when forced to retreat, obliged to flee to the Bass Rock in the Firth of Forth. It was from there that James attempted to reach France by ship, a voyage interrupted off the Yorkshire coast by English vessels who consigned him to the custody of Henry IV of England.

When the ailing Robert III died on 4 April 1406, he already knew that his successor was in the hands of the kingdom's enemies.

Another prisoner

When we think of the first part of the reign of James I of Scotland it is even more than with the similar experiences of David II a matter of tracing the implications of absentee monarchy through two parallel stories: one is the tale of a King of Scots in English custody; the other relates Scottish developments, a narrative mainly shaped by the ambitions of those running the kingdom in his enforced absence.

Prison works?

James's English captivity may have had its compensations. For from his capture in 1406 until he was finally crowned at Scone in May 1424, he greatly improved his education and developed many accomplishments that, when the Renaissance was spreading across Europe from its Italian roots, the most sophisticated rulers were increasingly beginning to display. Ultimately James came to embody this new ideal of cultured and cultivated kingship. An able writer, poet and musician, this peculiar royal literary career in exile was crowned by a work known as *The Kingis Quair*, a semi-autobiographical poem which reflects philosophically upon life's uncertainties and consolations and shows the influence of James's English contemporaries, above all Geoffrey Chaucer. This text is now numbered among the greatest achievements of medieval Scottish literature.

Politics inside Scotland proved particularly challenging. The Duke of Albany, James's uncle who had already had James's brother David killed, ruled as governor (not regent) until his death in 1420. Albany was then succeeded as both duke and governor by his own son Murdoch Stewart.

The elder Albany's tenure was marked by forceful attempts to challenge the growing power of the Lord of the Isles. He also made periodic efforts to defend Scottish interests against the English, including besieging Berwick in 1417 and commanding a force sent to France two years later. Albany even had the distinction of overseeing the foundation of the kingdom's first university at St Andrews, established under Bishop William Wardlaw in 1410.

Whether Albany tried very hard to bring about James's release is, however, unclear. After all, it was scarcely in his interests to do so. James's release only came about after the elder Albany's death and because he had become close to Henry V, accompanying him on French campaigns and even marrying one of Henry's cousins, Joan Beaufort.

The younger Albany's life, as well as his rule, was then cut short by James's return. On 24 May 1425 he and two of his sons were executed at Stirling by the newly crowned king, having been convicted of treason. James was assisted by the fact that the Albany faction, strong supporters of the French alliance, were weakened both numerically and politically by the defeat of a Scottish army at Verneuil-en-Perche in August 1424. James also had a power base among Scots who had visited him in England, which helped him re-assert his authority on his return.

James's subsequent reign, beginning when he was already 30 years of age, was broadly successful. Diplomatically he plotted an independent course, allying with France in 1428 (and betrothing his daughter to the French dauphin) but avoiding having to wage war by also signing a truce with England. In addition, enemies and rivals at home felt the full force of James's authority. He clipped the wings of the Albanys' allies, such as the Douglases, and reined in traditionally disobedient regional leaders, like Alexander, Lord of the Isles, defeated and forced to submit at Holyrood Abbey in August 1429. So effective was James initially that for some time there was little meaningful opposition.

Continuing tensions within the Stewart family itself, however, eventually proved James's undoing. This time the problem was the direct legacy of Robert II's complicated private life. In 1348 Robert had belatedly married his mistress Elizabeth Mure, James's grandmother, in an attempt, endorsed by Parliament in 1371, to legitimize their nine children, including the future Robert III. But after Elizabeth's death the king had married Euphemia, daughter of the Earl of Ross. This marriage had produced a further two sons. It was therefore always open to Euphemia's male offspring to claim the crown as Robert's descendants through the only unambiguously legitimate line.

Down the drain

On the night of 20 February 1437 James I's lodgings in the Blackfriars' monastery at Perth were attacked. He attempted to escape through a sewer but, unfortunately, he had recently lost tennis balls down it and ordered it blocked up. The desperate king was duly cornered and stabbed to death. The assassins were under orders from Walter Stewart, Earl of Atholl and son of Robert II by Euphemia Ross, who subsequently endured three days of hideous torture before his execution – far worse even than the standard butchery of hanging, drawing and quartering – in the hope of deterring anyone else from daring to kill a King of Scots.

When this dispute caused James's murder, his own son James, not yet seven, inherited in the most difficult of circumstances. The resulting minority, necessitating yet another prolonged Guardianship, gave Scotland only further instability and factional infighting.

The fiery king

The early years of James II, nicknamed 'fiery face' because of a red birthmark on his cheek, were dominated by shifting alliances among those who surrounded the young king and sought to govern in his name.

In this situation the Douglases, whose interests had been closely intertwined with those of the Bruces and the Stewarts since Robert I's time, were inevitably prominent. It was thus no surprise when Archibald Douglas, 5th Earl of Douglas, became lieutenant-general and regent. But after Douglas's untimely death from a fever in 1439, things deteriorated rapidly as various rivals scrambled to replace him.

William, Lord Crichton, the Chancellor, exercised considerable influence. So too did Sir Alexander Livingston, warden of Stirling Castle where James resided. Both wanted to curtail the power of the Black Douglases and to advance their own families' interests. The 6th Earl of Douglas and his brother were duly murdered. A co-conspirator was James Douglas, Earl of

Avondale, great-uncle of the leading victim whose title he then conveniently inherited as 7th Earl.

Guess who's coming to dinner?

Invited to supper with James II in Edinburgh Castle on 24 November 1440, William Douglas, Earl of Douglas, and his younger brother David, suddenly found a black bull's head, the symbol of death, presented at the table. They were swiftly overpowered, subjected to a brief mock-trial and beheaded by Crichton and Livingston in front of the presumably horrified 10-year-old king. The grisly episode came to be known as the 'Black Dinner'.

This barbaric act was typical of the mixture of extreme violence and naked ambition among near relations that characterized the mid-15th-century elite. But what happened next was no less predictable. The Livingstons made common cause with William, 8th Earl of Douglas, Avondale's son, and turned against Crichton, in a brazen double-cross.

The chronic factionalism was not ended even by James's growing independence as an adult. Understandably he resented the Black Douglases' domination. James's decision to confront the 8th Earl at Stirling Castle on 22 February 1452, accusing him of plotting to seize power, ended with a characteristic royal loss of temper and several of James's servants helping stab Douglas to death. Allegedly 26 wounds were counted on the corpse.

Subsequently, James gradually reduced the Douglases' overbearing power. So potent had been their influence, especially in the south, that James proceeded carefully, sometimes removing the properties and titles of major offenders, at other times rewarding and trying to win over their allies. By 1455 the 9th Earl was in English exile, leaving James effectively in control of Scotland for the first time.

Unfortunately his reign, despite all these intriguing signs of a royal assertiveness not matched for more than a century, came to an unexpectedly early end. Besieging Roxburgh Castle on 3 August 1460 in an attempt to remove the last vestiges of the English occupation, he died when a large cannon exploded beside him. Killed in a ball of flames that superstitious contemporaries considered had been foretold by his fiery birthmark, James was just 29 when he was laid to rest at Holyrood.

Like father, like son

James II's son and heir, James III, experienced even greater difficulties.

He inherited as a minor: historians disagree over his date of birth but he was certainly not yet nine when succeeding. Before reaching adulthood his family relationships had deteriorated to such an extent that his reign saw continuous instability. His attempts to assert authority and reduce the power of his leading subjects were therefore doomed from the start. That James III would die young and violently – at the hands of near-relations and rebellious magnates – ought to have surprised no one.

Endemic factionalism, a problem exacerbated by the tendency for different groups to jockey for position in the absence of a strong adult ruler, was vividly displayed during James's early years. Mary of Guelders, his Dutch mother, initially presided as regent, and helped Scotland temporarily reclaim Berwick from England by supporting the Lancastrians during the Wars of the Roses. But following her death in 1463 a number of regents shared responsibility, including James Kennedy, respected Bishop of St Andrews, who died in 1465, and his brother Gilbert, Lord Kennedy, both of them grandsons of Robert III.

Soon, however, power fell into the hands of Robert, Lord Boyd. A descendant of one of Robert I's close allies, in 1466 he managed to abduct James into the custody of his brother Sir Alexander Boyd and persuade Parliament to make him sole Guardian. So confident was Boyd that he even had his own son created Earl of Arran and married him swiftly to James's sister. The teenaged king, meanwhile, was betrothed to Margaret of Denmark. Orkney and Shetland were pledged to Scotland against a dowry never subsequently paid: perhaps unintentionally, Boyd had extended the kingdom to the Northern Isles.

As had happened with his father, however, the adult James III reacted strongly against these encroachments on his power. By 1469 Sir Alexander Boyd had been executed for treason and Lord Boyd had fled. Yet there was little sign that James knew how to exploit his new-found authority. He sought an English alliance, underpinned by a plan to marry his second son James, Earl of Ross. But this outraged most of the Scottish nobility, adamantly hostile to England. James's taxes, applied rapaciously to people not accustomed to such exactions, also damaged his relationship with vested interests.

> 'It is ordained, advised and concluded by our sovereign lord and his three estates assembled in this present parliament, that peace [should] be made with England if it can be had with honour [and] without inconvenience, and that the alliance and marriage previously appointed be observed and kept in all points by our sovereign lord, if [Edward IV], king of England, will do the same for his part...'
>
> Acts of the Scottish Parliament (1482)

James III's greatest difficulties, though, were with his own immediate family – especially his brothers Alexander, Duke of Albany, and John, Earl of Mar. The latter died suspiciously in 1480 and Albany fled to France to escape questionable charges. There he joined with Edward IV, who had also fallen out with James, and took part in the English invasion of 1482: this damaged James's prestige by re-taking Berwick. It was during this campaign that James, leading an army to defend his kingdom, instead found himself arrested at Lauder Bridge by disaffected nobles and imprisoned in Edinburgh Castle while Albany established his own government under English protection.

The king, though, was lucky in his allies. The Earl of Huntly, married to James's aunt, played a leading part in successfully challenging Albany's regime which many Stewart loyalists could not stomach. Albany was expelled and James's power restored by 1485. But his underlying unpopularity remained.

James continued to make overtures to England, annoying many Scots. He rewarded his own favourites (or 'familiars'), like the notorious Thomas Cochrane, lynched by James's victorious enemies at Lauder Bridge. He ignored the interests of many great magnates, such as Huntly, whose support went largely unrewarded. Worst of all, he seemed uninterested in traversing the kingdom to administer justice – a key obligation for a medieval king.

Contemporaries responded to weak government in ways that made sense within a feudal society. The vulnerable signed 'bonds of manrent' with the powerful to provide military service in return for protection. Individual landowners also increasingly built defensible 'tower houses'. James's inadequacies were clearly at odds with what was expected – and demanded – of a King of Scots. Many of his most prominent subjects must have heaved a sigh of relief when news came of this divisive figure's death at the Battle of Sauchieburn, fought close by the hallowed field of Bannockburn, on 11 June 1488.

Key idea: Tower Houses

Tower houses appealed to feuding late-medieval landowners' interest in fortified habitations. Self-contained with high stone walls built on a narrow square or L- or Z-shaped base, with battlements, gun-loops and other defensive features, hundreds were eventually built, like Scotstarvit in Fife and Affleck Castle in Angus. By 1600, however, with the use of gunpowder and siege cannons widespread, they were militarily obsolescent, reflecting only a craze for imposing-looking residences that declared their occupants' ancestral status and power.

James in fact died as he had lived, warring against powerful noblemen aligned with elements of his own family – in this case his eldest son, James, Duke of Rothesay, a 15-year-old whom the king, in a fatal misjudgement, had marginalized in favour of his brother the Earl of Ross.

Pride before a fall

James IV, the beneficiary of Sauchieburn, was the greatest king since Robert I. Arguably he was also among the most successful rulers of medieval Scotland.

He took the finest traits of his Stewart predecessors and blended them with his own unique strengths. The result was a ruler with political judgement, personal bravery and genuine charisma as well as considerable intellectual abilities and cultural sophistication.

Like James I, he was a Renaissance prince – though his contributions were of even wider and more lasting benefit. Scottish printing started when the bookseller Andrew Millar and the merchant Walter Chapman received letters patent in 1507 to set up shop in Edinburgh's Cowgate: the first books, mainly poems and including Blind Harry's *Wallace*, appeared the next year. James himself was also impressively multilingual, speaking German, French, Latin, Italian and Flemish, as well as Gaelic and Scots.

By an Act of Parliament in 1496 he commanded the nobility to have their sons educated in Latin and law – the first of several measures by Scottish governments to improve literacy and raise formal educational standards (and in the process undermining Gaelic-speaking oral culture among the Highland elite). His great Bishop of Aberdeen, William Elphinstone, founded that town's first university in 1495, naming it King's College: at a time when England had only two universities, Scotland, with Glasgow having been added to St Andrews during James II's reign, already had three.

Most importantly, a group of talented poets known as the 'Makars' (i.e. makers or creators) were associated with James's court. They included William Dunbar, responsible for the deep reflection on mortality *Timor Mortis Conturbat Me* ('The fear of death affrights me') and the obscene and humorous *The Flyting of Dunbar and Kennedie* (whose reputation spread rapidly after Millar and Chapman published it), and Gavin Douglas, Bishop of Dunkeld, whose magnificent Scots version of Virgil's *Aeneid* was the first complete vernacular translation of a classical masterpiece undertaken in northern Europe.

Another of James's enduring legacies was his enthusiasm for the latest architectural fashions.

Crowned heads

Visitors to St Giles's Cathedral in Edinburgh and King's College Chapel, Aberdeen, should look up at the unusual stone crowns that take the place of conventional spires or steeples on the main towers. They were constructed in James IV's time and capture not only the Renaissance architectural exuberance of the reign but also the sense of growing royal authority and Scottish cultural self-confidence. A similar feature at St Michael's in Linlithgow, another church with strong Stewart associations, was dismantled in 1821 for fear of collapse, but in 1964 a lightweight timber and aluminium crown replaced it.

It is to this that we owe Scotland's great Renaissance royal buildings at Edinburgh, Stirling, Falkland and Linlithgow: Stirling in particular, where James had several structures erected that survive to this day, remains powerful testimony to his commitment to placing his kingdom, previously a cultural backwater, closer to the cutting-edge of contemporary European style. He also built the royal palace of Holyroodhouse, adjacent to the old abbey, which would be the main focus for Scottish politics and government not only in the 16th century but also, once again, in the 21st.

James's political conduct was notably well-considered – dramatically so after his father's ineptitude. He won a far better reputation for active kingship, delivering justice firmly and fairly throughout the country. In 1493 he was even able to revoke the Lordship of the Isles, thereafter in the crown's possession: symbolizing James's unprecedented control, the last independent holder of the title, John MacDonald of Islay, was exiled to the Lowlands.

James also maintained acceptable relations with England for most of his reign, signing the Treaty of Perpetual Peace with Henry VII in 1502 but also creating new dockyards and developing Scotland's navy: in 1511 the famous *Great Michael* was launched – at 240 feet long and displacing 1,000 tons, Europe's largest ship.

Given James's wisdom and prudence, it is ironic that his reign should have ended prematurely after a single bad decision. With the outbreak of a new Anglo-French war, he agreed to invade England under the terms of the French alliance. This was a catastrophic error. Confronted by the Earl of Surrey's army at Flodden Field in Northumberland on 9 September 1513, the Scots, although more numerous, were utterly routed, over-confidently advancing across boggy terrain and being felled en masse by English arrows and cannonballs at a distance and then by English billhooks at close quarters. Between 5,000 and 10,000 Scots perished.

Nine earls – Argyll, Bothwell, Caithness, Cassilis, Crawford, Errol, Lennox, Montrose and Rothes – were killed. So too were the Archbishop of St Andrews, the bishops of Caithness and the Isles, two abbots, the French ambassador, and numerous other noblemen, their heirs, clan chieftains and lairds.

James himself lay dead on the battlefield. It was the most one-sided battle yet fought between the two old enemies, conducted on a scale hitherto not seen. Not just a king's reign but also a kingdom's elite – long lamented as the 'flowers of the forest' – had been destroyed in an afternoon.

> 'Dool and wae for the order sent oor lads tae the Border!
> The English for ance, by guile wan the day,
> The Flooers o' the Forest, that fought aye the foremost,
> The pride o' oor land lie cauld in the clay.'
> Jean Elliot, *The Flowers of the Forest* (1756)

The waning of the Middle Ages?

Historians disagree over when the medieval period ended.

1492 and Columbus's 'discovery' of the New World is a strong candidate if lasting global impact is the test. 1453, the fall of Constantinople to the Turks, terminating the eastern Roman

Empire, has its advocates. 1517, when Luther initiated the Reformation, is another plausible contender. And in a British context there is 1485, the year of the Battle of Bosworth Field, whose victors, the Tudor dynasty, ended feudal challenges to royal power and created the modern English state.

For Scotland, however, no such convenient date exists. 1513 saw the unnecessary deaths of a king and much of the kingdom's leadership. But the turbulence of the previous two centuries meant that the resulting minority, regency and disorder were scarcely novel. Nor did new kinds of politics and government emerge: 16th-century Scotland remained a feudal society prone to periodic and sometimes successful aristocratic assaults on royal authority.

Yet this is to miss an important feature of the next 30 years. For key trends that would dominate for another 300 years, and help define modern Scottish history, now began to impose themselves – albeit for reasons largely unconnected with James IV's demise.

James V was just 17 months old when he succeeded. His mother Margaret Tudor, sister of Henry VIII, served as regent for a year until she married the Earl of Angus (a Red Douglas). The role was then taken on until 1524 by John Stewart, Duke of Albany, his father's cousin, the French-born son of Alexander, Duke of Albany, and James's own heir at that stage.

The regency proved contentious. Partly the problem was personal, with rival individuals seeking advantage. But another cause of tension was the hostility of Angus towards Albany, who represented French influence in Scotland. The result was conflict.

Margaret's regency was ended by Albany's seizure of all James IV's children in 1514, forcing her to flee to London. Angus and Margaret's relationship, however, deteriorated, and she subsequently made peace with Albany. In 1524, when James V was 12, Margaret had Albany removed, but Angus was able to persuade Parliament to appoint him Guardian. After 1525 Angus was effectively running Scotland, helped by James Beaton, Archbishop of St Andrews, until James escaped, sided with his mother and had Angus exiled to England in 1528.

Throughout the first half of James V's reign Scotland therefore suffered from the same chronic factionalism and internal family feuding that had scarred James III's time. Yet after freeing himself from Angus's control there was actually a greater resemblance to James IV. He was a Renaissance prince: he built imaginatively at the royal palaces; he patronized playwright Sir David Lyndsay of the Mount and composer Robert Carver; he even played the lute.

James also faced down challenges from the outlying regions. In 1532 he inaugurated the College of Justice, a central judicial institution to develop and administer laws. James himself toured Dumfriesshire, Galloway and Ayrshire, overseeing the trial and execution of outlaws such as Johnnie Armstrong of Staplegordon and of notorious 'Reivers' such as William Cockburn of Henderland. In the Highlands congenitally disobedient figures such as the MacDonald and Maclean chieftains submitted rather than face the consequences from a determined monarch.

Key idea: Reivers

Reivers (from *rēafian*, Anglo-Saxon for 'to steal') were armed and mounted raiders who exploited the remoteness and weak law enforcement of the disputed Border zone to engage in robbery and extortion. The modern English term 'blackmail' derives from their distinctive practice of demanding money from victims to halt further raids. In a mainly pastoral region, livestock-rustling was a particular reiving speciality.

James's drive to strengthen royal authority was also reflected in his religious policies. This was an increasingly critical area, with the Reformation proving so divisive not only between nations but also, perhaps especially, within individual European societies. Scotland, with strong cultural, educational and intellectual ties to France, Germany, England and the Low Countries, where Protestant activities were concentrated, was unsurprisingly exposed to the new ideas from an early stage.

James's response to Protestantism was severe, reinforced by his personal piety and devotion to Catholic orthodoxy. There were executions. Patrick Hamilton, for example, a Lutheran who returned from France and Holland, was tried by Beaton and burned at St Andrews in 1528. Six years later James personally presided over the incineration of two more heretics outside Edinburgh Castle.

James also dealt confidently and competently with England and France – with lasting significance. He maintained the Auld Alliance and in 1537 and 1538 married two French wives in quick succession (the first had died tragically on arrival in Edinburgh). The second was Mary of Guise, a favourite of the King of France, and she bore James two sons, who died in infancy, and one daughter, Mary. Peace with England was encouraged by his English mother and it was only after her death in 1541 that, as Anglo-French relations cooled and Henry VIII's attacks on Catholicism repelled the devout King of Scots, James renewed hostilities.

As for his father this was to prove fatal. The Scots were beaten at Solway Moss on 24 November 1542. James, not present, duly took to his bed in Falkland Palace. Evidently seriously ill as well as just depressed, he died unexpectedly on 14 December, aged just 30.

James was succeeded by Mary, just six days old. As queen she would be overwhelmed by the violent social and political forces the Reformation unleashed. And ironically, because of her own intimate connections with the French court, she would unintentionally trigger Scotland's rupture with France and its reconciliation – even its eventual royal union – with England.

This, above all, is why we can say that with the dramatic reign of Mary, Queen of Scots, the modern history of Scotland begins.

Fact check

1 Which dynasty succeeded the Bruces in 1371?
  a Stewart
  b Canmore
  c Plantagenet
  d Tudor

2 Who was 'the Wolf of Badenoch'?
  a the Earl of Buchan
  b the Red Comyn
  c the Black Douglas
  d Robert II

3 Who won the Battle of the North Inch?
  a England
  b the Camerons
  c the Duke of Albany
  d Clan Chattan

4 Who ordered the murder of King James I?
  a Walter Stewart, Earl of Atholl
  b the Duke of Rothesay
  c King Henry VI of England
  d Elizabeth Mure

5 Who was called 'fiery face'?
  a the Earl of Atholl
  b the Earl of Douglas
  c King James II
  d Lord Crichtoun

6 Where was King James III killed?
  a Perth
  b Sauchieburn
  c Aberdeen
  d Huntly

7 What was a 'Makar'?

   a a poet

   b a painter

   c a priest

   d a soldier

8 Where was King James IV killed?

   a Stirling

   b Perth

   c Falkland Palace

   d Flodden Field

9 Which Lutheran convert was burned in 1528?

   a George Wishart

   b Patrick Hamilton

   c John Knox

   d Andrew Melville

Dig Deeper

Stephen Boardman, *The Early Stewart Kings* (East Linton, 1996).

Michael Brown, *James I* (Edinburgh, 1994).

Christine McGladdery, *James II* (Edinburgh, 1990).

Norman MacDougall, *James III* (Edinburgh, 1992).

Norman MacDougall, *James IV* (Edinburgh, 1989).

Jamie Cameron, *James V* (East Linton, 1998).

Reformation and rebellion

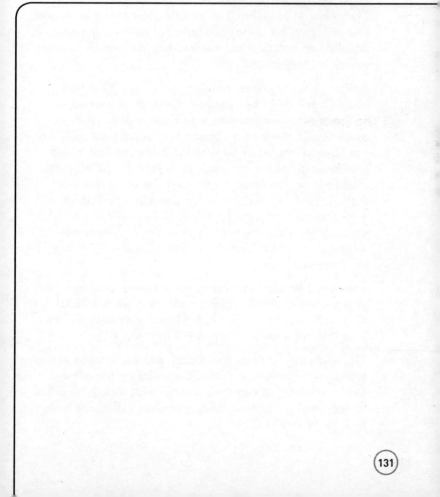

Two queens and two regencies

Along with Mac Bethad who won and lost Scotland's crown and 'Bonnie Prince Charlie' who failed to reclaim it, Mary, Queen of Scots, is one of the three best-known figures in Scottish history. A heroic royal trinity, they were elevated to tragic victimhood because their own flawed characters, along with cruel misfortune, ultimately swept them to defeat.

Mary's early reign was once more, as so often with the unlucky Stewarts (or Stuarts, as they were re-spelled under the influence of Mary's French associates), dominated by minority and regency. For 12 years Scotland was ruled in her name by James Hamilton, 2nd Earl of Arran, James II's great-grandson and Mary's heir. In 1554, her French mother, Mary of Guise, became Queen Regent. But Guise's rule provoked growing opposition. A crisis of authority therefore existed when Mary finally came to govern in her own right.

Religion was the gravest problem. Arran was Protestant, and on 1 July 1543 he signed the Treaty of Greenwich, restoring peaceable relations with England and agreeing that Mary should in due course marry her cousin, Henry VIII's son Edward (the future Edward VI). Henry, of course, had recently imposed the Reformation, while Edward was being raised a pious Protestant. In Scotland, however, closer ties with England, especially ones creating a joint monarchy, were predictably unpopular. Cardinal Beaton, who backed the traditional alliance with Catholic France, also opposed a scheme that would clearly have placed Scotland decisively in the Protestant camp.

Beaton had already tried unsuccessfully (based on a forged will of James V) to claim the regency and was closely associated with the Solway Moss debacle. But he was eventually able to have Parliament annul the treaty late in 1543.

This understandably angered Henry VIII. But worse was to follow. Arran embraced Catholicism, aligning himself with Beaton and Mary of Guise. Henry responded with the so-called 'Rough Wooing', applying military pressure to force the Scots to fulfil the treaty's terms.

There were successive invasions. In 1544 the Earl of Hertford attacked Edinburgh. Three years later, on 10 September 1547, 'Black Saturday', to the east of the capital, the Scots were defeated at Pinkie, again by an army commanded by Hertford (now Duke of Somerset and the infant Edward VI's protector). In 1548 the English captured Haddington, devastating the surrounding countryside. All the while Mary of Guise kept the young Queen of Scots safe by moving her from fortress to fortress.

England's aggression, rather than weakening the Scots' resolve, had the opposite effect. Accordingly on 7 July 1548 they signed a new treaty promising the marriage of Mary to Prince François, the dauphin. The next month Mary sailed for France. During the next 13 years Mary was reared as a French princess and as a consort fit for the occupant of the French throne, transforming her into an essentially French rather than a strictly Scottish monarch in the eyes of many of her own subjects. This mutation had unforeseen but dramatic implications when she finally returned to Scotland as queen.

Mary's time in France was at least not wasted. She emerged a poised, confident, accomplished and widely admired figure, recognized for her linguistic proficiency and artistic skills as well as for her grace and beauty. What she did not acquire, though, were any real political skills or insights.

Nor did she learn much about Scottish society and politics. This was a crucial failing, especially as scepticism about the Guise regency, which placed Frenchmen in charge of key government offices and relied on the visible presence of French soldiers in Edinburgh, intensified quickly after 1554. At the same time, and intertwined with anti-French feeling, pressure from a growing Protestant faction for religious reform, a demand backed by powerful noblemen and by energetic preachers, was increasing.

In France this may have appeared not to matter. Mary's position at the heart of the French state seemed secure. In 1558 she married François. On 10 July 1559, when Henri II died and her husband was crowned, she became Queen Consort of France.

Adding to the complexity of her position, however, was her Tudor ancestry. For Mary now also became the focus of long-standing French claims to the crown of England which, with her cousin Elizabeth, a Protestant, on the English throne, was regarded in Paris as being held unlawfully by a heretic. Mary and François were duly presented in French propaganda as England's legitimate monarchs – something that from the outset undermined the relationship between the Catholic Queen of Scots and the Protestant Queen of England, with ultimately lethal effects for one of them.

Events soon took an unexpected turn. By 5 December 1560 Mary was already a 17-year-old widow, François having died of a cerebral abscess. His brother Charles succeeded and Mary was suddenly without an obvious French role.

In Scotland, too, developments were spinning out of control. Mary's mother died in June with her regime and its French backers facing open rebellion. This was led by disaffected Scottish aristocrats who called themselves the Lords of the Congregation – the religious connotations of the name indicating their Protestant affiliations – who had allied with Queen Elizabeth and wished to end French and Catholic domination of Scottish affairs. Fronted by the earls of Argyll, Glencairn and Morton, this group signed a covenant in December 1557, binding themselves to each other and to God for the defence of the Protestant cause.

This opposition movement also had a dangerously popular, public dimension. By 1558 Protestant preachers, most famously John Knox, a follower of the French reformist theologian John Calvin, had been urging comprehensive change on the Scottish Church. Attacks on religious sculpture and stained glass, symbols of what radical Protestants denounced as Catholic idolatry, had broken out in towns like Perth, encouraged by the inflammatory sermons delivered by Knox and his colleagues. More importantly but less visible, individual Protestants across the country, some wealthy and influential but many humble and obscure, were rejecting the authority and structure of the unreformed Church, getting for themselves religious ministers who had enthusiastically embraced reformed ways.

The Scottish Reformation, in other words, was already happening by stealth. Among Mary of Guise's last acts as regent had been an attempt to confront this problem by demanding that Protestant preachers meet her at Stirling to receive firm instruction. But this only worsened the situation. The Lords, whom Arran formally joined in September 1559, seized the initiative. By Christmas 1559 they had taken Edinburgh, having first ejected French troops from Perth.

In the last six months of her life Guise was therefore in desperate difficulty. The more obviously dependent her regime became on French military resources, the less legitimacy it enjoyed. It also became easier for her opponents to recruit support, not least from England. French forces did push the Lords back to Stirling in January 1560. But the timely arrival of an English fleet in the Forth and then of an English army soon led the French to fall back on the port of Leith.

The outcome was the Treaty of Edinburgh, signed by the Lords on behalf of Scotland. This effectively ended the 'Auld Alliance', made the Scots and English allies, allowed the calling of a Scots Parliament which Protestants would dominate and also promised peace between England and France. Guise's convenient death clearly helped matters. Mary, Queen of Scots, refused to endorse it but could do nothing to prevent it.

Widowed and marginalized at the French court and with her mother dead, Mary came back to Scotland. But as she arrived at Leith on 19 August 1561, the circumstances could hardly have been less encouraging.

A revolution of faith

For most countries where the Reformation occurred, historians struggle to disentangle the material and political self-interest of Protestantism's supporters from their sincerely held spiritual convictions. Scotland is no different. And Mary's opponents were a decidedly mixed bunch.

Some, like Arran and some Lords, were clearly interested in restoring their own earthly power at the expense of the Stewarts and their French allies. Others, energized by Knox's famously volcanic pulpit performances or by contact with one form or another of the new theology, were genuinely concerned to revolutionize not just the Church and its practices but also Scotland's people and Scotland's government. They wanted a more 'godly' society, ahead of what they believed were the last days, the final clash at the end of time between God and Satan. Catholicism and Papal authority, seen in this light, were not only irrational and immoral. To many, they were positively diabolical.

In this context Mary's Catholicism could not be anything but deeply troubling. With so many having converted to Protestantism, including not just Arran but also her own illegitimate half-brother James Stewart, created 1st Earl of Moray by Mary in 1562 and a key early ally, her religious stance was difficult in the extreme. Wisely, and heeding Moray's guidance and that of William Maitland of Lethington, her secretary and closest advisor, she chose initially to compromise.

A small ball game

No one could have imagined that hitting a ball with a stick towards a hole, a game played on the sandy seaside 'links' at places like St Andrews as long ago as the 12th century and enjoyed by Mary during her troubled Scottish reign, would have evolved into a lucrative spectator sport as well as attracting mass participation internationally. The 2010 Open Championship at St Andrews was alone worth at least £80 million to the economy. Four other Scottish links currently host the Open – Carnoustie and Muirfield on the east coast, Troon and Turnberry on the west – while spectacular golf courses such as Gleneagles and Dornoch are among the world's most hallowed.

Mary therefore appointed several Protestant nobles to the Privy Council. She agreed to restrict Catholicism to her private chapel while tolerating the de facto triumph of Protestantism in the public domain. There seems little doubt that Mary would have preferred to re-impose the old faith. But this was no longer an option. Her military and political weakness, and the fact that she was an inexperienced female ruler dependent upon older male advisors who mostly had different religious opinions, meant that this was simply not possible.

This is why the Scottish Reformation rooted itself strongly during Mary's personal reign, even though she discouraged its most extreme manifestations. Parliament formally declared an end to Papal jurisdiction in Scotland and accepted Calvin's Confession of Faith, though Mary did not ratify these moves. Anti-Catholic measures proposed by Edinburgh's town council were also blocked. And despite Knox's rhetoric, to which Mary was personally exposed on occasion, her own religious preferences were at least tolerated, providing she did not threaten her subjects' Protestantism.

The number of reformed clergy, and the number of Scots attracted to Protestant theology and practices, continued to grow. A particularly important milestone was the move in 1561, led by Knox and endorsed at Privy Council, to require a school in every parish – the intention being, of course, that elementary education should include clear instruction in the new faith.

> 'Well then, I perceive that my subjects shall obey you, and not me; and shall do what they list and not what I command, and so must I be subject to them and not they to me... but ye are not the Kirk that I will nurse. I will defend the Kirk of Rome, for, I think, it is the true Kirk of God.'
>
> Mary to Knox (1561)

If she could do little to prevent the rising tide of Protestantism, a more fruitful focus for Mary's efforts at this time seemed to be the English succession. For with her cousin Elizabeth unmarried and childless, it was widely assumed that the next ruler of England would have to be nominated. In Scotland, though significantly not in England, it was also presumed that Mary was the most likely nominee.

This issue understandably dominated Anglo-Scottish relations throughout Mary's reign. She tried to secure Elizabeth's endorsement. Elizabeth, suspicious of Mary's motives and in particular of her Catholicism, was equally determined not to grant it. For her part Mary refused to approve the Treaty of Edinburgh, which would have meant renouncing her own claim to be already the legitimate Queen of England. Neither woman would budge. Both were strong-willed enough to think that they might eventually browbeat the other into submission.

Mary's hopes of the English crown were also dealt a major blow by her pursuit of a new husband. In order to placate the English and reassure them about her accommodation with Protestantism, the last thing she should have done was consider Don Carlos of Spain, a prominent European Catholic – which is precisely what she did in 1563, though without success.

Only slightly less damaging was her actual marriage in 1565 to her cousin Henry Stewart, Lord Darnley, whose religious affiliations were notoriously ambiguous. Elizabeth was particularly alienated by this union because, since Darnley too had a claim to the English throne, it looked like a clumsy attempt to reinforce Mary's case to be Queen of England.

The queen of hearts

The Darnley marriage marks the end of the first and more successful part of Mary's Scottish reign and the onset of the greater difficulties that would ultimately destroy not only her credibility but also her rule.

One immediate consequence was that Moray and several of the other Lords, fearing Darnley might increase Catholic influence at court, decided to challenge Mary's power. The so-called Chaseabout Raid in late August 1565 was unable to rally sufficient forces and it fizzled out, forcing Moray into English exile. But it was a worrying sign, as Mary's earlier accommodation with the Protestant nobility began to unravel.

Another unhelpful development was Darnley's behaviour. He alarmed many of Mary's previous supporters by demanding greater political authority when strictly he was only her consort. He was also centrally involved in the killing of David Rizzio, an Italian private secretary and musician at her Holyroodhouse court, in March 1566. Rizzio had become a favourite of Mary and a certain amount of salacious gossip had emerged about the exact nature of their relationship (not least because the queen was pregnant with the future James VI). Darnley's jealousy fuelled the suspicion of many Protestants that immorality was, as they had feared, rampant in the court's Catholic culture.

Unsurprisingly, his role in blackening Mary's reputation and in the dastardly murder of her close friend also destroyed her relationship with her husband, the father of her baby son.

Darnley's ambitions, meanwhile, proved lethal. His disdain for other people of rank made him dangerously unpopular. Mary's own private affections had also turned to a new man, James Hepburn, 4th Earl of Bothwell. The result was another sensational murder in the queen's circle. On 10 February 1567 Darnley died in highly suspicious circumstances in an explosion at Edinburgh's Kirk o' Field. Bothwell, at whom fingers naturally pointed, was believed to have supplied the gunpowder, while many saw the queen's own hand in the affair. It would be hard to think of an episode less likely to quell suspicions among her opponents that Mary was a dangerous and deceitful woman who simply could not be trusted.

What little was left of Mary's active rule in Scotland can be swiftly described.

A hasty marriage to Bothwell, further incrimination in many people's eyes, took place on 15 May. And although performed in the Protestant fashion, this ceremony proved the spark that ignited the tinderbox. The Lords, suspicious of the married couple's intentions and sensing an opportunity to strike, raised another rebellion. At Carberry Hill near Musselburgh on 15 June they confronted forces loyal to Mary and Bothwell.

In return for permitting Bothwell to escape, Mary was imprisoned on the island in Loch Leven in Fife. But a more decisive turn of events was the discovery five days later of the so-called Casket Letters, widely thought to confirm Mary's involvement in Darnley's murder. Bothwell was declared guilty and a bounty put on his head. An outlaw, he died ten years later, insane and friendless, in a Danish jail.

Proof positive?

Allegedly found in Edinburgh Castle in 1567 and presented by Moray to Queen Elizabeth, the Casket Letters comprised eight notes in French from Mary to Bothwell, a love poem by the queen and two marriage contracts. Collectively they indicated Mary's adulterous attachment to Darnley's killer as well as her prior approval of the crime. But was the discovery of this incriminating material simply too convenient? There was great controversy among 18th-century historians, who, noticing certain linguistic peculiarities, mostly pronounced them clever forgeries. Today, opinion remains divided, with many claiming that, although certainly tampered with, their guilty substance was real enough. Unfortunately the originals disappeared in the 1580s and only supposed English copies survive, so we will never know.

Mary, who miscarried twins in the succeeding weeks, was finally forced to abdicate on 24 July 1567. Her only surviving child by Darnley, the one-year-old James, was proclaimed King of Scots, under Moray's regency.

Despite an attempted fight-back the following spring, when Mary escaped from Loch Leven and her supporters fought an unsuccessful engagement at Langside near Glasgow against Moray's army, her troubled reign was effectively over. By the summer of 1568 she had fled to England. There, as a focal point for Catholic opposition and with an unrenounced claim to Elizabeth's throne, she ought not to have been entirely surprised to find herself under arrest.

A long imprisonment followed. At an early stage there were English demands that she be investigated for complicity in Darnley's murder. Later there were accusations that Mary had been active in various plots, with the aid of foreign Catholic powers, to take the English crown. The culmination came with the Babington plot by English Catholic aristocrats in 1586. Implicated by letters unwisely written in her own hand that were intercepted by Elizabeth's spies, Mary was put on trial at Fotheringhay Castle in Northamptonshire.

Found guilty of treason against Elizabeth, she was sentenced to death. And although her cousin hesitated before signing the death warrant, Mary was beheaded on 8 February 1587.

A divisive Queen

Later generations would remain bitterly divided over Mary. For the first 200 years, when conflict between Protestants and Catholics remained crucial, attitudes were determined mainly by religion: to Protestants from Knox onwards she was an immoral and dishonest tyrant justly overthrown by the defenders of Scottish and British liberties but for Catholics she was more sinned against than sinning, a pious martyr for the faith. From the mid-18th century onwards, however, as religious tensions lessened, an appreciation of Mary's human qualities, together with a greater awareness of the challenges she faced, became more typical. She has more recently been seen as a tragic victim of her own failings, as an ill-starred romantic heroine – even a feminist icon – who fell foul of a hostile male-dominated world. There is every reason to believe that future ages will continue to re-interpret Mary's enthralling story according to their own lights.

Two kings in one?

With Mary's son James we enter a decisive new phase in Scotland's history.

In the later middle ages, English kings' claims to rule the Scots had been the main force behind the kingdom's development. The result was regular cross-border conflict and, though clearly the opposite of what was intended, reinforcement of the Scots' powerful sense of their own distinctiveness. James VI's reign partially reversed these trends. Inheriting his mother's claim to Elizabeth's throne, the King of Scots himself became King of England in 1603, re-styled thereafter as James VI and I. His so-called Union of the Crowns – by which one individual ruled the two separate kingdoms – laid the groundwork for his descendants to complete the process of forming a single British state.

Contemporaries were perplexed by James and later ages have also found it difficult to get to the root of the man. For his life is full of contrasts and apparent contradictions. A fiercely proud Scot, he died a much-loved King of England. He was the clearly Protestant son of a pious Catholic mother who allowed the persecution of the old faith while quarrelling regularly with the more aggressive supporters of the new. He was a devoted husband and father who also liked the company of good-looking men, leading to inevitable speculation over his sexual orientation. He faced upheaval and rebellion in Scotland in his youth yet somehow emerged later as 'Good King James', a ruler long remembered for the stable government he provided. He displayed great learning and culture but was a robust personality whose Scottish origins and coarse manners easily offended delicate English sensibilities. No wonder it has sometimes been tempting to see James as two completely different monarchs, the division lying geographically at the border and chronologically in or around 1603.

In truth many of the paradoxes of James VI and I stem from the challenging circumstances of his childhood. First, his mother had probably connived at his father's murder while he was a baby. She had subsequently been absent and was eventually executed by the cousin to whose throne James himself aspired. James was also the heir to a ruler who in the white heat of the Reformation crisis had been on the wrong side in the eyes of many of her most influential subjects. Finally he had succeeded not just as an infant but actually as the result of a coup d'état. Its leaders had used him as a figurehead providing cover for their actions. They had also tried to turn him against his mother and to impress upon him his complete reliance on their own goodwill and support. Tensions and contradictions were hardly surprising in a man whose character and approach to kingship were forged in such testing conditions.

Particular emphasis needs to be placed on the effects of James's unusual upbringing. Cruel circumstances not only denied him parental contact and affection. They also placed him in the hands of his mother's enemies. As a result James's education was controlled by the famous George Buchanan: Europe's greatest-living Latin poet and a scholar of international repute,

Buchanan was also a militant propagandist for the coup of 1567 and a zealous convert to Protestantism.

Buchanan's teaching was exceptionally intellectually rigorous. It exposed James to some of the most advanced political and cultural ideas. It also helps explain his sincere lifelong love of literature, learning and the arts – once in London he would become Shakespeare's patron and also sponsor that timeless monument to the English language, the *King James Bible*. But his teacher was also a harsh taskmaster. James was beaten into submission: when the Countess of Mar thought Buchanan's violence excessive, his tutor reportedly snapped: 'Madam, I have whipped his arse: you may kiss it if you please.'

Such severity allowed James to be force-fed not only Protestant teachings but also Buchanan's revolutionary notions about the duty of patriotic subjects to resist over-mighty (but especially Catholic and therefore godless) tyrants. Indeed, James's childhood seems to have been one long programme of deliberate indoctrination by his mother's opponents. Rather indicating what they had in mind from the outset, Knox, Mary's nemesis and still the country's leading Protestant preacher, even gave the sermon at the baby's coronation at Stirling in 1567. The intention was clearly that James should eventually be left in no doubt about the strict limitations placed on him by God – and in Scotland by God's chosen lieutenants on earth, the reformed clergy.

The last king in Scotland

Regency formed a familiar part of the complex set of problems affecting James's early years. Unavoidable in 1567, with the king barely a year old, the struggles for power that had traditionally surrounded regencies in Scotland were nevertheless made even worse by the uniquely revolutionary circumstances of James's accession. Moray, the designated regent, lasted not three years before being shot dead at Linlithgow in 1570 by James Hamilton, a Catholic supporter of the Queen's Party, as Mary's allies were known. The assassin was the nephew of John Hamilton, Archbishop of

St Andrews, who was opposed by Knox and the Protestant movement. The murderer escaped to the Continent but the archbishop, nominally still Scotland's senior cleric, was hanged for his complicity.

A succession of regents followed – their short tenures a reminder of the violence and instability for which Scotland was notorious. Matthew Stewart, 4th Earl of Lennox, Darnley's father and thus the king's grandfather, was next: he survived barely a year before dying from wounds inflicted by Mary's supporters at Stirling. John Erskine, 17th Earl of Mar, followed Lennox but was likewise dead within the year, this time falling victim to a suspicious poisoning in which all the evidence pointed at the dead man's host, James Douglas, 4th Earl of Morton. The latter was a Lord of the Congregation, had participated in Rizzio's murder and had subsequently helped force Mary's abdication. It was thus no shock when Morton himself acquired the regency, a role in which he served until his execution in 1581 – ostensibly for involvement in Darnley's assassination but as much because his power had become too great for other leading noblemen to bear.

The Morton regency, by far the longest-lasting of James's minority, proved of wider importance for three reasons.

First, it saw the final defeat of the Queen's Party. This was important, and only occurred when, with English help, the government re-captured Edinburgh Castle from Mary's die-hard partisans in 1573. James, once he took effective charge around 1584, therefore enjoyed real legitimacy, despite his mother still being alive. This in turn allowed him to shore up his authority in the time-honoured fashion, by confronting challengers and suppressing disorder.

Second, Morton's last years witnessed the emergence of James's French cousin Esmé Stewart, soon, to native irritation, created Duke of Lennox. Like some of Mary's liaisons, this relationship isolated the monarch from other allies, particularly as Lennox enjoyed considerable power – it was he who brought about Morton's demise.

The third key development that emerged during Moray's regency, closely connected with first two, was the successful entrenching of the Reformation in Scotland – which would have lasting consequences. Protestant ideas, supported personally by the courtiers and other leaders who had overthrown the French-backed Guise regime and who had then brought down Mary's government, were steadily imposed over much of the Scottish Church and most of its people. If the coup of 1567 was indeed a revolution, then its motivating ideology, to which everyone was now required to subscribe, was unquestionably Calvinism.

Calvinist theology, strongly advocated by Knox and his allies in the early 1560s but for obvious reasons not formally endorsed by Mary's government, was finally approved on James's behalf in 1572. Calvin's Confession of Faith became thereafter the official definition of acceptable religious belief in Scotland.

Yet Calvinism also brought with it some rather more practical implications that were less easily translated from the city republic of Geneva to the kingdom of Scotland. Above all, it meant trying to create an entirely new and highly controversial form of church organization known as Presbyterianism. In place of the familiar oversight of bishops and archbishops appointed by the crown – Episcopalianism, or Episcopacy, as it is called – Presbyterianism required a complex structure of church courts leading from each parish's 'kirk session' up to a national General Assembly, each level staffed by so-called 'presbyters' (in practice a mixture of ordained clergy and small landowners or 'heritors') and together supervising every significant aspect of religious, moral and social life.

The main result would, of course, have been to place the Church effectively beyond royal control. This, understandably, was not something that James's advisers, let alone the king, could countenance, and the Black Acts, passed in 1584, expressly confirmed his right to appoint bishops to govern religious affairs.

'Our sovereign lord and his three estates of parliament statute and ordain that Patrick, archbishop of St Andrews, and others, the bishops within this realm using and exercising the function and authority of bishops, with such others as shall be constituted the king's majesty's commissioners in ecclesiastical causes, shall and may direct and put order to all matters and causes ecclesiastical within their diocese, visit the kirks and state of the ministry within the same...'

Acts of the Scottish Parliament (1584)

This unresolved issue over the control of a broadly Calvinist church was the main problem with which James wrestled during his personal rule. Things were certainly not helped by the emergence of an assertive younger generation of radical clergy, led by Andrew Melville, a brilliant scholar and inspirational leader at Glasgow and then St Andrews universities.

Melville, like several leading Presbyterian clerics, tended to view James as merely an arrogant and over-ambitious layman who had forgotten his subordinate place as just one of Christ's many sinful followers. In one famously undiplomatic outburst in 1596, Melville gripped the royal sleeve and told James to his shocked face to remember that 'ye are God's silly vassal' ('silly' being colloquial Scots for 'weak' or 'feeble'). To be fair, James gave as good as he got from the fundamentalists, responding to one ear-bashing from a minister, whose sermon against royal authority the king found especially unpalatable: 'I will not give a turd for thy preaching.'

In 1592 Melville and his supporters in Parliament even achieved the Golden Act, which partially reversed the Black Acts and formally endorsed Presbyterianism in the Scottish Church – though on James's insistence the appointment of bishops continued as before.

We should also be careful not to overstate the differences between James and even the most militant Protestants. It was true that he tolerated prominent Catholics, like his favourite George Gordon, 6th Earl of Huntly, forgiven for his violent activities in the north-east and even, astonishingly, for open rebellion against the king himself in 1593–4: such leniency was hardly calculated to impress Presbyterian observers. But James was nonetheless a godly Protestant king who agreed with the Calvinist radicals on many points – such as on burning witches (there was a spate in the early 1590s) and on the importance of education (Edinburgh University was founded in 1583, and Marischal College, Aberdeen, a decade later).

By this time, however, James's Scottish reign, despite his on-going tussles with the Presbyterians, was dominated by one factor above all: the long-anticipated death of Elizabeth and the resulting vacancy on the English throne. James had harboured ambitions since his childhood. And with the passing years, as Elizabeth failed to marry or nominate an heir, the prospect of becoming King of England more and more preoccupied him. The inevitable finally happened on 24 March 1603.

With Elizabeth's passing, the English Privy Council offered James the crown. Gratefully accepting, he prepared to ride from Edinburgh to London, to begin a new chapter not only in his own life but in that of the kingdom of Scotland.

Fact check

1 Who ruled on Mary's behalf from 1542 to 1554?
  a the Earl of Arran
  b Mary of Guise
  c Cardinal Beaton
  d the Earl of Hertford

2 To whom was Mary first married?
  a Henry Darnley
  b the Earl of Bothwell
  c Philip of Spain
  d François of France

3 Who was the main Calvinist preacher in Mary's Scotland?
  a Cardinal Beaton
  b Patrick Hamilton
  c John Knox
  d George Wishart

4 Who were the Lords of the Congregation?
  a Presbyterian clergy
  b Protestant noblemen
  c Church attendees
  d A court faction

5 Who arranged the murder of David Rizzio?
  a Henry Darnley
  b the Earl of Bothwell
  c John Knox
  d Cardinal Beaton

6 Name James VI's tutor.
  a John Knox
  b the Duke of Lennox
  c George Buchanan
  d Andrew Melville

7 Who led the Presbyterians in James's adult reign?
   a Andrew Melville
   b George Buchanan
   c the Earl of Arran
   d John Calvin

Dig Deeper

Jenny Wormald, *Mary Queen of Scots* (London, 1988).
Jane Dawson, *Scotland Re-formed, 1488-1587* (Edinburgh, 2007).
Gordon Donaldson, *All The Queen's Men* (London, 1983).
I. B. Cowan, *The Scottish Reformation* (London, 1982).

11

Two crowns united

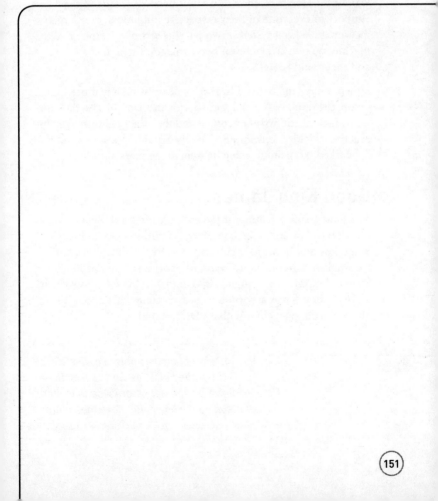

The accidental inheritance

The most important point to bear in mind about the Union of the Crowns – important because it created problems that dominated British politics for the next century and more – was what it was not. For when James VI also became James I, in no real sense were Scotland and England themselves brought together.

They remained, as they had always been, two separate kingdoms. There were still two peoples and two nations with deep-rooted identities and longstanding antagonisms; two parliaments, with contrasting histories and traditions; two markedly different Protestant churches, though neither now commanded the support of everyone in their respective kingdoms; two largely incompatible legal systems; two parallel sets of governmental machinery; two armies; even two coinages (the pound sterling and the pound Scots).

So what happened after Elizabeth's death was only a personal union, the result of the biological accidents that had seen the same individual inherit first the Scottish and then the English crown. In practice its wider constitutional and political implications had to be worked out painfully, step by step, in the years ahead.

Good King James

The most striking feature of James's rule after 1603 was his re-location to London – the largest and wealthiest city in his two kingdoms and home to their most powerful political institution, the English Parliament at Westminster. At a stroke this rendered Scotland physically a kingless kingdom. On his sole return visit in 1617, James was surprised to hear genuine hurt about his absence from poets like William Drummond.

> 'Ah! why should Isis only see thee shine?
> Is not the Forth, as well as Isis, thine?
> Though Isis vaunt she hath more wealth in store,
> Let it suffice thy Forth doth love thee more...'
> William Drummond, *The River of Forth Feasting* (1617)

Drummond's poetic discussion of James's residence beside the Thames (known up-river as the Isis) rather than the Forth hinted strongly at wounded Scottish pride at the king's preference for life in the English capital. But the choice had practical implications too. When it was still impossible to ride between Edinburgh and London in much less than 14 days and so took the best part of a month for any meaningful two-way communication, the very nature of James's rule was seriously affected by his sheer remoteness from Scotland. Inevitably he became much more detached from Scottish events.

Another source of friction was James's attempts to harmonize the two kingdoms. For the self-styled first King of Great Britain (as he declared himself in 1604, to widespread irritation), this made sense not merely in terms of personal vanity but as a solution to the political havoc that continuing differences would cause for someone with obligations to both sides.

Symbolically James experimented with a single flag, merging the Scottish cross of St Andrew with the English cross of St George: this was finally introduced for shipping in 1606, though over continuing opposition from English and Scottish critics. More important was James's successful promotion of a scheme that saw his subjects in each kingdom granted the legal right of naturalization in the other: in effect, a common Anglo-Scottish citizenship emerged.

In 1605 he also established a joint commission to oversee the Borders, or the 'Middle Shires' as they were now called in deference to James's view that he ruled over a single polity. This was an especially wise move given this wild upland region's notoriety for lawless behaviour. Inside the first year the commission had hanged 79 offenders, the notorious Armstrong family was exiled to Ireland and by the 1620s reiving had been largely eradicated. More generally, James bore down on the traditional practice of blood-feud between kin groupings as a form of rough-and-ready justice.

James also tackled the Highlands, the part of mainland Britain that least conformed to the kinds of behaviour expected by a London-based ruler for whom south-east England increasingly defined the norms. The Statutes of Iona were imposed in 1609.

In a striking attack on the distinctive foundations of Celtic culture, they banned the bards – the singers of traditional oral songs and poems – whose words inspired Highlanders to emulate the heroic deeds of their ancestors. They also required chieftains to educate their sons in Lowland schools (further undermining the Gaelic language).

James also made sure to have a significant number of Scottish allies with him in London. The arrival of some of Scotland's leading aristocrats displeased their English counterparts: soon there were 158 Scots in paid royal employment, each taking up a position previously occupied by members of England's elite. But this did at least help maintain James's relationship with the ruling families of the country he had left behind.

Not content with creating a genuinely Anglo-Scottish court, James even wanted to bring about the formal political unification of the two kingdoms, as he told the English Parliament in 1604 and again in 1607. But his hopes were dashed. Accustomed to debating in person in the Scots Parliament, really just a gathering of people whom James knew, he could not use the same device to overawe the much larger House of Commons and House of Lords, England's separate, well-established and often independent-minded chambers. When Westminster threw out James's scheme, suspicious that it threatened English identity and interests, he was angry but could do nothing about it.

Clearly union still had severe limits.

The church militant

It would not have surprised James that the Scottish Church remained a major problem even when he was resident in London.

In organizational matters, an uneasy compromise continued. The Church contrived somehow to be simultaneously Presbyterian, having the necessary hierarchy of courts, and Episcopalian, with the king's bishops, who generally tried to be tactful and inoffensive, working closely with those elected bodies. Indeed, historians have generally been impressed by the surprising harmony of this hybrid arrangement, noting how it only imploded once monarchs lacked James's established personal authority in Scotland as well as his intimate first-hand knowledge of Scottish conditions.

But in other policy areas James remained on a collision course with the Presbyterians, a trajectory that eventually produced the controversial Five Articles of Perth. These were regulations on worship and religious observance which, although compatible with moderate Protestantism and with English practice, outraged James's Presbyterian critics when he tried to impose them in Scotland.

The General Assembly duly rejected the Articles in November 1617. Furious, James had them proclaimed publicly by the Privy Council in October 1618. And it took considerable pressure and political manoeuvring from James and his officials to secure the Scots Parliament's approval in 1621. The whole episode, with James underestimating the degree of resistance to his plans, was a classic illustration of the problem of absentee monarchy, with the ruler detached from local events and increasingly unable to read the very obvious signals about serious trouble ahead.

When he died in 1625, James VI and I was in many ways as much of an enigma to those who surrounded him as he had been when he first emerged from his peculiarly intense and restricted childhood – as a rough-tongued bully but also an international diplomat and peacemaker; a sincere supporter of the Reformation who bickered constantly with his fellow-Protestants and had numerous good Catholic friends; an experienced and generally flexible politician who could still make appalling mistakes.

His successor Charles I, who inherited the challenging legacy of the Union of the Crowns, was a delicate and prudish man who lacked some of his father's cruder vices. Crucially, however, he also lacked James's winning charisma, his political astuteness, and, not least as things turned out, his good fortune.

The native who was a stranger

One of the many ironies of Charles's rule, given the disasters that subsequently unfolded in his relations with the Scots, is that the future king entered the world in 1600 every inch a Scottish prince, at Dunfermline, with its enduring associations with the Canmore dynasty and where the Bruce himself lay buried. By a further quirk of fate, Charles was even baptized at Holyroodhouse by a Presbyterian minister. Yet no other Scottish monarch would ever betray such suicidal ignorance about the nature and limitations of his power in Scotland, particularly in questions of Church and faith.

A key explanation for Charles's behaviour as king again lies in a peculiar childhood. First, Charles was not born to rule. Only the sudden death of Prince Henry in 1612 turned a sensitive younger son into an ill-at-ease future monarch desperate to live up to the rich promise displayed by his popular but tragically lost sibling. Second, Charles had disabilities, including a limp (possibly from rickets in infancy) and a speech impediment that never left him. His adult obsession with status and his inability to absorb constructive criticism both look like the results of an underlying lack of confidence and of a desire to compensate – perhaps over-compensate – for these handicaps. The same factors also make good sense of Charles's arrogant decision to run England personally from 1629 onwards without calling a Parliament to Westminster where his opponents and critics might congregate.

A further trait that Charles I possessed, in this case much like his father, was a taste for the arts and learning. Mainly this was a good thing. The wonderfully human triple-headed portrait by Van Dyck is probably how we now most often remember Charles's appearance; he knighted Rubens, who decorated the ceiling at the new Banqueting House in Whitehall; and, as a connoisseur with impeccably progressive tastes, he made the royal collection of paintings Europe's greatest concentration of top-class contemporary art.

More troublingly, however, Charles also acquired an intense interest in theology and church history. As a result, he learned to view these deeply controversial matters from the doctrinaire perspective of an intellectual purist rather than that of a pragmatic ruler. This was to prove a catastrophic flaw in Charles's approach as monarch, particularly in relation to the Scottish Church.

Arguably Charles's greatest weakness, however, was simply the result of 1603. For he was the London-based monarch not only of England but also of the distinctive, distant and – to Charles at least – largely unknown kingdom of Scotland. He paid his only adult visit, for an inexcusably late Scottish coronation, fully eight years after actually succeeding, in 1633. And like James in 1617 he heard a welter of complaints, articulated once more by anxious loyalists like Drummond, which again reflected the tensions created by absentee monarchy.

> 'Here, could thy Prince still stay,
> Each month should turn to May;
> We need nor star, nor sun,
> Save him, to lengthen days, and joys begun...'
>
> William Drummond, *The Song of the Muses at Parnassus* (1633)

All of these problems converged as Charles attempted to deal with the most difficult and contentious policy area of all: the forms of worship and internal organization of the Scottish Church.

It would have seemed far-fetched as Charles paraded proudly through the streets of Scotland's capital in 1633 in a splendid coronation pageant. But in the final analysis, these issues would literally be the death of him.

Fact check

1 Who was William Drummond?
   a a Presbyterian clergyman
   b a courtier in London
   c a Scottish poet
   d a Scottish general

2 Where were the 'Middle Shires'?
   a the Hebrides
   b the northern Highlands
   c the Anglo-Scottish border
   d Galloway

3 What did the Five Articles of Perth do?
   a Weaken Presbyterianism
   b Re-introduce Catholicism
   c Ban Gaelic
   d Imprison opponents

4 Where was Charles I born?
   a Edinburgh
   b Whitehall
   c Windsor
   d Dunfermline

5 What was Charles's hobby and passion?
   a Football
   b Golf
   c Horse-racing
   d Art

6 When was Charles crowned in Scotland?
   a 1617
   b 1625
   c 1633
   d 1637

Dig Deeper

Maurice Lee Jr, *Government by Pen: Scotland under James VI and I* (Urbana, 1980).

Roger Lockyer, *James VI and I* (London, 1998).

Jenny Wormald, 'James VI and I: Two Kings or One?', *History* (1988).

Alan MacDonald, *The Jacobean Kirk, 1567-1625* (Aldershot, 1998).

The conflict of the Covenant

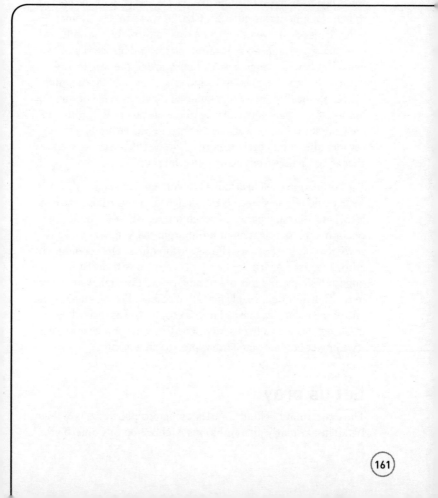

Clumsy beginnings

The personal and political calamity that was Charles I's reign as King of Scots gave out a number of early signals that all was not well. These should have indicated that a monarch poorly informed about Scotland was stumbling unwittingly into avoidable disagreements with important interest groups. But the signs were ignored.

One error that caused immediate and lasting friction was the Act of Revocation of 1625. In one sense, this was unremarkable. At the end of their minority adult monarchs had traditionally annulled all grants of lands and offices previously made in their name. These were then re-assigned or, more likely, a fee was paid by the holders to maintain the status quo. But Charles was scarcely a minor when James died, even though he was still strictly just under the customary age limit for revocation of 25. And his legislation was audaciously wide-ranging, stretching back all the way to 1540. Clearly this was intended to include the huge number of grants of ecclesiastical property to secular landowners made during the Reformation, Charles's aim being to use the proceeds to better fund the Church. To families whose ownership was being threatened decades after it had been acquired, however, this was provocative, alienating Charles from many powerful people.

The coronation itself also stoked discontent. For the royal visit in 1633 could not have been better designed to anger Presbyterians. Henrietta-Maria, Charles's French queen, was a Catholic and celebrated mass privately in Edinburgh: the king was inevitably suspected of, at very least, Popish sympathies. The ceremony too echoed the Five Articles of Perth: ornately dressed clergy, including English bishops, and lots of kneeling before the altar, were red rags to the Calvinist bull, visible hints that Scotland's new king was not one of them. Finally, one of James's proposals was revived by his idealistic, theologically obsessed son. This was for a new English-style prayer book to standardize practice in worship.

Let us pray

The mastermind behind Charles's religious policies was William Laud, his scholarly and ambitious Archbishop of Canterbury, who, like a number of other theologians in Holland and England, favoured Arminianism, a substantially modified version of Calvinism.

Key idea: Arminianism

Arminiamism suggests that it is because God knows we will have faith in Christ that He predestines us to salvation, rather than, as Calvin had taught, God giving us that faith only because He has already chosen us. We are liable to look at these words and not see much difference. But to contemporary Presbyterians, versed in the fine theological details and passionately committed to Calvin's insistence that their spiritual destiny rested entirely and exclusively with God's grace rather than with their own decisions, the shift of emphasis in Arminianism was certainly ungodly, seemingly crypto-Catholic, and perhaps even directly diabolical in origin and intent. Taken together with the Arminians' general bias towards episcopacy and royal authority in the church, this struck at the heart of what most Scottish Presbyterians believed their own Reformation – the triumph of God's elect – had achieved.

From this point onwards the ability of Charles's religious reforms to generate not merely heated academic debate but profound public hostility and outright physical resistance becomes more intelligible. Despite what was later claimed, the new prayer book, distributed in 1637, was mainly drafted by the Scottish bishops. But it was certainly corrected and approved by Laud and Charles. And it was an open secret that Laud's Arminianism was the driving force behind a document, which, his Scottish opponents pointed out, had been approved neither by a Scots Parliament nor by a General Assembly.

The rebellion began at a service in St Giles's Cathedral on 23 July 1637 when, it is said, Jenny Geddes, a local market trader, hurled a stool at the minister while accusing him of leading a new Catholic form of worship: 'daur ye say Mass in my lug?' ('dare you say mass in my ear?'), she supposedly asked.

Entertaining though the story is, it is, like so much else in Scottish history, a colourful mixture of hard fact and later embellishment.

Geddes herself is not named in any near-contemporary source. There is also real doubt that she spoke those particular words. Yet the commotion does indeed seem to have been begun by a woman. And whoever it was who cast the first stone, the vast exposed glasshouse of Charles's prayer book and the Arminian reforms now came under attack – so much so that a degree of co-ordination surely lay behind the campaign. Certainly the hostility was both widespread and ferocious.

Edinburgh was in ferment, the Privy Council at one point seeking refuge at Holyroodhouse. The changes nearly saw one Glasgow clergyman torn limb from limb. The Bishop of Brechin took to sporting a pair of loaded pistols when performing communion in the new style.

Large-scale petitioning also occurred. Most importantly, a hostile organization emerged late in 1637 called the Tables, led by the earls of Rothes and Montrose. The Lord Advocate, the leading Scottish law officer, advised a climb-down but Charles refused. Indeed, his response, typically convinced that boldly asserting royal authority would unnerve his opponents, was simply to stand firm and issue proclamations demanding obedience.

Joining with God

The Presbyterians' reaction was revolutionary. Meeting at Greyfriars' Church in Edinburgh for three days from 28 February 1638, the Tables oversaw the mass signing of what they called the National Covenant – drafted by the lawyer Archibald Johnston of Warriston and the Fife clergyman Alexander Henderson. Copies were also sent for signing across Scotland. Its text was immensely significant, for it bound the signatories to each other and to God and to fight their king's religious programme.

'This is the great marriage day of this nation with God. I ask all of you to sign this document and pledge to maintain our true religion.'
Archibald Johnston of Warriston (1638)

Soon a sizeable proportion of the population had taken this oath. They were careful, however, not explicitly to denounce Charles: indeed, the Covenanters professed loyalty, claiming that they only opposed the king's advisers.

Charles, privately convinced that he would need to fight what he recognized was effectively a rival Scottish government, allowed a General Assembly at Glasgow in November 1638. This strongly Presbyterian gathering again proved violently hostile. It abolished episcopacy and deposed the remaining bishops. It also repudiated the new prayer book (in a revealing rhetorical flourish it was accused of being 'heathenish, Popish, Jewish and Arminian' – as though anything could be such different things at once).

Charles rejected these decisions, even though, with the ambitious Presbyterian nobleman Archibald Campbell, 8th Earl of Argyll, emerging as the Tables' leader, it was now a national government in all but name. He prepared a royal army in northern England and moved it towards the border. The Covenanters gathered arms and prepared their defences.

So began the Bishops' Wars. Led by Alexander Leslie, a battle-hardened Scottish veteran of the recent Continental wars, and by the Earl of Montrose, the Covenanters' superior forces successfully blocked Charles's advance near Berwick in June 1639. Rather than fight at a clear disadvantage, Charles conceded further negotiations, and permitted meetings of the General Assembly and Scots Parliament. The former predictably repeated the Glasgow decisions; the latter also declared episcopacy abolished and agreed to end royal control of parliamentary business. Charles again was indignant and unmoved.

Key idea: Mercenaries

Long before national conscription, when governments often simply wanted the best possible personnel, foreign soldiers and commanders were widely recruited. Scots, from a poor society with limited career opportunities but, because of its relative violence and instability, a reputation for courage and military know-how, were employed as mercenaries in exceptionally large

The second phase of the Bishops' Wars saw Leslie's army advance on Newcastle and Durham in August and September 1640, which they occupied as Charles's feeble forces melted away. This humiliation finally compelled Charles to call a new English Parliament, the first for 11 years and the body of angry and frustrated MPs who would shortly themselves begin a civil war against him.

The Scottish dimension to the final months before open warfare broke out in Britain was in one sense minimal. Covenanting forces remained in northern England until late in 1641, doing no real physical damage but causing the king huge embarrassment. Charles gambled on yet more concessions – unerringly offered, as was his way, just too late to be convincing or effective, and probably in any case calculated to shore up his position in England, which remained his priority, by giving ground in Scotland, which ultimately mattered less. To this effect he spent the period from August to November 1641 in Edinburgh during which he accepted the recent decisions of the General Assembly and Scots Parliament. Leslie also became Earl of Leven and the Earl of Argyll a marquess.

Charles's ploy failed, however, because events were now spiralling wildly out of control at Westminster. The king and his English opponents, divided over his religious policies but also over the proper relationship between crown and Parliament, were soon at daggers drawn.

On 22 August 1642 Charles I raised his own standard at Newark in Nottinghamshire: England, at least, faced civil war. How would the Scots, still antagonistic to the same ruler, respond?

Allies against the king

The Scots' approach to the English conflict was complicated by pronounced differences of opinion among Charles's Scottish opponents. In particular, not all were willing to join with England's parliamentarians, much less risk provoking civil war in Scotland itself, especially given the concessions the king had made.

Another issue was Ireland. For decades Scots had been settling there under royal encouragement. A rising in 1641 by Catholics, with massacres of Protestant immigrants and vicious reprisals by both sides, therefore became an acute problem for the Covenanters, who quickly despatched an army to Ulster to help protect Scottish settlers.

In the event the Scots only properly committed themselves after the English Parliament formally asked for assistance. Crucially, however, this request came with a proposal: in return for Scottish help, Presbyterianism could become England's official church settlement.

A formal treaty, the Solemn League and Covenant, was agreed in September 1643, though Presbyterianism was alluded to rather than explicitly mentioned. This was because many English parliamentarians were actually Independents, favouring a radical Protestantism allowing individual congregations to follow their own consciences: as the Scots would later realize, people like this – the as-yet-unknown Oliver Cromwell was one – thought that rigid discipline imposed by Presbyterian church courts was no better than rigid discipline imposed by the king's bishops.

With this somewhat vague but promising-sounding agreement in place, the Committee of Estates, the Scottish parliamentary body that now ran the country's affairs, entered the English war.

Importantly, however, there were also Scots fighting actively on the king's side. The most prominent was Montrose, who had quarrelled with Argyll, the leader of Clan Campbell and the Covenanting aristocracy's dominant figure. Indeed, Montrose saw royal authority as a necessary bulwark against either Presbyterian dictatorship or outright anarchy. He was assisted by Alasdair MacColla, a Catholic and Gaelic lord from the Hebrides with strong connections among the MacDonalds of both western Scotland and northern Ireland and a deep hatred of the Campbells.

The period between 1643 and 1645 therefore saw something of a paradox. In England the Scottish Covenanters, with their greater military experience, proved a vital aid to Parliament, playing a key role in its greatest victories. Most famously, at Marston Moor outside York on 2 July 1644, a force of 14,000 Scots under Leven and 11,000 Englishmen commanded by Lord Fairfax crushed the king's roughly equal-sized army: Charles thereafter abandoned northern England, previously an important area of strength.

But in Scotland itself things were quite different. Montrose, made a marquess by Charles in 1644, humiliated the Covenanting regime in its own backyard. Less than two months after Marston Moor, the army of Montrose and MacColla, a motley assortment of Highlanders, Irishmen and Lowland Royalists, defeated a superior force of Covenanters at Tippermuir near Perth; 12 days later they repeated the feat near Aberdeen; and the following February they defeated a larger number of Campbells at Inverlochy in the Highlands. As if this were not enough, three more stunning Royalist victories followed: Auldearn, Alford and Kilsyth, all fought and won in the summer of 1645.

Confident, determined and flexible, Montrose and MacColla formed a formidable partnership that cut a swathe through the military resources of the Committee of Estates, some of whose members had by August 1645 sought refuge in Berwick. Montrose, seemingly dominant in Scotland, was appointed Lord Lieutenant and captain-general by a grateful king.

'He either fears his fate too much,
Or his deserts are small,
That dares not put it to the touch
To gain or lose it all.'
Marquess of Montrose, 'My Dear and Only Love' (1640s)

But Charles's weakness in England soon undercut his unexpected strength north of the border. Having defeated Charles at Naseby on 12 June 1645, the main Covenanting army was able to spare David Leslie, another of the Scots' veteran commanders, to return home. Leslie surprised Montrose on the misty morning of 13 September at Philiphaugh near Selkirk in the Borders, defeating his Highlanders and, in the aftermath, massacring Irish women among the Royalist camp followers (the killing of Irish people engaged in the fighting in mainland Britain being a particularly repellent feature of the period).

This one setback shattered the newly minted myth of Montrose's invincibility, which in any case had never made him widely popular. In particular, his reliance on imported Irish troops and on Catholic Highlanders, together with his being a former Covenanting turncoat, had always limited his appeal throughout Presbyterian and Lowland society.

Leslie then executed a successful mopping-up operation. By September 1646 Montrose had fled to Norway. Charles, defeated in a longer and bloodier civil war than anyone had ever expected, appeared finally to have run out of options.

Covenanted kings

If Montrose's meteoric campaign of 1644–5 took everyone by surprise, what happened next in Scotland was even less predictable.

We have already seen how the Solemn League and Covenant had originally promised the spread of Scottish-style Presbyterianism to England. The Westminster Assembly of Divines had even convened in 1643 to devise a uniform system of church government and common services for both kingdoms. By 1646, however, its members had failed to deliver.

The main problem was that the Independents, especially strong in Cromwell's New Model Army, which had acquired the upper hand in England by winning the war for Parliament, rejected the Scots' vision of hierarchical authority imposed on all believers through Presbyterianism. An agreed Calvinist statement of belief and form of worship emerged – the Westminster Confession of

Faith, still used today by the Church of Scotland. But the gulf over church government proved unbridgeable.

The resulting acrimony had seismic implications. It split England's Presbyterian parliamentarians from their increasingly dominant Independent comrades. This offered Charles, a prisoner of the New Model Army by 1647 but with no final peace agreed, the chance to re-open the war against a now-divided enemy. More extraordinary still, the rupture between Parliament and the Scots created the thrilling possibility – inconceivable in 1638 or 1642 or even 1645 – of Charles doing a deal with the Covenanters and using Scottish military power against Cromwell and the radicals who had captured the English parliamentary leadership.

The result was a secret agreement in December 1647, known as the Engagement. Charles would impose Presbyterianism on England himself in return for Scottish support. Many Covenanters, including Argyll, Leven and Leslie, disliked it, either on principle or out of suspicion about Charles's motives, and so did not participate. It fell to the king's kinsman and supporter, the Duke of Hamilton, to lead a Scottish army.

The second civil war in England began early in 1648 in south Wales and in Kent, as Royalists and some English Presbyterians rose against Cromwell. For his part Hamilton marched south in July with 20,000 men under his command. This was met by Cromwell and just 8,000 men near Preston. But in a complicated three-day engagement on 17–19 August the numerically superior Scots were easily beaten. Hamilton was captured and subsequently executed.

The strategic and political consequences, however, were far-reaching. Preston effectively strangled the second civil war at birth, simultaneously proving to Cromwell that neither Charles nor the Presbyterians could be trusted. This left the New Model Army and the Independents in total command. The Engagers' failure therefore had a quite unintended (and, to most Scots, unwanted) outcome, hastening the culmination of England's crisis that came with Charles's beheading on 30 January 1649.

Charles's death changed everything and it changed nothing. It was and remains a great constitutional turning-point. Even if never repeated, it firmly established a new understanding of the relationship between ruler and ruled in England – a reigning monarch being tried as a traitor to the people and put to death for his crimes.

In Scotland, however, it did little that the Engagement had not already done. In particular, it commenced the Scottish reign of Charles II, the late king's son and heir. Though in a Dutch exile, he was duly proclaimed king by the Scots Parliament on 5 February 1649. But like his father, the new ruler found there were strings attached: specifically, a requirement to embrace Presbyterianism throughout Britain and to sign the Covenant himself.

This was not easy to accept, and while negotiations proceeded slowly he encouraged Montrose to land in Orkney to apply a little pressure to the Scots. This cynical ploy went badly. Montrose, lacking support, was defeated at Carbisdale in Sutherland on 27 April 1650 by an army loyal to Argyll and the radical Covenanters. Hiding with Neil Macleod of Assynt, who betrayed him, Montrose was conveyed to Edinburgh where he was tried and hanged by the Covenanting government.

With no other alternatives now available, Charles II accepted the Covenanters' terms and returned to Scotland in June 1650. Cromwell and the New Model Army, however, were alert to any sign of Stuart revival. On 3 September 1650 they smashed the much larger Scottish army led by Leslie, now fighting for the king, at Dunbar to the east of Edinburgh. The capital was soon securely in English hands. Prisoners from Dunbar were marched off to Durham, perhaps 3,500 dying en route or in captivity.

Formally signing the Solemn League and Covenant, Charles II was crowned at Scone on 1 January 1651. But it was a hollow victory. The king despised and mistrusted his Scottish allies. And they had already effectively lost control of their country to Cromwell. Charles II was able to persuade them to mount one last desperate attempt to defeat Cromwell. The broader strategic aim was to invade England and bring together an unlikely grand alliance, rousing English Presbyterians and old Royalists to fight alongside the Scots, all on behalf of a Covenanted king.

Charles's Scottish army, closely monitored by Cromwell, got as far as Worcester where on 3 September 1651 it was destroyed. Leslie was fortunate only to have to spend the next few years in the Tower of London; the king, after hiding up an oak tree, escaped to France.

A strangely constructive dictatorship

Substantial Scottish resistance to Cromwell was now largely over. Edinburgh was already firmly under English control. General John Lambert defeated the last significant Scottish force at Inverkeithing in Fife on 20 July 1651, opening up the way northwards; and then General George Monck, who had fought for Charles I in the Bishops' Wars but was now a respected subordinate and friend of Cromwell, had taken Stirling, Perth and Dundee – in the latter case storming it when it held out for King Charles, killing 800 citizens in the process and burning every vessel in the harbour. A few remote strongholds – the Bass Rock in the Forth, Dunnottar Castle perched on its Kincardineshire cliff top – were reduced in the coming months.

Scotland, for the first time since Edward I, found itself by late 1651 an occupied country, governed by an English administration using overwhelming military force. The way was therefore clear for Cromwell to resolve the key problem in Anglo-Scottish relations since 1603. But he did so, and was uniquely free to do so, at the point of a republican sword.

Precious stones

Scotland's royal regalia, now on display at Edinburgh Castle, have had a colourful history. Comprising a crown, a sceptre and a sword all made between 1490 and 1540, they were used at coronations up to Charles II's at Scone in 1651 but never since. Under Cromwell's occupation – he successfully destroyed the old English regalia as hated symbols of monarchy – they were hidden by Royalists first at Dunnottar Castle, then in Kinneff parish church, and later were placed for safe keeping in a box in Edinburgh Castle ... and promptly lost. They were finally rediscovered by Sir Walter Scott in 1818.

In October 1651 Cromwell issued the Tender of Union – 'tender' suggests merely an offer but it was definitely not one that the Scots, who were not consulted, would be able to refuse. Under its terms Scotland would cease to be independent. A single expanded Commonwealth would come into existence, with a Parliament at Westminster in which Scotland would have 30 representatives. All forms of Protestantism (Episcopalianism excepted) were to be tolerated.

Small-scale resistance to Cromwell's regime continued. At least until 1655, when Monck finally quashed all remaining appetite for Royalist adventurism, there were local risings and minor engagements that indicated significant levels of opposition to occupation by the English republic. Charles's principal agent was the Earl of Middleton, an able soldier, assisted by the Earl of Glencairn. But disagreements between Charles's supporters, together with the government's military strength, made this insurgency more a serious irritant than a grave counter-revolutionary threat.

Meanwhile the Cromwellian regime was busy reforming the reach and efficiency of government – again without consultation. As commander-in-chief until 1655 and thereafter as the dominant figure in Cromwell's hand-picked Council of Scotland, Monck could actually re-shape the country's politics and administration as he saw fit. And historians have generally agreed that he chose well.

> 'A man may ride all Scotland over with a switch in his hand and £100 in his pocket, which he could not have done these 500 years.'
> Thomas Burton, *Diary* (1650s)

Justice and taxation in particular were better run: 'honest general George', as he became known, proved more impartial than any native Scot had ever been and much more effective in enforcing Scots law for the benefit of almost everyone. As chance would have it, the competent and conscientious Monck would also do more than anyone else to bring the Cromwellian dictatorship and the English republic to a close.

As the military commander in Scotland, he became the key figure who, after Cromwell's death and the accession of his insubstantial son Richard in 1658, decided to throw his considerable weight behind a return to full parliamentary decision-making and, eventually, a Stuart restoration. Marching a select force from Coldstream on the border on 1 January 1660 – these men, previously Royalism's sworn enemies, would soon become the king's prestigious 2nd Foot Guards, today's Coldstream Guards – Monck arrived in London, helped reinstate Parliament and began negotiations for Charles II's return.

In that very specific sense the Restoration throughout Britain had direct origins in a small Berwickshire village. This did not, however, guarantee that Charles II would be welcomed with open arms by everyone in Scotland.

Fact check

1 What did the Act of Revocation do?
  a Annul land grants
  b Abolish Presbyterianism
  c Suspend Parliament
  d Penalize Catholics

2 Who was William Laud?
  a Archbishop of St Andrews
  b Bishop of Glasgow
  c Earl of Leven
  d Archbishop of Canterbury

3 Where did rebellion against the new prayer book allegedly start?
  a Greyfriars' Kirk
  b St Giles's Cathedral
  c St Machar's Cathedral
  d Westminster Abbey

4 Who drafted the Covenant?
  a Johnston and Henderson
  b Argyll and Montrose
  c Charles and Laud
  d David Leslie

5 Who assisted Montrose in his victories?
  a the Earl of Leven
  b the Earl of Argyll
  c Alasdair MacColla
  d the Duke of Hamilton

6 By which agreement did the Scots switch sides and support Charles in 1647?
  a the Covenant
  b the Resolution
  c the Revocation
  d the Engagement

7 Where did Cromwell destroy the Covenanters' army in 1650?
- **a** Dunbar
- **b** Marston Moor
- **c** Naseby
- **d** Tippermuir

8 Who ran Scotland under Cromwell?
- **a** John Lambert
- **b** the Duke of Hamilton
- **c** the Earl of Middleton
- **d** George Monck

Dig Deeper

Maurice Lee Jr, *The Road to Revolution* (Urbana, 1985).

Allan Macinnes, *Charles I and the Making of the Covenanting Movement, 1625–1641* (Edinburgh, 1991).

David Stevenson, *The Scottish Revolution, 1637–1644* (Newton Abbot, 1973).

David Stevenson, *Revolution and Counter-Revolution in Scotland, 1644–1651* (London, 1977).

Frances Dow, *Cromwellian Scotland* (Edinburgh, 1979).

A restoration and a further revolution

A merry monarch has the last laugh

The Restoration was a major turning point in British history.

It marked the failure of a radical constitutional experiment and the end of a period of unprecedented political upheaval. The republic was over. But, because of what had happened since 1642, monarchy too would never be the same again.

There were also differences between what the Restoration meant north and south of the border, with important implications for what happened next.

First, although Royalists naturally insisted that Charles II's reign had begun at the precise moment of his father's death in 1649, he had never been crowned King of England. In Scotland, however, Charles's coronation had occurred a decade earlier. He had also had the opportunity, during some difficult first-hand experiences in 1650–1, to form a distinctly unfavourable impression of many of Scotland's leaders.

Second, Charles returned to become, as English monarch, the supreme head of the Church of England. Conveniently this reflected his Episcopalian preferences. In Scotland, though, as a consequence of his dealings in 1650, Charles was now that most unlikely (and uncomfortable) of creatures: a Covenanted king. The problems created by this crucial difference were worsened by the fact that Charles never saw Scotland again, reverting to the absentee rule that had generated so much mutual misunderstanding between the Scots and both his father and his grandfather.

On 1 January 1661 a Scots Parliament convened. An early result was the Act Rescissory which voided all legislation since 1633 – as if the laws of the Covenanting revolution and Cromwellian occupation had never happened. Middleton and Glencairn, helped by their support for Charles in the 1650s, held sway.

Some of the business of the restored royal government was personal. There were wrongs to right and scores to settle. The Marquess of Montrose's remains were reassembled and paraded solemnly through Edinburgh for re-burial in St Giles's Cathedral on 11 May 1661. His old nemesis, however, received the opposite treatment just 16 days later. Argyll was convicted of treason for collaborating with Monck's occupying forces and he was now beheaded. Interestingly, the two enemies were eventually joined in death as they had been in life, Argyll today lying in St Giles's, his tomb directly facing Montrose's.

Johnston of Warriston, joint author of the National Covenant and scourge of royal government, was similarly singled out. Hiding in France, he was handed over and tried for treasonable collusion with the regicide regime. Warriston was hanged in Edinburgh in June 1663 and his severed head placed on a spike on the city's Netherbow.

Aside from chilling retribution against prominent individuals, the Restoration government, coming after the long reign of the Covenanters, had far bigger fish to fry, especially in religious matters. In September 1661 an intention to restore Episcopacy was proclaimed. By 1662 bishops had also been reinstated, the Presbyterian courts abolished and all clergy required to repudiate the Covenant.

This was doubly controversial. Episcopalianism was an anathema to many Presbyterians and especially to hardcore Covenanters. But it was the accompanying sense of betrayal that made things worse. A monarch who had embraced the Covenant had now gone back on an oath taken before God – not only demonstrating untrustworthiness but also committing an act of sacrilege.

The new leaders of the Episcopalian church were despised for the same reasons: James Sharp, who became Archbishop of St Andrews, was especially reviled by former Covenanter allies as an unprincipled traitor.

Opposition was widespread. Many Covenanting parish ministers either had to be ejected for refusing to accept the new requirements or simply walked out. Those who left, however, did not vanish into thin air. Instead they often re-appeared as independent preachers at 'conventicles'. It therefore soon became clear that, rather than achieving uniformity and effective royal control of Scotland's Church, the government had simply created what was in effect a worryingly militant and entirely unofficial strand of Presbyterianism.

Key idea: Conventicles

In the period after 1661 many Covenanters and ejected ministers held their own services in conventicles – illicit congregations meeting out in the fields of southern Scotland. The practice was troubling in its radical religious complexion and strictly illegal. It was also politically threatening because attendees were frequently armed and the gatherings therefore had an essentially paramilitary character.

Middleton was chiefly responsible and to him should be attributed much of the blame for what followed. But by 1664 he had been eclipsed by John Maitland, 2nd Earl of Lauderdale (and 1st Duke from 1672), a former Covenanter who had helped negotiate the Engagement in 1648 and who had been imprisoned under Cromwell. As secretary of state, Lauderdale, a skilled political operator, was able to dominate Scottish affairs, although he was, of course, also left to deal with the bitter legacy of Middleton's policies.

Lauderdale, it appears, had not favoured the ruthless re-imposition of Episcopacy. But this did little to help make the government and its religious policies more palatable. Indeed, in 1666 open warfare erupted in the form of the Pentland Rising by armed Covenanters. They were defeated by the Royalist cavalry officer Tam Dalyell at Rullion Green near Edinburgh on 28 November. Severe punishments followed – hanging for dozens; banishment to the English colonies in the New World for others. Yet this only supplied new martyrs to keep the radical flame of the Covenant burning.

'Killing Time'

Under Lauderdale genuine attempts were made to modify the Restoration religious settlement. In particular he was associated with a more balanced approach. Concessions were offered, aimed at wider opinion, while seeking to isolate and eliminate more extreme opposition.

In the late 1660s some moderate Covenanting clergy were re-embraced and, under what were termed 'indulgences', retained in their parishes – to the annoyance of the more doctrinaire bishops. An indemnity was granted to former rebels. So confident was Lauderdale that this would draw the Presbyterian opposition's teeth that he felt able to have the Parliament of 1669–70 pass the Act of Supremacy. This made Charles II the head of the Scottish Church and made attending conventicles punishable by death.

This two-pronged strategy continued into the next decade. Late in 1672, for example, another 80 Presbyterian clergy received parishes. Yet this approach always had its limits, given that hostility to Episcopacy remained widespread in the south.

Conventicling also flourished. It was probably this that eventually led Lauderdale to favour a return to repression. Accordingly, the Privy Council issued decrees in 1674 against unlicensed gatherings. Even then Lauderdale tried to interest the bishops in balancing harshness with further targeted concessions. Neither side, however, wanted compromise.

A tougher line thus became even more necessary. This reached its epitome in 1678 when Lauderdale recruited 5,000 soldiers, mainly from the reliable Episcopalian and Catholic clans of the north and west. Known as the Highland Host, they were quartered in the Covenanter-dominated south-west, to deter conventiclers from armed activities. Unfortunately it soon proved counter-productive.

On 3 May 1679, riding from Edinburgh to his St Andrews home, James Sharp was assassinated by Covenanters on Magus Muir in Fife. The murder of Scotland's leading cleric was a sensational event. The perpetrators were soon tried and executed, but again they became martyrs to the cause.

Charles's government now faced not merely civil disobedience but low-intensity civil war. Another indication of the problem's extent was offered at Drumclog in Lanarkshire on 1 June, where 200 conventiclers defeated government forces under James Graham of Claverhouse. The victorious radicals were exhilarated at having struck a body blow against an ungodly government – against the Anti-Christ, as some irreconcilables saw Charles II's regime. But their triumph was brief.

On 22 June Claverhouse, assisted by Charles's illegitimate son the Duke of Monmouth, smashed them at Bothwell Brig in the Clyde valley. As after Rullion Green, severe punishment caused lasting Presbyterian resentment: a thousand Covenanters were imprisoned wretchedly in Edinburgh's Greyfriars' churchyard. There followed what became known, thanks to its meticulous documenting by Robert Wodrow, an 18th-century clergyman and historian with strong Covenanting sympathies, as the 'Killing Time' – a period of intensified state persecution of committed Presbyterians. Some resisted to the end, arguing not only for non-submission but also for the violent overthrow of a king whom they reckoned was doing the work of Satan.

The most significant of the diehards were the armed followers of the field preacher Richard Cameron, from Falkland in Fife, known for his fiery temperament and extreme views. The Sanquhar Declaration, read out at that Dumfriesshire town on 22 June 1680, which painted Charles as a godless usurper, was little short of an open declaration of war.

> '... we, for ourselves, and all that will adhere to us as the representative of the true Presbyterian Kirk and covenanted nation of Scotland, considering the great hazard of lying under such a sin any longer, do by these presents, disown Charles Stuart, that has been reigning, or rather tyrannising, as we may say, on the throne of Britain these years bygone, as having any right, title to, or interest in, the said Crown of Scotland.'
>
> The Sanquhar Declaration (1680)

As things transpired, Cameron was killed in an encounter at Airds Moss in Ayrshire just a month later. But the Cameronians, and their leader's uncompromising Protestant ideals, lived on.

Soldiers and psalms

Cameron's disciples, arch-enemies of royal power, had a paradoxical afterlife. On 14 May 1689 at Douglas in Lanarkshire, his former followers agreed to fight for the new government and became the 26th Foot, later The Cameronians (Scottish Rifles), under the command of William Cleland. Thereafter they retained peculiar Covenanting traditions: recruits received bibles, carried weapons on church parade, posted sentries and held open-air conventicles, while officers never toasted the monarch's health. In the late 20th century as the British Army shrank The Cameronians very unusually requested disbandment rather than dilute this unique heritage by merger with any other regiment. It was therefore as late as 14 May 1968 that Cameron's men, at one last conventicle at Douglas with Cleland's sword present, finally marched proudly into history.

Ill-health and royal doubts about his effectiveness had by now cost Lauderdale his position. His place was taken by the king's younger brother James, Duke of York. Residing in Edinburgh from October 1679 and serving as the figurehead for Scottish policy until March 1682, he has subsequently acquired much of the blame for the Killing Time. Also closely associated with the cruel misdeeds carried out in Charles's name between 1681 and 1685 were Dalyell ('Bluidy Tam' to his many enemies, who whispered that he played cards with the Devil) and the charismatic but ruthless Claverhouse.

That military commanders in particular took the leading role in disciplining people in matters of religious observance might seem strange. But the Scottish Privy Council, horrified at conventicling's revolutionary potential, had authorized summary execution for anyone possessing unlicensed weaponry or refusing the oath of allegiance to the crown. Officials who despised the Presbyterians therefore had a free hand in rooting out disloyalty by terrifying whole communities into submission.

Some of the victims became widely known, not least because Wodrow's writings depicted several unforgettable martyrs. John Brown of Ayrshire died in May 1685 in front of his children and pregnant wife, allegedly shot by Claverhouse himself for rejecting the oath. Even more heartrendingly, that same month Margaret Wilson, an 18-year-old Covenanter, and Margaret McLauchlan, her elderly companion, were tied to stakes on the beach at Wigton and left to drown in the incoming tide of the

Solway Firth: there is even a marvellously affecting 19th-century painting of the scene by John Millais – though some historians insist the women's awful sentence was never in fact carried out.

There is scope also for arguing over the numbers killed and over where responsibility ultimately lay. But there is no doubt that the Killing Time traumatized many who lived through it. It poisoned the minds of subsequent generations against the late Stuart kings. And it further radicalized some Presbyterians in their rejection of the crown's power in matters of Christian faith and religious conviction.

A king much misunderstood?

On 6 February 1685 Charles II died and James, Duke of York, succeeded him as King of England, Scotland and Ireland.

James had already spent the best part of three years in Edinburgh. Essentially he had been in exile from acute political tensions in London over his likely succession, as an avowed Catholic, to Charles II who, though a prolific father of bastards, lacked a legitimate child. As a result, when he became King James VII and II, he knew Scotland better, and certainly had more extensive personal connections there, than any monarch since James VI.

The most complex of kings

James VII's previous residence at Holyroodhouse has several implications for a rounded assessment of the man. One is that his genuine interests in learning and the arts led him to endorse or directly to contribute to the establishment of several key Scottish cultural institutions that are still with us today – the Advocates' Library (now the National Library of Scotland), the Royal College of Physicians, and the posts of Historiographer-Royal and Geographer-Royal. James's involvement in enlightened developments of this kind is all the more perplexing because so many people's opinion of him has been coloured by the accusation that he was also the evil genius behind the Killing Time. Yet this view of James probably owes as much to hatred and suspicion of Catholicism as it does to what is known about his personal role in

As king James tried to encourage toleration of those unlicensed conventicles held in private houses: after all, unlike the large-scale armed gatherings out in the fields, they were obviously no threat to peace and order. He was also willing to pardon any who would say the words 'God bless the king' – though given the intense zeal of the more extreme Covenanters, takers were few and far between.

But we cannot exonerate James from all charges. He was a man and a prince of his time. And his occasional flexibility on questions of loyalty, obedience and religious belief did not extend anything like as far as we might want in the 21st century. He made some serious mistakes, such as the Act pushed through the Scots Parliament at the start of his reign making attendance at conventicles or harbouring their participants a capital offence. Another error was his plan not merely to achieve toleration for Catholicism but actually to re-establish it in Scotland and England on at least an equal footing with Protestantism.

How difficult it would be to fulfil such contentious objectives was shown in the year of James's succession. For in June 1685 occurred the co-ordinated rebellions that in England were raised by the Duke of Monmouth and in Scotland by the 9th Earl of Argyll, the latter the son of the executed Marquess and Covenanting leader. The new king's religious preferences provided more than enough opportunity for both men to claim that they were simply the righteous defenders of Protestantism.

The risings, as it happened, went badly. Monmouth and Argyll quickly shared the same experience of defeat, capture and execution. In Scotland the outcome confirmed that James enjoyed sufficient support, especially among the Highland clans, to see off comparatively easily an under-resourced challenge from a Protestant nobleman. Yet the episode should also have been a warning – a reminder that his devout Catholicism, his desire to give his faith official status, and his already toxic relationship with radical Presbyterianism, together left his sovereignty open to challenge.

Developments in Edinburgh soon bore this out. For James's commitment to promoting Catholicism even divided his leading advisors. James Drummond, 4th Earl of Perth, the chancellor, an Episcopalian and then Catholic convert, was encouraging. But William Douglas, 1st Duke of Queensberry, a Protestant and lord treasurer (who later claimed James had offered him £20,000 to convert), was horrified. Anti-Catholic rioting in 1686 further underlined the scale of the problem for a monarch seeking to reverse the single most important consequence of the Scottish Reformation in what had until recently been an explicitly Covenanted kingdom.

James VII and II also had problems persuading the Scottish and English parliaments to approve toleration both for Catholics and for those Protestants who rejected the official churches. In the end he simply declared those measures lawful by royal proclamation. Accordingly in February 1686, Scottish Quakers and Catholics were allowed to worship at home. Twelve months later moderate Presbyterians received the same right. James also freed Scottish Catholics from various legal restrictions imposed at the Reformation. But the political damage inflicted by appearing to confirm that this was indeed an aspiring absolute monarch bent on overriding parliamentary processes and imposing his own religious vision by extra-constitutional means outweighed any possible gains for James among these policies' individual beneficiaries.

The not-so-glorious revolution

The backlash, when it came, had its focus in London rather than Edinburgh. For it was James's English subjects who first concluded that their king had made himself dispensable and that they needed to find an acceptable way of getting rid of him.

This was the genesis of what in England was and is known as the Glorious Revolution of 1688. It was 'glorious' not least because it was quick and cost few casualties – for the English, at least. In Scotland and Ireland, dragged along in England's wake, the process of replacing a bad king with a good one was neither smooth nor peaceful.

Not for the first time, the immediate trigger for crisis was the royal succession. Since 1685 it had seemed that James, without a male child, would be succeeded by Mary, one of his Protestant daughters by his first wife. But on 10 June 1688 James and his second wife, a Catholic, finally had a son, James Francis Edward, opening up the likelihood of a permanently Catholic monarchy. This being intolerable to many in England, particularly in view of the royal policy of seeking to re-establish Catholicism as an official religion, leading members of the Whig and Tory factions in Parliament decided that it had to be prevented.

An approach was made to William, Mary's husband and leader of the Dutch republic. Like his wife William was a grandchild of Charles I and third in line to the throne before the new royal baby was born. He was also not merely a Protestant but the emerging leader of the grand European alliance of Protestant states against Louis XIV of France: as a proven ruler with the right religion and the right blood flowing through his veins, William's credentials as a replacement for his father-in-law were obviously strong.

In November 1688 William landed in Devon and over the next few weeks England gradually fell in behind him. Many towns declared their support. Leading allies of James deserted. A couple of very small military engagements were fought, both won by William's forces. And when told that William could not guarantee his safety (clearly the aim being to encourage him to flee rather than have to fight him and then worry about what to do with him), James conveniently left London in early December and headed for France, in effect abdicating and creating a vacancy instead of standing and fighting for his throne.

A Convention – a parliamentary gathering not formally authorized by the reigning sovereign – then gathered at Westminster to hammer out a response. In February 1689 this body duly declared William and Mary joint monarchs of England. In Scotland, where English events had been observed with understandably keen interest, the revolution took a completely different shape. The

Scottish Privy Council hurried to declare for William as soon as James had fled. But a Convention also met in Edinburgh to decide what should be done following their king's abrupt departure from Britain. The Scots' options were narrowed by letters received in March 1689 from both James and William: the former threatened reprisals for disloyalty while the latter was tactful and hinted at concessions to the Convention in return for support.

On 4 April the Convention voted to end James VII's reign – in itself a dramatic moment in Scottish history since it involved accepting the principle, already implicit in Queen Mary's deposition in 1567 and long advocated in George Buchanan's political theories, that Scotland's parliamentary representatives could terminate the reigns of the country's monarchs. This decision was justified by reference to the Articles of Grievances in which the Convention listed James's faults and accused him of defaulting on his obligation to observe the kingdom's laws and constitutional customs.

> 'The settling of the monarchy and ancient government of this Kingdom admitting no delay, we did upon the eleventh instant proclaim Your Majesty and your royal consort, King and Queen of Scotland ... and humbly to present the petition or claim of right of the subjects of this Kingdom, as also to represent some things found grievous to this nation, which we humbly entreat Your Majesty to remedy by wholesome laws in your first Parliament.'
> Letter from Scottish Convention to William of Orange (16 April 1689)

They also issued the Claim of Right, which set out the conditions on which replacement monarchs would be accepted. The crown was offered to William and Mary on those terms. They formally became co-sovereigns of Scotland on 11 May 1689.

Yet this was not the end of the matter, since the Convention certainly did not speak for all shades of opinion. It had been dominated by Presbyterians only because Episcopalians refused to participate after mid-March 1689 in what they saw as an illegitimate process concocted by people determined to remove a lawful king and replace him with a usurper. Given their deep attachment to hereditary monarchy as much as to a church governed by the king's bishops, most Episcopalians put loyalty to the king, and their previous oaths to uphold his divine right to rule, ahead of their own religious reservations as Protestants about James's Catholicism.

This decision, principled but naive, allowed the Presbyterians, James's bitterest opponents, to make the running in Edinburgh. Having abandoned the constitutional machinery to the Presbyterians, the Episcopalians became the main contributors to a new opposition movement committed to reversing the revolution by force. Its Scottish members became known as the Jacobites – from *Jacobus*, the Latin for James. Claverhouse, now Viscount Dundee (and henceforth known in song and story as 'Bonnie Dundee'), took the lead in making Jacobitism militarily effective, raising support among those Highland clans who had previously been bulwarks of James's power. What resulted was a specifically Scottish civil war over how to respond to a British revolution initially conceived and pushed through in the southeast of England.

Dundee's forces fought a successful engagement on 27 July at the strategic point of Killiecrankie, in the pass on the Tay that carries the main road from the Highlands down towards Perth. Facing Hugh Mackay, the commander of Presbyterian forces loyal to William, the Jacobites won a stirring victory. But in a disastrous moment Dundee himself was hit by a single musket shot and died on the battlefield.

Without his skill and talismanic status, James's supporters were fatally weakened. This was proven on 21 August when a second battle took place at nearby Dunkeld: this time the Jacobites failed to dislodge a much smaller occupying force of Williamites and Cameronians led by William Cleland – at 28 already a veteran of Drumclog and Bothwell Brig – who died in the fighting. The Jacobite clansmen thereafter fell back on their Highland heartlands where in a third battle at the Haughs of Cromdale, fought in Speyside the following spring, they were defeated and their forces dispersed.

In effect, therefore, the revolution had been resolved in Scotland, albeit by a quite different route, and with broadly the same outcome as in England. William and Mary were monarchs. James and his allies had been removed from power. The dependence of the crown upon parliamentary approval was clear. Catholicism had been defeated and Protestantism saved.

As the next 15 years proved, however, the situation was actually far more complicated, and the circumstances more difficult for Scotland, in particular, than this superficial description makes it sound.

When William met Mary

As we have seen, William II (or William III in his English style) was, in a sense, a very modern kind of king. This was especially so in Scotland, where he was crowned only after being endorsed by Parliament. And even then William only ascended the throne because he accepted – or at least he finally did early in 1690 through gritted teeth after being threatened with non-payment of taxes – a series of explicit conditions intended to make him govern as a constitutional ruler.

Yet a number of difficulties peculiar to Scotland had also been inherited from before the revolution. These continued to cause William serious problems.

First, like his predecessors since 1603, he ruled from London, and there was no doubt where his priorities lay. Indeed, William became the first (though not the last) King of Scotland never even to see the country at all. This meant that his Scottish policies were often ill-informed. Royal decision-making remained peculiarly prone to misreading clear signals from Scotland, generating mutual suspicion between crown and people.

Second, the revolution created as many problems as it solved. Above all, the fact that the Presbyterians were the new regime's principal backers and that the Episcopalians remained attached to the exiled Catholic dynasty meant that William faced a contradiction. He understood Calvinism: most Dutch, like most Scots, had embraced it following the Reformation. But he disliked Presbyterianism, preferring the firm royal control of the Church that only Episcopacy offered. William's reign was therefore marked by tensions between what he really wanted and what was achievable given the nature of his own Scottish support.

This divergence was clearly seen from April 1689 onwards. For the Presbyterians predictably sought to extend the revolution into the Church. This they accomplished with the help of the Convention, and then the succeeding Parliament, which passed laws that it must have seriously pained the new co-sovereigns to ratify.

Most important was the Act of Settlement of 1690, abolishing the entire paraphernalia of Episcopacy, including bishops, bishoprics and the doctrine of royal supremacy. A Presbyterian system of church courts, wholly independent of the crown and the government, replaced it (and survives even now). Parliament in addition endorsed the Westminster Confession of Faith as the legal basis of a thoroughly Calvinist theology for the post-revolutionary Church of Scotland.

It also abolished 'patronage', the crucial but contentious right of landlords, town councils, universities and the crown itself to appoint suitable candidates – usually safe, politically inoffensive clergy – as parish ministers. A radical Presbyterian alternative was imposed. Individual parishes would now make these vital decisions for themselves, increasing the chances that enthusiastically Calvinist candidates would be successful. In the same spirit of enforcing strict adherence to Presbyterian principles, the Scots Parliament even set up 'visitations' to ensure the university professoriate embraced the new order.

Not surprisingly, these measures triggered a substantial turnover in manpower. Around 200 Episcopalian ministers either left their parishes voluntarily or, in Covenanting districts, were aggressively 'rabbled' – hounded out – by local Presbyterians because as 'non-jurors' they refused to take the Williamite oaths. Some professors (all but one at St Andrews, for example) suffered the same fate and were replaced with more compliant alternatives. It is easy to see how this purge drove new members directly into the arms of Jacobitism: persecution is often a useful recruiting-sergeant for resistance movements.

The 1690s, even though the preceding revolution had established the modern principle of government by consent, were therefore distinctly illiberal. Much of the unpleasantness was caused by Presbyterians seeking revenge for crimes previously committed against them, especially in the Killing Time. They also wanted to avoid a counter-revolution. The problem, however, was that understandable caution easily breeds needless paranoia.

In such a situation even the slightest appearance of dissent can generate extreme repression. One notorious instance was the trial and hanging of Thomas Aikenhead in 1697, an Edinburgh student charged with making a joke about the Christian doctrine of the Trinity.

The massacre of several dozen of the MacDonalds in Glencoe on 13 February 1692 by government-supporting Campbell soldiers acting under ambiguous orders from John Dalrymple, the Lord Advocate, was another shocking example.

Murder under trust

Supposedly justified because the MacDonalds were slow to take the Williamite oaths, the killings in Glencoe attracted lasting outrage. Partly this was because the victims had unwittingly offered refuge and hospitality to their killers amid a winter blizzard. But it was also because government officials were clearly implicated in a heinous crime for which no one was punished. The setting – a gloomily magnificent glen with towering snow-capped mountains and deep defiles all too easy to romanticize – added a backdrop fit for melodrama to a shocking human story.

Also adding to the grimness of William's Scottish reign were the 'seven ill years'. At what turned out to be the coldest point in the 'Little Ice Age' from which average temperatures have since steadily risen, successive weather-induced harvest failures and consequent famines struck from 1692 onwards. Scotland's primitive agricultural and commercial systems were implicated, though this too was a wider problem: a third of Finland's population died, for example. But events in the faraway Baltic were not much noticed. What mattered was that nearby England and Holland had avoided disaster while perhaps 15 per cent of Scots starved to death and many others migrated to Ulster to escape the catastrophe.

The famines therefore highlighted a broader difficulty. This was Scotland's chronic economic under-development, especially compared with England. The Act of Parliament in 1695, which established the Bank of Scotland (whose branches are still a familiar sight in Scottish towns), was one part of the response – an attempt to create a financial institution to kick-start growth through lending. The Education Act of 1696 also arose from similar progressive instincts, finally delivering the parish school system earlier Presbyterians had sketched out.

The Darien scheme was yet another contribution to the country's urgent modernization. An Act in 1695 founded the Company of Scotland Trading to Africa and the Indies, the intention being to establish the Scots in lucrative colonial trading of the sort that had manifestly boosted the English, French and Dutch economies. The focus was to be a commercial outpost at Darien in Panama.

The whole venture, however, was badly planned and poorly executed. Darien, never properly surveyed, was in malarial rainforest. The first shipload of settlers in 1698 was dead before the second arrived. The territory was also claimed by Spain. Madrid complained to William, who needed peaceable relations with them while fighting Louis XIV. The man who was also King of Scotland therefore declined to support the Scots' scheme, while the English, who saw Darien as a cheeky attempt to steal their own trade, refused to help.

The consequences were drastic. So poor was Scotland that around one-quarter of the cash in the kingdom had been pooled together and invested. Darien's failure thus dealt a devastating blow to the nation's liquid capital. It also severely damaged national confidence in the viability of genuinely independent economic and foreign policies.

This was how Scotland entered the 18th century. The structural disadvantages of the existing regal union were increasingly difficult to ignore. And, conscious of their economic backwardness as well as of their political weakness, many influential Scots were starting to think that fundamental change was imperative.

The far-reaching consequences of this realization form the subject of the next chapter.

Fact check

1 What did the Act Rescissory do?
   a   annul Covenanter laws
   b   depose Charles II
   c   ban Presbyterianism
   d   proscribe enemies

2 Who became Archbishop of St Andrews after 1660?
   a   Andrew Melville
   b   the Earl of Lauderdale
   c   the Earl of Glencairn
   d   James Sharp

3 What were 'conventicles'?
   a   Charles II's courtiers
   b   Illegal Presbyterian services
   c   Catholic gatherings
   d   English soldiers

4 Who documented the sufferings of the 'Killing Time'?
   a   Robert Wodrow
   b   John Claverhouse
   c   Tam Dalyell
   d   James Sharp

5 Who were the Cameronians?
   a   Catholic rebels
   b   Royal troops
   c   Armed radical Covenanters
   d   Episcopalian clergy

6 Where was 'Bonnie Dundee' killed?
   a   Dunkeld
   b   Bothwell Brig
   c   Killiecrankie
   d   the Haughs of Cromdale

7 What did the Act of Settlement of 1690 do?
   a Impose Presbyterianism
   b Ban Catholicism
   c Forfeit James VII
   d Endorse William II

8 Where did the Company of Scotland establish its Darien colony?
   a Guinea
   b India
   c Jamaica
   d Panama

Dig Deeper

Julia Buckroyd, *Church and State in Scotland, 1660–1681* (Edinburgh, 1980).

I. B. Cowan, *The Scottish Covenanters, 1660–1688* (London, 1976).

Ronald Hutton, *Charles II* (London, 1989).

Alastair Mann, 'Inglorious Revolution' in *Parliamentary History* (2003).

Wout Troost, *William III, the Stadt-Holder King* (Aldershot, 2005).

Union and Jacobitism

The national crisis

The intertwined political and economic misfortunes of the late 17th century may have forced many Scots to look forward with growing anxiety. The immediate cause of the changes that would soon transform Scotland's relations with England, and in their own way be a genuine attempt to resolve the Scots' numerous difficulties, was in fact much more short-term.

With neither William and Mary nor the latter's younger sister Anne having produced an heir, the question quickly arose as to who should eventually succeed. Two factors lent this special urgency in English eyes. One was the existence of James Francis Edward Stuart, the Jacobite claimant who, on his father James VII's death in 1701, enjoyed significant support, particularly in Ireland and parts of Scotland. The second was the international situation: Louis XIV, at war with England, was providing a base and active encouragement for James – the Old Pretender, as he became known.

All of this made it imperative that the destination of the English crown be settled clearly, neatly – and promptly. The Act of Settlement, passed at Westminster in 1701, duly decreed that Anne's successor as Queen of England would be Sophia the Electoress of Hanover, a German Protestant princess and, crucially, a granddaughter of James VI and I.

The Scots were not consulted. Politicians in Edinburgh were livid at having once more been ignored on a matter with vital consequences for Scotland. Given the increasing anxiety about their own peripheral status, the insensitive way in which this matter had been handled by the English confirmed all of the Scots' worst fears about their complete irrelevance in London's eyes.

The response was two pieces of legislation, the first being the Act Anent Peace and War ('anent' being a Scots legal term for 'concerning'). Passed in 1703, this stated that after Anne's death no Scottish ruler should declare war or otherwise determine Scottish foreign policy without the express approval of the Scots Parliament. This would stop them from automatically being forced to co-operate with future strategies developed by and for English interests.

The second measure was the Act of Security. In this case Anne refused royal assent in 1703 when the Scots Parliament first approved it but it became law the next year when the Scots declined to grant further taxes unless the crown relented. By this act Scotland reserved the right to select its own successor to Anne from among the eligible Protestant candidates but that this should not be Sophia unless specific concessions were made by the English – essentially guarantees of free trade and access to England's colonies.

London, not surprisingly, reacted badly to what it saw as Scottish blackmail, effectively holding English foreign policy and the British succession to ransom. Worse, the Scottish legislation hinted that the northern kingdom might host a rival dynasty with a claim to England's throne and that the Scots' assertively independent diplomacy could undermine London's hard line against Louis XIV.

Westminster retaliated with the Alien Act of 5 February 1705, which was little more than an ultimatum. Cunningly it threatened the Scots with the reverse of what they had been demanding – the ending of free trade with England in key exports like cattle, sheep and coal – unless they either repealed the Act of Security or entered negotiations for a full political union. The latter, as English politicians well knew, by creating a single parliament, would secure both a unified foreign policy and a common royal succession in perpetuity.

Initially the Scots were appalled by this aggressive attitude. But they were also keenly aware that their under-developed economy was utterly dependent on trade with England. Without this, a country already unable to feed its population in the bad years would be even worse off. Accordingly, the Scots Parliament finally agreed to commence discussions with a view to forming a constitutional union between the two kingdoms.

An arranged marriage

The ensuing debate in the Scots Parliament was energetic, acrimonious and deeply fascinating. It had two distinct phases. The first, late in 1705, focused on selecting Scotland's negotiators – critical to the potential for any agreement with England. The second, at its peak between November 1706 and January 1707, revolved around the draft treaty those negotiators brought back. Both debates revealed how complex and contradictory were the arguments both for and against union.

Opponents were numerous and diverse. There were hardened Jacobite enemies of the Hanoverian succession like George Lockhart of Carnwath, the sole anti-unionist negotiator. There were old Williamites like Andrew Fletcher of Saltoun, whose eloquent hostility is remembered and honoured by Scottish Nationalists even today. All of the doubters were intensely patriotic Scots. Some were also loudly Anglophobic. Many were concerned that union with a much larger and more powerful country meant Scotland still being ignored whenever key decisions were being made.

Certain vested interests also opposed union for their own reasons. Arguments were heard, backed by petitions, that Scotland's manufacturers and royal burghs would be ruined by superior English competition. Lawyers complained that Scotland's distinctive legal system would be lost. Others objected that Presbyterianism would be jeopardized by the powerful position of the (essentially Episcopalian) Church of England.

Collectively these criticisms almost certainly enjoyed majority support in the country at large – though this mattered little since Scotland was not a democracy and Parliament alone would be making the decision.

Pro-unionists such as Sir William Seton of Pitmedden and the 2nd Duke of Queensberry also saw union from different perspectives. Some were primarily motivated by fear of the alternative: further poverty, further marginalization. Those of a sunnier disposition optimistically looked forward to peace and plenty with the Scots finally being granted a seat at the top table, as part of a Protestant, commercial superpower on the world stage. Again, self-interest was decisive for some. In particular, disappointed Darien investors were tempted by an English offer of compensation built into the draft treaty.

Significant numbers of pro-unionists were also swayed by bribery: titles and money were undoubtedly offered so as to change minds (the 4th Duke of Hamilton, for instance, acquired an English dukedom, while sceptical noblemen owed cash by the crown suddenly received assurances about repayment). It is common – though not necessarily fair – also to see the English offer of free trade and funds to pump-prime the stagnant Scottish economy as just another form of bribery. After all, Scottish parliamentarians with business interests clearly anticipated benefiting disproportionately.

Partly because of the gradual movement of key individuals from the anti- to the pro-camp, with bribery often but not always implicated, the parliamentary votes were ultimately won by the unionists. The Treaty of Union, implemented on 1 May 1707, therefore tells us much about what the dominant groups in each country most wanted.

Scotland received numerous concessions, mainly but not exclusively economic, necessary to get the treaty through the Edinburgh Parliament: free trade, access to the colonies, promises on taxes, Darien compensation, use of the pound sterling plus guarantees of continuing independence for the Church and legal system. For England, however, union delivered the Hanoverian succession and a single parliament: these were what really mattered to London, preventing future uncertainty over the crown and foreign policy.

Scotland had at the stroke of a pen finally ceased to be an independent self-governing nation. So too, at least in theory, had England. A new and larger state, Great Britain, had been invented, as well as a new Parliament at Westminster, with 45 Scottish MPs in the House of Commons and 16 Scottish noblemen in the Lords. But there had been surprisingly little prior discussion on many of the other implications not covered in the treaty's mere 25 articles. There is even a plausible argument that Scottish history ever since has been mainly about working out the details required to make it work in ways that the two countries might find acceptable.

In the short term, however, the political unity envisaged in 1707 faced one major obstacle with particularly deep Scottish roots.

For Jacobitism, rather than dying back because of the agreement on the Hanoverian succession, flourished with a vengeance in the years immediately afterwards. And it did so in a new and potent guise, as the main vehicle for Scottish anti-Unionism.

We obviously need to ask how this happened and why.

Flogging a dead horse?

Few subjects have attracted more attention or rooted themselves more firmly in Scotland's modern culture than 18th-century Jacobitism. Virtually no one has not heard of 'Bonnie Prince Charlie'. Ironically, however, it remains hard to know just how substantial and potentially viable this movement really was in the years after 1707.

One aspect that tends to obscure Jacobitism's real extent was its secrecy – wise for people facing execution, imprisonment or exile if discovered. Some prudently held back, reluctant to show their true colours until victory, and hence immunity, seemed certain. Others, by contrast, enthusiastically embraced the cause, but for the wrong reasons: they hankered after personal advancement, thirsted for revenge for a personal slight, or simply craved the excitement and glory that rebellion offered. A few found deliberate ambiguity extremely useful – such as drinking to the health of a monarch without specifying which one was intended. Mixed motives and inconsistent behaviour were therefore typical of the movement at all times.

> *Weel may we a' be,*
> *Ill may we never see;*
> *Here's to the King*
> *And the gude companie.*
> Jacobite toast (anonymous)

What we can say is that Jacobitism was definitely stronger in certain quarters. Highlanders, with their rigid social hierarchies, attachment to the Stuarts and longstanding suspicion of Lowland and English governments, were especially attracted. So were many Tories throughout Britain. After all, they harboured ideological reservations about the 1689 revolution and were frequently treated badly by Anne and the first two Georges. Scots, too, were generally more likely to be taken with the Stuarts' loudly trumpeted Scottish associations.

Catholics, sharing the Pretenders' faith, were an obvious constituency, though they were in fact disappointingly few in number in 18th-century Scotland: this explains why Ireland produced so many prominent Jacobites. Episcopalian non-jurors, far more numerous, likewise became supporters in many cases because they would not break their previous oaths to defend James and his heirs as God's anointed.

Finally, the Old Pretender's promise to abolish the Union should have been unconvincing given the Stuart dynasty's obsession before 1689 with unifying their kingdoms. But in Scotland this argument exerted, as it was meant to, a powerful pull on the heartstrings of many who were not reconciled to what they saw as the great national betrayal of 1705–7.

Rising ... then falling

It was no accident that March 1708, shortly after the Union's implementation, saw the first of several major attempts to raise a Scottish rebellion. Unfortunately for them, a parallel uprising in northern England, where much was expected of the significant Catholic minority, failed to get off the ground. And with the Royal Navy in close attendance, the government's intelligence networks having got wind of the plans, a French naval commander sensibly declined to put the Old Pretender ashore in Fife, where strong support had been anticipated among the county's Episcopalian gentry.

The 1715 rising ('the 'Fifteen' in the customary Jacobite shorthand) was no more successful – and for similar reasons. It was led by the 6th Earl of Mar, an opportunistic and widely distrusted former supporter of the Union who had fallen out with George I (who, with the prior death of his mother Sophia, became Britain's first Hanoverian monarch in 1714).

This whole venture aimed, again with French backing, to take advantage of widespread concern, particularly acute in Scotland, at the accession of a German prince. Mar's standard was raised at Braemar on Deeside on 6 September. Several leading north-eastern aristocrats like the 10th Earl Marischal and clans such as the Mackintoshes and the Camerons loyally converged. The plan was to take Edinburgh while others rose simultaneously in the Borders and in England.

Much of Scotland, however, was hostile. Many Lowland burghs and Presbyterian noblemen were appalled at the prospect of civil war being unleashed by an ambitious Catholic usurper with the connivance of France's absolute monarch. They roundly condemned the Pretender and his supporters. Worse, Mar himself (mocked as 'Bobbing John' for having switched sides) proved neither confident nor competent.

He dallied for more than two months with his army of 10,000 before finally being confronted at Sheriffmuir on the road from Perth to Stirling by the 2nd Duke of Argyll's 4,000 soldiers on 13 November. The tactical outcome after a short fire-fight was unclear. But the strategic consequences were unmistakable. Argyll commanded the road south and Mar retreated to Perth to lick his wounds.

With the northern English rising also suppressed and foreign allies discouraged by Mar's uninspiring performance, James's landing at Peterhead as late as 22 December rather missed the point. The momentum necessary to recruit further supporters had not been achieved: the rebellion was stillborn. In February 1716 a disappointed Pretender, unable to be crowned James VIII and III, boarded a ship back to France at Montrose, accompanied by Mar.

Government punishment for the brazen treachery by certain landowners was in fact comparatively gentle. Viscount Kenmore, active in the botched English rising, was executed. Some rebels were deported to the American colonies. A few Scottish peerages, like the earldoms of Seaforth and (predictably) Mar, were legally annulled. Several landed estates owned by the guilty were forfeited to the crown.

Westminster also passed a Disarming Act imposing fines for the illegal possession of weaponry by Highlanders – except by the Independent Highland Companies now being raised under trusted landowners to police the region. One result with longer-term implications was the formation of what later became the Black Watch, the British army's first Highland regiment.

In the next two decades George Wade, appointed commander-in-chief in North Britain, spread his 240-mile network of roads across the Highlands, the basic features of which are often still visible alongside major routes like the A9 and A82. Military strongholds such as Fort Augustus were strengthened and garrisoned to deter rebels and nip trouble in the bud.

As things turned out, however, the most significant development had occurred overseas. The Treaty of Utrecht, Louis XIV's death and the long regency of the Duc d'Orléans reduced France's interest in fomenting discord. The Old Pretender himself moved to Rome, where he became instead a pawn of the ambitious Spanish monarchy.

In the short term this new Continental connection produced yet another Jacobite plot with a strong Scottish flavour, the comically abortive invasion of 1719. This began, exotically enough, with the arrival of two frigates, filled with 300 Spanish soldiers and Jacobite exiles such as the Earl Marischal, at Loch Duich in the far north-west, originally intended as a useful diversion for a major assault on the southern English coastline. Owing to bad weather, however, the main invasion was abandoned, leaving this intrepid little band in a remote Inverness-shire glen very much alone.

They were not alone for long. A government force under General Joseph Wightman marched out from Inverness to engage them in Glenshiel on 10 June. Within hours the invasion was stopped in its tracks and many of the Spanish imprisoned – further evidence, for those willing to accept it, of Jacobitism's complete dependence upon fragile co-operation between generally half-hearted foreign allies and a tiny core of active native supporters prepared to risk their own lives against forbidding odds.

Just as international diplomacy had marginalized Jacobitism, it was only changes in the wider European scene that eventually revived it. The War of the Austrian Succession, which after 1740 set Britain once again against France, led the adult Louis XV to rediscover his country's traditional interest in the disruptive potential of the Pretender's claims. The emergence of the Old Pretender's Italian-born son and heir Charles Edward – the 'Young Pretender', 'Bonnie Prince Charlie' – was an added bonus. For it provided a credible and articulate leader who would play the central part in the most audacious Jacobite plot of them all: 'the 'Forty-five'.

The last best chance

Once again, the best-laid schemes were dogged by limited resources, unrealistic expectations and some rank bad luck. In particular a French invasion of the English coastline was cancelled following a Channel storm in 1744 (a staple of Williamite and Hanoverian propaganda being that God supplied 'Protestant winds' to thwart Catholic attacks). This ended plans for a multi-pronged assault. Yet, typically confident in the face of a setback that would have deterred a wiser strategist, Charlie pressed on with the Scottish part of the project, certain that victory was still achievable.

Charlie first set foot on Scottish soil on Eriskay in the Outer Hebrides on 23 July 1745, accompanied by the famous 'Seven Men of Moidart' who came with him from exile. But it was at Glenfinnan on the mainland on 19 August that the campaign began. Here, in the traditional Scottish summer rain and mist, Charlie oversaw an armed gathering of supportive clansmen, led by the Clanranald MacDonalds.

Revealingly, however, many Jacobite sympathizers were absent. The Catholics on the island of Barra, for example, sent no one. Some with the power to rally others, like MacLeod of MacLeod, suspecting that this was merely an invitation to commit suicide, refused to participate. One pivotal chieftain, Donald Cameron, known as 'Gentle Lochiel' and a respected veteran of previous risings, was only eventually persuaded by Charlie's insistent smooth talking.

The assembled force made impressive progress. Passing swiftly south, at Perth they recruited Lord George Murray, an experienced soldier, brother of the government-supporting Duke of Atholl and the perfect military commander for Charlie's enthusiastic but diverse army. The threat they posed to the British state, still very much focused on the Continental war, dawned too slowly. It was only when 2,400 men under Murray routed General Sir John Cope's force of largely inexperienced new recruits in ten minutes on 21 September at Prestonpans near Edinburgh, where they surprised their opponents by appearing from the wrong direction, that the government sat up and took notice.

After partying long and hard through October in Edinburgh (the Highlanders living up to their reputation for knowing how to have a good time), Charlie and his army eventually took the high road to England, the inevitable next step if they were serious about placing James VIII and III on his rightful thrones. By now two separate government forces had been hastily assembled. But Murray cunningly avoided both, marching through Lancashire and even collecting a few additional recruits from among Manchester's Catholics before arriving at Derby.

At this point London was just 127 miles away. Some wealthy residents began packing their belongings for a retreat to the country, fearing the imminent arrival of lawless Highlanders. There was also a run on the Bank of England, unmistakable evidence of anxiety. Informed opinion really did think that a stunning Jacobite victory, against all the odds, was a serious possibility.

What no one expected was that at Derby a fateful decision would be taken in the Jacobites' camp. Murray and several other advisors had long been wary of the prince's excessive optimism. The failure to recruit many English supporters only increased their scepticism. So too had the continuing absence of the substantial French assistance Charlie had repeatedly promised. Government intelligence had also convinced the Jacobites' leaders that another sizeable and well-equipped army actually lay between them and London, making further progress perilous.

Ultimately these considerations prevailed. Charlie found himself outvoted. On 5 December ('Black Friday') the Jacobites decided to fall back on Scotland for the winter, with a view to a renewed offensive in the spring.

The retreat was orderly. Despite skirmishes with government troops in Lancashire and Westmorland, the Jacobites maintained their discipline. At Falkirk on 17 January, they even defeated another government force under General Henry Hawley, using a classic Highland charge backed by lashing wind and rain. Next month they were back on the familiar terrain of the Highlands.

Unfortunately for them, the government's main army, under the command of George II's third son, the Duke of Cumberland, had avoided the arduous winter march northwards. Four of Cumberland's 16 infantry battalions were actually Scottish, including the 1st Foot (subsequently the Royal Scots) and Royal North British Fusiliers (later the Royal Scots Fusiliers), recently withdrawn from the Continent to deal with the domestic threat. Conveyed by ship to Aberdeen, rested, well-fed and properly equipped, they kept their powder dry and waited for the moment to strike.

Appropriately, it was yet another misjudgement by Charlie, over-ruling Murray and his advisors, which led the Jacobites to square up to Cumberland's army on the exposed and boggy high ground of Culloden Moor to the east of Inverness. Here, on 16 April 1746, after exchanges lasting barely an hour, perhaps 2,000 of Charlie's bravest and most loyal followers lay dead in the heather. Subjected on disadvantageous terrain to the overwhelming firepower available from disciplined professional musketry backed by emplaced artillery, the military substance of Jacobitism was simply obliterated.

The Butcher and some bills

The aftermath was even more devastating. Cumberland, having fought what he considered a civil war against traitors rather than a conventional campaign against honourable foreign opponents, discouraged leniency. Fleeing Jacobite soldiers were cut down. Suspects, genuine or imagined, were rounded up. Blameless non-participants living in the wrong places had their houses burned down.

This is why the king's son is now generally reviled as 'Butcher Cumberland'. But the Presbyterian, Lowland majority saw things very differently at the time, with the shock of the rebellion still fresh in their minds. A relieved University of St Andrews awarded Cumberland its chancellorship for having imposed order on impending chaos. The freedom of Glasgow was also bestowed by the grateful civic authorities.

Longer-term responses included new laws at Westminster. Rebel titles like the earldom of Cromartie and property like Cameron of Lochiel's estates were forfeited. The Act of Proscription of 1746 banned the wearing of tartan, other than by government forces, and also forbade unauthorized weapons to Highlanders. The Heritable Jurisdictions Act of 1747 swept away the wide-ranging judicial powers of Scottish landowners which had given them an unusually firm grip on their tenants and potentially an effective tool for raising rebel armies. This last measure attracted furious opposition – it applied to all landlords, not just Jacobites, and arguably breached the Treaty of Union's protection of Scotland's legal peculiarities. But the large English majority in Parliament, which considered these feudal powers oppressive and dangerous in a modern society, carried it anyway.

A miscarriage of justice?

Colin Campbell of Glenure, a government agent responsible for the Jacobite Stewart family's forfeited Appin estates, was killed by a sniper's bullet on 14 May 1752. James Stewart, an associate of the likely culprit Allan Stewart, who had escaped, was convicted as an accessory by a Campbell-dominated jury overseen by the 3rd Duke of Argyll and hanged. As a murder mystery with no satisfactory resolution the case retains great fascination. It was also notorious proof of the continuing power of feudal landowners over local Scottish justice – notwithstanding the reforms of 1747.

Jacobitism's long-term fate was everything that Parliament could have wished. Above all, the errors of the 1745–6 strategy, the bitter fruits of the defeat at Culloden and the final realization that sufficient support was simply never going to materialize had at last destroyed its credibility. Nor did Charlie's unattractive response – a painful, self-pitying descent into alcoholism and abusive behaviour before his death in Italy in 1788 – encourage even his most dogged former sympathizers to continue putting their lives, careers and properties on the line for him. The passage of time also undercut Jacobitism's plausibility: Scots who could even remember James VII and an Episcopalian Church were rare by the late 1740s, and wanting to turn the clock back six decades increasingly seemed not just unrealistic but also worryingly eccentric.

Not all reasons for abandoning Jacobitism, however, were negative. After all, the virtues of Hanoverian Britain were becoming ever clearer, especially to the wealthy and well-connected. By the 1750s commercial developments, many linked to involvement in English and colonial markets, were rapidly enriching Scottish property owners in ways of which their grandfathers could never have dreamed: jobs for sons in India or the Royal Navy, profitable exports to Virginia, marriage to an English heiress or a big townhouse in London or Edinburgh could all transform opinions about the status quo.

Some with strongly Jacobite backgrounds rehabilitated themselves quickly: certain forfeited privileges, like the earldom of Seaforth for the Mackenzies, had already been recovered by the 1770s. Several rebel dynasties went even further, raising government regiments, like the 78th or Fraser Highlanders – established in 1757 by Simon Fraser, the son of Lord Lovat, an incorrigible Jacobite who ten years before had become the last man to be beheaded on Tower Hill in London for his part in the 'Forty-five'.

Such units quickly proved their worth, serving with high-profile distinction overseas. When at Quebec in 1759, as he won Canada for Britain, General James Wolfe, an English veteran of Culloden, engaged the French troops, he had under his command many former Scottish enemies, still dressed in tartan but now fighting courageously and victoriously beneath the Union flag. No more dramatic illustration of Jacobitism's neutralization – or of the new loyalty of virtually all Scots to Britain, Unionism and the Hanoverians – could be imagined.

Adjusting to new realities

For many English observers after the Union, when they looked at Scottish politics – which, to be honest, few did very closely – all that they tended to see was Jacobitism. It goes without saying that this was unfair: at no time were most Scots supporters of the Pretender; and the large majority of those with power were solidly Presbyterian, Unionist and Hanoverian.

Yet every Jacobite rebellion was undeniably centred on Scotland. The Pretenders, too, positively flaunted their Scottish ancestry. And there was no doubt that much of the military muscle was provided by tartan-clad clansmen and their chieftains. Accordingly, the notion that the Scots were enemies of peace and civil order, and that they favoured the kind of absolute and arbitrary government associated with the exiled Catholic line of the Stuart dynasty rather than the limited parliamentary monarchy and the rule of law confirmed in 1688–9 and continued under the Hanoverians, lingered long in suspicious English minds.

This prejudice still influenced British politics even after Jacobitism was dead. It explains the government's consistent refusal between the 1750s and the 1790s to allow the Scots, like their English partners, to form an armed militia of citizen volunteers to defend their coast against French attack. This issue was like a sore tooth for two generations of post-Culloden Scots. It was an ever-present reminder that the English still did not really trust them. Indeed, it demonstrated a residual fear in London that the collective noun for a group of Scottish civilians bearing guns was a 'rebellion'.

Related concerns about true Scottish motives also lay behind the unpleasant controversy of the early 1760s when John Stuart, 3rd Earl of Bute, was prime minister to the new king, George III. For Bute was a Scot – the first after the Union to shin to the top of London's greasy political pole. To English people opposed to what they believed were the king's plans to increase his own influence over Parliament, his chief advisor's Scottishness was a gift. John Wilkes, the celebrated radical activist, had immense fun at the prime minister's expense, continually suggesting that Bute wished to undermine traditional English freedoms by helping George introduce absolute monarchy. Wilkes's magazine *The North Briton* – the name reminded English readers where the main danger to English liberties lay – proved a potent weapon in the propaganda offensive against what many saw as the threat posed by influential Scots.

Bute, however, was only the highest-profile offender. Another important consequence of the Union was that large numbers of Scots soon acquired well-rewarded positions outside Scotland that would otherwise have been enjoyed by Englishmen. By the late 18th century, the commissioned ranks that ran the British army had a markedly Caledonian hue: one-quarter of infantry officers were Scottish in 1794 and perhaps 40 per cent of colonels commanding regiments. Scots also dominated in India – holding at least half of East India Company jobs in Bengal, the most lucrative posting, by the 1770s – as well as in the American and Caribbean colonial administrations.

Individual Scots even reached the upper echelons of England's leading domestic institutions – one became Archbishop of York, another Lord Chief Justice, yet another Lord Chancellor – despite the fact that Scotland retained its own church and legal systems that were still effectively closed to English entrants. Scottish politicians performed a similar trick in Parliament: 120 Scots were MPs for non-Scottish seats just between 1790 and 1820.

All in all, it was easy for English critics to conclude that the Union, rather than seeing a powerful nation of around 5 million people absorb a smaller and weaker country of just 1 million, had in fact allowed the elites of the poorer country to capture the richer one for themselves.

This, then, was the stereotype to which the Scot now seemingly conformed in British life, at least as far as anxious English commentators were concerned. Ambitious, dictatorial and ruthless, he was also grasping, clannish, conspiratorial – and unnervingly successful. It is worth pointing out, however, that the reality of politics in post-Union Scotland itself was rather more mundane, not to say parochial. Indeed, a form of Scottish politics continued after 1707, and in many respects it did not really fall substantially into line with English patterns for more than 100 years.

Partly this was because many aspects of Scotland's old politics survived 1707 intact. In particular, the voting system in force until 1832 was the one inherited from the old Scots Parliament. This was far more restrictive than the procedures used to elect MPs in England.

In 1788, for example, there were fewer than 3,000 eligible voters across all of the Scottish counties (the equivalent figure in England, still not very generous but nonetheless vastly better, approached 250,000). These county electors, qualified to vote because they held the rights in feudal law to a very substantial parcel of land, returned 30 MPs. In most Scottish burghs, meanwhile, which elected the remaining 15 Scottish MPs, the voters, exclusively comprising the members of each town's governing council, were normally barely into double figures.

Naturally the survival of such distinctive electoral practices regularly produced uniquely Scottish electoral controversies – generally settled in the Scottish courts under Scots law.

The oddities of Scotland's electoral law together with the tendency of these tiny electorates to succumb to direct personal manipulation by candidates and their backers allowed those with both the expertise and the motivation to do so to control Scottish politics in their own interests. Usually, because of the system's legal complexity, this meant Scottish lawyers or those who retained the services of Scotland's finest legal minds.

For the period from 1707 until the 1750s the winners in this obscure but rewarding game were the 2nd Duke of Argyll and his brother the Earl of Ilay (latterly 3rd Duke). Allies of Sir Robert Walpole and the Whig party in London, the Argylls worked closely with senior judges and with other major landowners across Scotland. This allowed them to control a large number of the country's contested parliamentary seats, to influence a great many Scottish MPs and so shape government policies as they affected Scotland.

Later in the century it was a lawyer working for himself, Henry Dundas, Lord Advocate and an associate of William Pitt the Younger, who effectively ran the country by pulling the same levers. The result was that he was half-jokingly known as 'King

Harry the Ninth' or 'The Uncrowned King of Scotland'. In practice it was again Dundas's relationships with local power-brokers that gave him control over elections and direct influence over two-thirds of Scottish MPs. Such power also made him a man of consequence in London and the holder of several major roles in the British cabinet.

There was also a succession of peculiarly Scottish political controversies, most provoking mystification in London at the alien ways of the Scots. A few were focused on Parliament but others involved public disturbances and public campaigning. On every occasion the English were forcefully reminded that Scottish politics had indeed survived the Union.

In 1713, for example, there was a failed attempt by Scottish peers in the House of Lords to have the Union annulled. This was in part because of anger at two recent pieces of Westminster legislation on Scotland that ignored assurances given in 1707 to protect Presbyterianism: the Patronage Act of 1711 took the right to appoint parish ministers away from local congregations and returned it to landowners; and the Toleration Act of 1712 gave Episcopalians the right to worship with impunity providing that they adhered to Church of England usages.

Similar grievances over alleged breaches of the treaty were involved in 1725 when there were riots in Glasgow over a malt tax – effectively a levy on whisky distilling – for which the local MP had unwisely voted. In 1736 it was Edinburgh's turn, as disorder erupted over the execution of smugglers whose disregard for the hated customs taxes imposed from Westminster had won them widespread sympathy.

Perceived threats to distinctive Scottish institutions and dislike of heavy-handed government interference continually provoked strong reactions. This invariably seemed to take London by surprise. In the early 19th century, for example, the adoption of English-style jury trials in Scottish civil cases proved unexpectedly contentious before being embraced. In 1826, meanwhile, Sir Walter Scott fronted a successful campaign against plans to stop Scottish banks issuing uniquely Scottish bank notes (a practice that, despite regular English criticism, no British government has yet dared end).

Not surprisingly, however, the most problematic political issue – reform of the restrictive and unresponsive political system itself – also played an important part in Scottish politics in the 18th and early 19th centuries.

Radicalism and protest

The principal cause of rising discontent was a sense that an irresistible force was increasingly coming into contact with an apparently immovable object. The latter was the electoral system – as we have seen, a leftover from pre-Union Scotland far narrower even than England's and denying all but a few thousand Scots the right to participate in representative politics.

What made this intolerable were the growing political aspirations of key excluded groups, especially middle-class professionals and business owners who were increasing in number as well as ambition. The problem became impossible to ignore by the 1780s, when in Scotland as in England there emerged serious efforts, led by influential people, to modify aspects of the voting system.

In 1782, for instance, smaller landowners in Caithness, Moray and Inverness-shire, themselves eligible to vote, organized unsuccessful campaigns aimed at ending some of the most blatant electoral manipulation by Scotland's great aristocrats. A committee also emerged the next year, mainly run by opponents of the government, to demand the extension of votes in the Scottish burghs – the preserve of town councillors – to all who were registered to trade freely in the town: this time Dundas and his friends at Westminster defeated the scheme.

It was the advent of the French Revolution in 1789, however, which gave a fresh language as well as renewed inspiration to the reformers. This was particularly so in Scotland, not least because progressive ideas were a notable feature of university teaching under liberal professors like John Millar at Glasgow and Dugald Stewart at Edinburgh: indeed, one free-thinking Scottish academic, William Ogilvie of King's College, Aberdeen, was an early advocate of that classic revolutionary principle, the common ownership of property (though his arguments were not much noticed at the time). Scotland therefore proved especially receptive to the sparks given off by dramatic French events, the flames further fanned by the English radical Tom Paine's *The Rights of Man* (1791), which circulated widely among all social classes.

Organizationally, the main vehicle for pursuing domestic constitutional reform was the Scottish Association of the Friends of the People, founded in July 1792 at the Fortune Tavern in Edinburgh. Shopkeepers, craft workers and other skilled workers were able to join, alongside the middle-class leaders. They found it the ideal focus for their demands for an end to corrupt electoral practices and a widening of the voting qualification. Demonstrations occurred in towns such as Perth and Dundee, and on the king's birthday in June 1792 there was a riot in Edinburgh, though the Friends' leadership carefully distanced themselves from actual disturbances.

Nonetheless, these developments, with the French Revolution descending from pious liberal idealism into the murderous Reign of Terror, steadily detached respectable opinion from a movement whose aims were destabilizing in dangerous times. What was left was an increasingly isolated group of radical activists like the celebrated Thomas Muir.

Muir, a lawyer and Glasgow graduate who had been influenced by Millar's lectures, became a hero for the cause. Tried for seditious libel in 1793 – the offence of fomenting political subversion – he was convicted in an elaborate show trial in front of an openly biased judge and transported to Australia. Less high profile campaigners, such as the radical English preacher and Dundee activist Thomas Fyshe Palmer, shared the same fate.

'I have devoted myself to the cause of The People. It is a good cause – It shall ultimately prevail – It shall finally triumph.'
Thomas Muir (1793)

So worried was the government that French violence might migrate to Britain because of the often-secretive activities of the radicals that detention without trial was legalized and unlawful gatherings prohibited. These measures formed part of what became known as the 'Dundas Despotism'.

Treachery in the capital

The discovery of the so-called 'Pike Plot' in 1794, a wildly implausible scheme to capture Edinburgh Castle and trigger a revolution in Scotland, seemed to justify the government's anxieties following the French Revolution. Robert Watt, a former government spy turned radical agitator, was eventually convicted of treason and executed. But he was the only Scottish fatality of the crackdown overseen by Henry Dundas, the lord advocate, and the threat of revolution seems to have been greatly overstated.

Small numbers of committed radicals remained active, but they tended to be weak and largely unconnected with the middle-class reformists who had made the cause respectable back in the 1780s. The best known in the 1790s, the United Scotsmen, argued for votes for all men – then an extreme and uncommon demand – as well as annual parliaments. They too were strong in the towns and among the workers. But their lack of clout and evident interest in bringing about what they thought would be a sympathetic invasion by revolutionary France, with which Britain was at war, as well as a failed insurrection that some of them attempted near Perth in 1797, kept them marginalized: George Mealmaker, a Dundee weaver and their leader, was convicted of sedition and despatched to Australia that same year.

One final point is worth making about this era. Because Scotland over the next two centuries, as we shall see, built for itself a powerfully radical, even revolutionary self-image, figures like Muir and Mealmaker and organizations like the United Scotsmen, who made demands that today seem unexceptional, have retrospectively attracted a great deal of historical attention. Indeed, they have frequently been depicted as typifying political opinion at the time.

But this is almost certainly wrong. The evidence suggests instead that very many of their contemporaries were politically conservative, loyal and patriotic. Statistically the Scots were twice as likely as the English to flock to join the Volunteer regiments that defended the coastline in the 1790s. And there is no reason to assume that Scottish conservatism, just because it did not express itself in rioting and plots, was any less sincere than Scottish radicalism, or that it should be taken any less seriously by historians.

For the next 20 years Britain's wars with revolutionary and Napoleonic France dominated the political scene. Any demand for significant change therefore risked seeming unpatriotic, even traitorous. But in the years of peace after 1815, in which unemployment and economic contraction added to the discontent, momentum built once more for constitutional reform, culminating in what became known as the Radical War of 1820.

The Radical War

In April 1820 a group of working-class Glaswegians, in the wake of the revolutionary Cato Street Conspiracy in London, went on strike and declared a provisional government in Scotland (though while a few allegedly talked of restoring 'the ancient Scottish Parliament' we need to avoid over-interpreting the anti-Unionist dimension because some of the instigators were English and the group's proclamation embraced England's tradition of Magna Carta, even appealing for support not from Scottish patriots but explicitly from 'Britons'). About 30 marched on the Carron ironworks in Stirlingshire, intending to seize weapons and establish a new order based on what they called 'equality of right'. They were stopped and dispersed by cavalry near Falkirk: this confrontation was later described as the 'battle of Bonnymuir', though this label seems a bit of a stretch given the small numbers involved and the fact that no one was actually killed and only four radicals were wounded in what in reality was a minor skirmish. The true retribution was judicial not military. Three ringleaders – Andrew Hardie, James Wilson and John Baird – were subsequently convicted of treason and executed. A further 18 were transported to Australia although all received an absolute pardon by 1835.

It is clear that government agents encouraged the insurrection of 1820 in a successful attempt to flush out suspected revolutionary elements in the radical movement. The outcome certainly helped deter campaigners for a time. But it could not and did not end the yearning for some kind of political reform, which eventually arrived throughout Britain in the early 1830s.

Fact check

1 Under the Act of Settlement of 1701 who was to succeed Queen Anne in England?
   a James Edward Stuart
   b Charles Edward Stuart
   c Sophia of Hanover
   d Frederick of Prussia

2 Who opposed the Treaty of Union?
   a George Lockhart
   b Sir William Seton
   c the Duke of Queensberry
   d the Duke of Roxburghe

3 How many Scottish MPs were sent to Westminster after 1707?
   a 20
   b 72
   c 50
   d 45

4 Who provided most Scottish support for Jacobitism?
   a Presbyterians
   b Catholics
   c Episcopalians
   d Hanoverians

5 Who led the 1715 Jacobite rising?
   a Bonnie Prince Charlie
   b George I
   c the Duke of Argyll
   d the Earl of Mar

6 Where was the 1745-6 rising defeated?
   a Falkirk
   b Prestonpans
   c Bannockburn
   d Culloden

7 Who was the first Scottish prime minister of Britain?
   a   the Duke of Argyll
   b   Henry Dundas
   c   the Earl of Bute
   d   Andrew Fletcher

8 Who was Thomas Muir?
   a   a radical reformer
   b   a liberal philosopher
   c   a government minister
   d   an English clergyman

Dig Deeper

Christopher Whatley, *The Scots and the Union* (Edinburgh, 2006)
Bruce Lenman, *The Jacobite Risings in Britain, 1689–1746*
(Aberdeen, 1995).
Alex Murdoch, *The People Above* (Edinburgh, 1980).
John Stuart Shaw, *The Political History of 18th-Century Scotland*
(Basingstoke, 1999).

Industry and Enlightenment

The shock of the new

If Scottish politics remained surprisingly little altered between the Union and the late 1820s, there were two critical ways in which Scotland became unquestionably different. One was its rapidly transformed social and economic condition, a process much more condensed than south of the border:

> '...the present people of Scotland [are] a class of beings as different from their grandfathers, as the existing English are from those of Queen Elizabeth's time.'
> Sir Walter Scott, *Waverley* (1814)

Equally, a country previously notorious for bigotry and backwardness was now known for its learning and sophistication. Scotland, indeed, had suddenly acquired an international reputation for intellectual brilliance.

> 'Really it is admirable how many Men of Genius this Country produces at present. Is it not strange that, at a time when we have lost our Princes, our Parliaments, our independent government, even the Presence of our chief Nobility, are unhappy, in our Accent & Pronunciation, speak a very corrupt Dialect of the Tongue which we make use of; is it not strange, I say, that in these Circumstances we shou'd really be the People most distinguish'd for Literature in Europe?'
> David Hume, letter to William Strahan, 1771.

Such dramatic changes in Scotland's society, economy and culture pose a very simple question: how on earth had this happened?

The fruitful soil

Any attempt to explain Scotland's post-Union transformation must begin with agriculture – the essential activity that fed, clothed and occupied the vast majority of Scots. Yet in no area of economic activity did the dead hand of the past lie more heavily on the shoulders of the present.

To start with, the geological and climatic circumstances were difficult. Scotland possesses much uncultivable upland, as well as many lower-lying landscapes where high acidity, often running to bog, makes cultivation challenging. Allied to the harsher weather conditions of the 'Little Ice Age', which bottomed out in the late 17th century, Scots who dreamed of extracting regular and bountiful returns from their native soil clearly faced considerable physical obstacles.

Human legacies further hampered progress. A low population density, limited urbanization and agricultural backwardness created a vicious circle. Unreliable harvests and meagre food surpluses kept population growth minimal and made non-agricultural activity precarious.

Feudal social structures and relationships similarly restricted progress. The famous 'runrig' system, where tenants cultivated fields in common, and widespread use of co-operative farming practices, guaranteed that change proceeded only through communal agreement and even then only at the pace of the slowest.

Clearly this regime was breaking down from 1650 onwards as landowners sought to improve productivity by adopting foreign innovations. But progress was insufficient to forestall the famines of the 1690s. Only the stimulation provided by increased exposure to English know-how and to the far greater demand from English consumers, reinforced by a slowly improving climate by the mid-18th century, eventually produced the transformation noticed by many observers, Scottish and foreign, by the early 19th.

Every aspect of Scottish farming had changed by 1800. The very nature of the land itself was physically altered by manure, liming and large-scale drainage and reclamation. Enclosure – adding fences or tree screens for protection from the ever-present winds and to create clear units of land for production – made the landscape look different: the modern 'patchwork quilt' effect familiar to modern observers in the Lowlands became the norm. New crops were also introduced. Peas, beans, turnips and potatoes, for example, varied the previous reliance on oats.

In upland areas it was forestry – and the beginning of attempts to replace the native Caledonian Forest, which had been shrinking under aggressive human intervention for millennia – that similarly caught the new commercial mood: the 4th Duke of Atholl, who died in 1830, planted 27 million new trees on his Perthshire estates. Elsewhere, complex rotation systems were applied to replenish the soil and maximize yields. Better ploughs, improved stone steadings (farm outbuildings) and enhanced domestic accommodation for farmers and resident workers also added to the sense of a tangible transformation underway.

Arguably most crucial of all, relations between landlords and workers were placed on a new footing. Farmers increasingly became single tenants, recruited for their skills. Encouraged to innovate, they paid commercially determined rents. Waged workers supplied additional labour, carrying out prescribed tasks as and when required.

Traditional labour-intensive communal farming swiftly disappeared. And by delivering generous surpluses like clockwork, there is no doubt that this new regime finally freed Scots as a whole from the age-old threat of starvation. But it also ended many people's direct involvement in food production. This in turn allowed a population shift from countryside to town and from agriculture to other economic activities. Indeed, mass migration was positively encouraged by landowners, as customary tenants lost their rights, their homes and their roles.

Towns and cities boomed. Glasgow grew from 32,000 people in 1755 to be the country's largest city with 147,000 people by 1821. Conversely, in some rural areas, like Peeblesshire, the population actually fell. Some historians argue that we might think of this great migration as the 'Lowland Clearances', as irresistible economic forces pushed people from rural central and southern Scotland into the crowded towns of the Central Belt as well as to England and North America.

History has certainly not been slow to recognize the 'Highland Clearances'. Yet this was really only the same experience of large-scale migration propelled by agricultural reforms – but given special emotional resonance because the collateral damage included the distinctive culture and society of Gaelic Scotland.

Undoubtedly the degree of change required to create commercially viable agriculture in these areas was greater. Here customary rights and a non-cash economy had been normal. The chieftain had been less a proprietor exploiting his assets than the wise and benevolent protector of his humble kinsmen. As a consequence, the introduction of written leases and money rents radically altered social relations.

Chiefs unsurprisingly were the big winners. The 'tacksmen', community leaders acting as middle-men between the lord and his people, lost out and quickly disappeared. The restructuring of the Highland economy unquestionably delivered impressive revenue growth: the average owner saw a 300 per cent increase in estate income between 1750 and 1800. Sheep farming, introduced in the inland glens so as to supply the expanding Scottish woollen textile industry, proved particularly lucrative. But it also entailed whole communities being moved – 'cleared' – either to the coasts or on to emigrant ships bound for North America.

Usually this was peaceful. It was frequently sweetened by the realistic promise of a better life, away from the hand-to-mouth existence and periodic famines of the Highlands' traditional economy. For many, however, it was an upsetting, and sometimes a brutalizing, experience. After all, people were required to leave their family homes and often their homeland for good. In certain cases, such as on the Countess of Sutherland's estates after 1806, tenants were definitely evicted forcibly in a notorious sequence of events that remain bitterly contested in Scotland more than two centuries later.

Tenants re-settled on the coast acquired a new way of life called 'crofting', designed by proprietors to make Highland society both sustainable and more profitable.

This way of life, however, as a supposed solution to the Highlands' age-old problems, turned out to have two major flaws, as we shall later see. It unwittingly exposed communities to some entirely new threats to their very existence. And it helped make relations between tenants and landlords even more toxic as the 19th century unfolded.

Filthy lucre

The first priority of those wanting to improve commerce and trade in post-Union Scotland was simply to overcome two critical deficiencies inhibiting business and investment: lack of cash, making buying and selling harder; and lack of credit, hampering the borrowing required for innovation or expansion. This is why the development of Scottish banking was so utterly vital to everything else that happened to the economy.

Building on the Bank of Scotland's foundation in William's reign, the Royal Bank of Scotland was chartered in 1727 under Lord Ilay's oversight. A series of major local institutions also soon appeared, including the Ayr Bank (which imploded spectacularly in 1772's financial crisis) and the Dundee Banking Company. As well as growing rapidly, the banking sector experimented with new products, now familiar, such as arranged overdrafts (the first granted by the Royal Bank in 1728) and their own paper banknotes (the Bank was the first private bank in Europe to issue them). Later, the world's first savings bank was opened at Dumfries in 1810 by the local Presbyterian minister, paying interest on ordinary people's deposits. And insurance – of both lives and property – also emerged as a key Scottish specialization. An economy once drained of liquidity because of Darien was, strangely enough, an international leader in financial services just a century later.

Improvements to the country's physical infrastructure were another key driver for trade. Authorized local markets in particular increased dramatically, further encouraging the production of agricultural surpluses for sale: astonishingly for a country unable to feed itself in the 1690s, Scotland by 1760 was even exporting excess grain to Norway.

The transport system was augmented to ease the movement of goods. New roads were built and others improved beyond recognition. John Smeaton's elegant bridge across the Tay at Perth, opened in 1771 and jointly funded by private donations and by government, became a symbol of the contemporary commitment to facilitating commerce, as did the Forth and Clyde Canal, which opened in 1790 and which Smeaton designed to carry waterborne freight right across the Central Lowlands.

Engineering success

The Scots' intensifying interest in transport also helps explain why some of them were responsible for landmark contributions to England's industrialization: Thomas Telford from Dumfriesshire became the greatest canal and bridge designer of the late 18th century, while John Loudon Macadam from Ayr will always be associated with his method for creating durable road surfaces from graded small stones – a technology that, when a modified pitch was later added, became known, in honour of its Scottish originator, as 'tarmac'.

The greater availability of manufactured goods because of industrialization proved another crucial stimulus to trade, especially in the retail sector. Imported goods either for domestic consumption or for further export, such as spices, silks, tea, coffee, sugar and tobacco, were equally helpful. Trade in these products, and above all in tobacco, which alone accounted for more than half of Scotland's total exports by 1760, was exactly the kind of activity that Darien had been intended to stimulate – controlling the movement of highly desirable commodities between the continents at a handsome premium.

These lucrative import-export businesses enriched Glasgow's merchants in particular. With their fine houses and newly bought country estates outside the city, some became known colloquially as 'tobacco lords'. The same profitability, however, also reinforced a mutually dependent relationship between Scotland's west coast and the slave plantations of America's eastern seaboard. This fact in turn raised profound moral criticisms in some parts of Scottish society as the 18th century progressed.

Dark satanic mills

The most significant long-term result of the commercial ties between Glasgow and America was to be the growth of cotton manufacturing, the activity on which early Scottish industrialization mainly rested. Indeed, the production of cotton goods in Scotland was only possible because the vital raw material, from a sub-tropical plant farmed in the American South, arrived by ship in the expanding Clyde ports – and Glasgow and Greenock especially.

Cotton industrialization had significant precursors. By 1750 Scotland was already familiar with what some historians call 'proto-industrialization' – especially textile production using spinning wheels and looms in workers' own homes, making linen wares out of locally grown flax. In fact, linen was an important source of part-time employment across the Lowlands and crucial to expanding Scottish trade and increasing exports in the first generation after the Union.

Cotton, however, was different. It was properly industrialized from the time the first mill opened at Penicuik outside Edinburgh in 1778. By the late 1780s large-scale manufacturing was converging on single-site factories where the workforce operated new thread-producing machinery such as the famous 'Spinning Jenny' and 'Crompton's Mule', recent English inventions. Initially these facilities were water-powered, hence their early location on rivers – such as at New Lanark on the Clyde and at Stanley on the Tay – which also provided convenient sites for related processes like dyeing and bleaching.

Once the first steam-powered mill was up and running in 1798, however, sites away from riversides quickly became viable. And by the 1830s mechanization of cotton production was even spreading at great speed to the more complicated weaving process – further lowering costs and increasing output, of course, as it finally threw the skilled handloom weavers out of work.

James Watt

Scottish industrialization produced several engineering heroes, none greater than James Watt from Greenock, who started out as Glasgow University's instrument-maker. The man whose name is used today for the standard unit of power, Watt is often wrongly credited with inventing the steam engine. His actual achievement, begun in Glasgow in 1765 and completed ten years later when working with the English entrepreneur Matthew Boulton in Birmingham, was to add a separate steam condenser to existing versions, greatly increasing efficiency and making their widespread industrial application economically irresistible.

Distinctive forms of cotton manufacturing also arose in some areas, as production, in another feature typical of full-scale industrialization, rapidly specialized and diversified: Paisley, near Glasgow, for example, lent its name to a complex new textile pattern that would unexpectedly return to fashion as late as the 1960s.

Taken together, these developments in power engineering and mechanical production increased output and profitability exponentially in an astonishingly short space of time: from 1780 to 1800, for example, the amount of raw cotton processed by Scotland's mills grew 14-fold. But these same factors, with

250,000 people employed in the textile industries by 1800, were also fundamentally altering workers' daily experiences and their relationships with employers and each other. Labouring for long hours at repetitive tasks, they operated under constant close supervision in a dedicated workplace for cash wages – and under threat of redundancy in business downturns or as further technological or organizational changes arose.

Comparable transformations were also underway in other industries. Woollens, for example, were important in certain districts, especially in Borders towns like Hawick and Galashiels. Here manufacturers turned fleeces into attractive mass-produced goods: 'tweed', a twilled woollen cloth named in the 1830s after the area's main river, soon became a characteristically Scottish garment material that was highly regarded internationally. This was only possible because of the scale of production that industrialization facilitated.

Coal-mining was less quickly revolutionized. It even took parliamentary legislation in 1775 and 1799 to end a system of indentured labour (found also in the salt-panning industry), which had made Scottish colliers an unusually powerful group but also severely reduced freedom of movement for what was in effect a hereditary workforce.

Technological change in mining was also slow. Primitive Newcomen steam engines had entered use around 1720, pumping water and circulating air. But more sophisticated power systems were only gradually applied to winding machinery so as to make possible deep-shaft mining. Even so, Scottish output, feeding the insatiable hunger of the steam engines, grew steadily. By 1800 the annual quantity dug had increased five-fold on a century earlier.

If one location above all others symbolized for contemporaries the essentially revolutionary scale and character of Scotland's industrialization it was the Carron ironworks near Falkirk in Stirlingshire. Here a combination of Anglo-Scottish business finance and expertise, the adjacent presence of both 'clayband' ironstone and substantial coal supplies, together with the copious power source and cooling potential of the River Carron, allowed the opening in 1760 of the largest industrial complex in 18th-century Scotland.

It was also for many decades Europe's largest ironworks. More than 2,000 people were employed in 1815. By this time the firm's famous 'carronade' cannons had allowed the British army and navy to defeat Napoleon, while its cast-iron baths and fireplaces adorned innumerable middle-class British homes.

A society in motion

The story of Scotland's population in this age of unprecedented socio-economic change is easily told – not least because this is the first period for which accurate contemporary statistics were gathered.

These tell us that the population grew from around 1 million in 1707 and 1.2 million in 1755 to 1.6 million in 1801 and 2.4 million in 1831. This would be noteworthy enough in a country that had never before had so many inhabitants and which had recently seen vicious famines kill tens of thousands. But some of the details buried within these data are also striking enough to bear closer examination.

For example, the main underlying trend was clearly not rising birth rates – these remained relatively static – but falling death rates: 30 people per 1,000 were dying each year in the 1750s but only 24 by the 1790s and 21 by the mid-19th century. Similarly, we can see that life expectancy at birth in Scotland was little more than 30 years in 1755 but then suddenly started on an upwards trajectory, passing 40 years by the 1840s.

Such figures clearly invalidate the belief, common among hostile observers at the time and lazily repeated ever since, that industrialization and urbanization brought only hardship and misery to ordinary men and women. They also provoke a series of further questions, not the least of which is why Scottish death rates actually began to reduce.

Again, the contemporary statistics are suggestive, revealing that the decline was overwhelmingly in infant rather than in adult mortality: put simply, children were becoming less likely to die at birth or shortly thereafter. This is a vital clue because it points to some of the more specific factors that surely lay behind the population's sudden growth.

One was the gradual spread from the 1730s onwards of inoculation against smallpox, previously the greatest child-killer of them all. Not everyone liked it or used it. Some Presbyterians even considered it sinful to thwart God's mysterious intentions. But where it was adopted it undoubtedly reduced infant mortality in particular.

Another advantage was the more varied and nutritious diet facilitated by agricultural improvement. Most Scots were now eating more and better food, again particularly benefiting the youngest and most vulnerable. Also important in all likelihood were improved living conditions in rural (though not, crucially, in urban) communities: cleaner and better-built homes again harboured fewer threats to the very young. We might further add that incomes generally rose faster than prices across this period, despite some short-term reversals. This too must have made life easier for the majority of adults and so for their children.

'Great chieftain o' the puddin' race'

Haggis is a sausage-like preparation of finely chopped sheep's offal, oats and spices, often served with 'neeps' (turnip) and 'tatties' (mashed or boiled potatoes). It is unclear where it originated (there are medieval English hints, while Scandinavian roots are sometimes claimed) but the Scots probably adopted it as a cheap, hot, filling meal for poor people in a cold and damp climate and by the late 18th century it was recognized as the national dish.

There were nonetheless considerable drawbacks to socio-economic change that we should not overlook. For rapid urbanization also generated cramped conditions where diseases like typhus and cholera could flourish. Increased localized mortality inevitably resulted: between just February and May 1832 cholera killed 660 people in Glasgow, caused primarily by unclean water in slum housing.

Moreover, society, as wealth grew, increasingly felt more divided. Animosity between 'clearers' and 'cleared' in the Highlands was unsurprising. But tensions also worsened elsewhere as the gap between the richest and the poorest widened and some groups suffered irreversible losses.

Irate traditional tenants, for example, like the 'Levellers' of Galloway who destroyed their landlords' newly erected enclosures in the 1720s, and the handloom weavers hit by falling wages and rising prices who mobilized in the Radical War of 1820, typified the resentments felt by many. The steady growth of working-class identity was another reaction. This re-energized reformist politics and brought the new and radical vocabulary of class antagonism to both industrial and political disputes.

A final dimension to changing social experiences in this period must also be mentioned. This was the combined effects of immigration and emigration on Scots at home and overseas.

In the first place, large numbers of Irish immigrants now arrived. A figure of 300,000 people between 1790 and 1850 is widely accepted, nearly all settling in Lowland towns and cities. They were to prove a useful source of cheap unskilled labour for 19th-century industries. But they also established a large Catholic community in a strongly Presbyterian country for the first time since the Reformation. As we shall see, this created significant social and religious tensions in succeeding generations.

At the same time, vast numbers of Scots were also leaving (which means, of course, that the contemporary growth in Scotland's population would have been far more dramatic but for these compensating losses). Perhaps 75,000 people crossed the Atlantic for good between 1707 and 1780 – 80 per cent probably from the Lowlands. Between 1821 and 1915, as the pace of emigration quickened, as many as 2 million more departed for North America, Australia and New Zealand.

Highland emigrants generally remained more recognizable once overseas, often leaving as entire communities. This was the case at Cape Breton in Nova Scotia, where Gaelic-speakers from Barra and South Uist put down lasting roots in 1775. It also happened at Cape Fear in North Carolina, where Argyllshire folk settled in the 1730s but then in the late 1770s found themselves fighting as Loyalists against the revolutionaries. This, together with the emotive connection with the Clearances in some cases, probably explains why Highlanders have tended to dominate most modern perceptions of historical Scottish emigration.

Yet the majority of Scots emigrants actually left as individuals or families from the Lowlands. The poor often worked as indentured labourers to pay off their fares. The better-off were able to hit the ground running. Most merged deftly into the melting-pot of colonial society, their Scottish origins soon signified only by their descendants' distinctive surnames. Some, however, acquired great prominence in their new homelands.

Nine of the first 13 state governors in the United States, for example, and every single member of the first Federal cabinet, had at least some Scottish ancestry. And some first-generation emigrants even played leading parts in the American Revolution: John Witherspoon, a Paisley clergyman who became president of the College of New Jersey, and James Wilson, a Fife lawyer who settled in Philadelphia, both signed the Declaration of Independence in 1776, placing themselves among the founding fathers of a new nation.

Politeness and the life of the mind

Significant cultural change was probably an inevitable side-effect of the extraordinary upheavals that were transforming the Scottish economy and Scottish society in the decades after 1707.

The landed elite were particularly affected. Assisted by their enhanced wealth and growing self-confidence, they increasingly knew England intimately, mingled with their English counterparts, and generally absorbed all kinds of subtle and not-so-subtle English influences: the 2nd Duke of Argyll, for example, the dominant chieftain in the West Highlands in the 1740s, was born and died in Surrey, had a mother from Suffolk gentry stock and two English wives.

Convergence, though less dramatically, was also happening more widely. Travel, trade and employment, after all, brought many ordinary Scots into regular contact with English people on both sides of the border. London-centred publishing in a standardized modern English further cultivated a common identity and a British-wide culture, especially among the literate majority.

Tongues and tales

There was a great revival of interest in Scots language and literature in the 18th century – because the break-up of settled rural communities and the harmonization of written and spoken English through printing, education and the wider effects of Union all threatened what remained of older Scottish ways of talking and writing. James Watson and Allan Ramsay who collected and printed old Scots poetry after 1707 and Sir Walter Scott who began his literary career gathering Border ballads for publication all helped keep these traditions alive for the future.

The potent contemporary propaganda of Protestantism and patriotism doubtless worked a similar unifying effect. At the five universities, specialist professorial teaching began, new subjects like history and modern literature were introduced and the latest English and European developments, including Newton's science and cutting-edge political and legal theories, were added to revised curricula. By 1750 Scotland had for the first time become an attractive destination for students from England and overseas.

The Scottish yearning for intellectual novelty also showed itself in the enthusiastic embracing of London literary fashion. The zeal with which Scots took to the popular magazines written by Joseph Addison and Sir Richard Steele, especially *The Spectator* (1711–12), was especially revealing. Their love of Addison's work was an early indication that literate Scots were becoming wedded to the brilliantly seductive vision of modern society that he projected. Like him, they wanted to create a new kind of community, prosperous and at peace with itself. People would use intelligent conversation and interaction to promote 'politeness' – meaning greater insight and understanding and mutual tolerance – for themselves and for others.

Some Scots by the 1720s, including some Presbyterian clergy, were certainly seeking to extend religious and intellectual freedom. Their aspirations were helped by the passage of time. The dogmatic and suspicious Covenanting ministers who had endured the Killing Time and then hanged Thomas Aikenhead for making a theological joke were fading away. A new generation of confidently liberal and Anglophile clerics was emerging. Tellingly, for men influenced by Addison's notion of politeness, they called themselves the 'Moderate party'.

The Moderates accepted the Patronage Act of 1711, which had returned power over parish appointments to secular landowners. Some in the Church, known as the 'Popular party' or the 'High flyers', long continued to reject this legislation. Many of its staunchest opponents even left altogether, forming their own permanent breakaway Presbyterian organizations – notably the Secession Church from the 1730s and the Relief Church from the 1760s. But the Moderates held firm, insisting that the national Church must obey the nation's law.

By the 1750s the Moderates, by dominating the General Assembly, had emerged as the Church's leaders. Self-consciously polite and strongly opposed to old-fashioned and dangerous religious prejudices, they helped make the Church more open-minded. Official harassment of Episcopalians and Catholics ended. Those with unusual opinions were protected from the traditional sanction of a heresy prosecution.

Some of the Moderates, indeed, became increasingly active in intellectual circles themselves – and duly faced sniping from the Popular party. William Robertson, for example, their acknowledged leader, was principal of Edinburgh University from 1762 and one of Europe's best-known and best-paid historians. His friend Hugh Blair, minister of St Giles, was another Edinburgh professor and an influential literary critic, whose greatest achievement was to provide encouragement and vital publicity for the emerging young Ayrshire poet Robert Burns.

The Bard

Burns, now Scotland's national poet, was a farmer who almost emigrated to America. His work, however, soon won him not just recognition but immortality, celebrated by Scots on his birthday, 25 January, at Burns Suppers. His poetry comprises Scots and

English verse on a vast range of themes, including romance, the countryside and religious faith. Each generation has claimed him as its own, the current fashion emphasizing his radical politics, proud Scottishness and unconventional love life. Burns remains the acknowledged property of almost all Scots, as a prominent English journalist found in 2008, provoking outrage by dismissing him as the 'king of sentimental doggerel'.

Robertson and Blair were central participants in what we now know as the 'Scottish Enlightenment' – the Scottish version of sophisticated 18th-century Western culture, characterized in most countries by scientific advances, philosophical free-thinking and progressive values. This development, with David Hume and his Moderate friends to the fore, was what had suddenly catapulted Scotland itself from cultural backwater to intellectual centre-stage.

Some of the Scottish Enlightenment was distinctively and vitally Scottish. In particular, because the king's government was accountable to Parliament and to the courts (where, to the astonishment of foreigners, it actually lost cases), the Continental Enlightenment's fervour for radical political change and hostility towards the oppressive role of churches and churchmen was less pronounced in Scotland (and in England). On the other hand the stark contrasts between Highland and Lowland society and the rapid contemporary commercialization of the economy made Scottish intellectuals like Adam Ferguson, a Gaelic-speaking Edinburgh professor, more fascinated than their European counterparts by the origins of cultural difference and by the causes and consequences of prosperity.

This richly stimulating context was actually a key reason why the Scottish Enlightenment registered such a wide impact outside Scotland. But another was that some of its greatest achievements provided answers to scientific and philosophical questions that were already being asked elsewhere.

Joseph Black, for example, another Edinburgh professor, had strong interests in industrial chemistry and successfully explained latent heat. He was also the first to isolate carbon dioxide (or 'fixed air' as he knew it). Black's friend James Hutton, meanwhile, progressed from expert in agricultural improvement to pioneering geologist: his work began the modern dominance of 'uniformitarianism', the assumption that the planet is the product of natural formative processes at work since its creation and still in operation.

Some of the Scots' most influential contributions came in the study of man's mind and social behaviour. Philosophy, the core of the traditional university curriculum, was an inevitable preoccupation in this vein, with David Hume, arguably the century's most original thinker, the leading Scottish exponent.

David Hume

Hume is widely seen as the greatest philosopher of the European Enlightenment. His most important work, *A Treatise of Human Nature* (1739–40), had limited impact in his own time because its arguments were so disturbing and Hume himself joked that it 'fell dead-born from the press'. Today, however, it is recognized as a founding work of modern philosophy. In the *Treatise* and in other later works Hume identified and explained the internal processes by which the mind perceives and appears to make sense of things. His conclusions were revolutionary. Above all, because the mind is completely dependent upon our senses, which are often unreliable, certain knowledge of things outside our own consciousness – even of their very existence – is not possible. Hume also rejected the orthodox belief about morality that an in-built human instinct naturally leads us to follow certain fixed rules of behaviour laid down by God. Instead he argued that morality simply means learning gradually by experience how to behave in such a way as to win other people's approval. He even insisted that many of the traditional arguments for belief in God were either illogical or lacked credible evidence. Unsurprisingly, a man with such subversive opinions failed to acquire professorships in universities still controlled by the Kirk and devoted to educating Scotland's parish ministers. Nevertheless Hume's wit, conversational skills and capacity for original ideas ensured that some of the leading clergymen of the Scottish Enlightenment were among his close personal friends.

Hume's friend Adam Smith, for many years a professor at Glasgow, also offered new insights in moral philosophy. But it was his subsequent study of economic change, forcing people to re-think their comfortable assumptions about the moral character of economic activities, which brought him fame and influence. Smith's main argument, running against the grain of much traditional Christian teaching, was that it is the self-interest of individuals that leads them to sell goods and offer services. The pursuit of private profit and not a benevolent concern for others is therefore what ultimately creates wealth and maximizes society's material wellbeing.

> 'It is not from the benevolence of the butcher, the brewer, or the baker that we expect our dinner, but from their regard to their own interest.'
> Adam Smith, *The Wealth of Nations* (1776)

Overall, the Scottish Enlightenment lacked a single theoretical standpoint. But its leading contributors typically assumed that extremely long histories interacting with highly specific cultural and environmental factors could explain most of the peculiar features of human societies. This insight was what made them important precursors to the 19th-century founders of the modern social sciences.

In literary and artistic terms the Scottish Enlightenment also brought Scotland and its culture to far wider attention than hitherto. Tobias Smollett and Henry Mackenzie produced some of the age's most entertaining novels, but it was Scott who from 1814 onwards offered some of the most popular and influential stories about Scotland ever written.

Scott-land

'Scott-land' was a one-word 19th-century joke that made a serious point. After early fame as a poet, Sir Walter Scott's extraordinary bestseller *Waverley* (1814), the first historical novel ever written, brought the Scotland of the 1745–6 rebellion dramatically back to life. *Heart of Midlothian*, *Rob Roy* and *Redgauntlet* are among his other novels to depict a seductive but old-fashioned Scotland dominated by the Highland mountains, imposing castles, scheming Jacobites, fervent Covenanters, amusing eccentrics, dogged heroes and lost causes. More than anyone else before or since, it was Scott who made the country seem irresistibly romantic.

The poet James Macpherson also achieved worldwide celebrity with his purported translations from the ancient Gaelic poet Ossian. These were a crucial inspiration for European Romanticism and Napoleon kept a copy with him on campaign. Even so, well-founded doubts persisted about whether they were genuine translations or had been substantially invented by Macpherson himself.

Not all aspects of the Scottish Enlightenment were concerned with the abstract. There were graphic and physical achievements too. The artists Allan Ramsay and Sir Henry Raeburn transformed the international standing of Scottish art with their celebrated portraiture. And William Adam and his gifted son Robert made signal contributions to British architecture in the fashionable neo-classical style: Charlotte Square in Edinburgh's New Town was to prove Robert's most striking and accessible legacy.

The New Town as a whole, which emerged from 1760 onwards, was deeply symbolic. It allowed the capital city finally to escape from the confines of the crowded medieval Old Town. It is also by far the most tangible monument to Scotland's progressive modernization as it was relentlessly pursued in the period from the Treaty of Union to the 1830s.

Fact check

1 What was 'runrig'?
   a a communal farming system
   b an enclosure
   c a tenancy
   d a new crop

2 When was Royal Bank of Scotland founded?
   a 1707
   b 1695
   c 1727
   d 1746

3 Which was Scotland's largest city in 1821?
   a Aberdeen
   b Dundee
   c Edinburgh
   d Glasgow

4 What was 'crofting'
   a animal grazing
   b a ploughing technique
   c a new Highland tenancy
   d adding fertilizer

5 What powered the early cotton mills?
   a water
   b electricity
   c steam
   d horses

6 What were the 'Moderates'?
   a academic philosophers
   b political reformers
   c liberal clergymen
   d a group of writers

7 Who pioneered geological science?
   a David Hume
   b William Robertson
   c James Hutton
   d Joseph Black

8 What was Sir Henry Raeburn?
   a a sculptor
   b a poet
   c a historian
   d a portrait artist

Dig Deeper

David Allan, *Scotland in the Eighteenth Century* (London, 2001).

T. M. Devine and R. Mitchison, (ed.) *People and Society in Scotland: Vol. 1—1760–1830* (Edinburgh, 1988).

Christopher A. Whatley, *Scottish Society, 1707–1830* (Manchester, 2000).

Christopher A. Whatley, *The Industrial Revolution in Scotland* (Cambridge, 1997).

Alexander Broadie, *The Scottish Enlightenment* (Edinburgh, 2001).

The long Victorian age

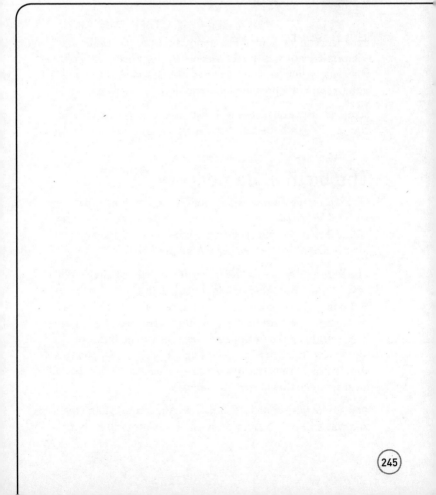

Change and stability

The Victorian age is conventionally regarded as one of success and tranquillity.

The British constitution was widely venerated, the monarchy popular and beyond reproach. The economy, directed by mutton-chopped entrepreneurs and overseen by prudent governments, boomed as never before. The *Pax Britannica* prevented major European wars. And a worldwide empire existed whose bounds got wider and wider. On this view the period saw a happy balance struck which, at least until things went disastrously wrong on 4 August 1914, made the British wealthy and contented as well as all-powerful.

Yet this is an unrealistic characterization of the Scottish experience in particular. The period between the 1830s and Victoria's death was in fact marked by unprecedented political changes, by further economic transformations, by social upheaval and by profound cultural developments.

Scotland, as we shall see, was fast becoming a quite different country from what it had been at the end of the Georgian era.

The birth of democracy

One reason why a misleading impression can sometimes be given of Victoria's reign is that the most fundamental of the political changes that re-shaped 19th-century Britain actually took place shortly before her accession in 1837.

The Reform Acts of 1832, implemented by Lord Grey's Whig government after more than a decade of public pressure and political campaigning, had dramatic effects in Scotland. Previously there had been just 4,500 Scottish voters; but by finally bringing the much narrower Scottish qualification into line with further-extended English practice, the changes enfranchised most well-to-do householders in the burghs and most small landowners in the counties.

At a stroke this created a Scottish electorate of 65,000. Of course, this was still only a fraction of the population. But that the vast majority of the new voters were middle-class nevertheless represented a shift in the balance of power. Government policies would in future no longer be dictated by the great landowners. Increasingly they would accommodate the views of urban Britain and the business classes.

Another seminal consequence, crystallized in the reinvention by the 1860s of the Tory Party as the Conservatives and the Whig Party as the Liberals, was the evolution of something like modern party politics. Beforehand, with many Scottish constituencies having just a few dozen electors, private relationships between candidates and individual voters were often decisive. Afterwards the sort of campaigning machinery that only mass-membership political parties can provide became necessary. Politicians were forced to court the newspapers to reach a wider public. In effect, prospective MPs and potential governments finally had to compete for the support of broad swathes of the electorate.

Man of the people

The emergence of modern politics in Victorian Scotland was exemplified by the famous campaign of 1879–80 in which William Ewart Gladstone, from a Scottish business family that had made its money in Liverpool and already twice Liberal prime minister toured the Midlothian constituency in which his father had been born. A series of packed public meetings heard his passionately argued speeches on the moral deficiencies of Disraeli's foreign policy. Gladstone in due course defeated the sitting Tory MP at the polls.

Sceptics at the time and since were, however, correct that the reforms of 1832 were limited in their extent. The signatories of the People's Charter in 1838 and of its subsequent revisions – demanding, among other things, votes for all men over 21, annual elections and equalization of constituency sizes – were only the most organized and articulate of the critics.

Chartism, as it became known, was a popular radical phenomenon throughout Britain, though it differed in character from place to place. It was especially potent in Ireland and in Wales, where open violence flared in 1839. But in Scotland it was associated with working-class Presbyterians from the Relief Church and the Secession Church. And they were noted for using peaceful meetings and the arts of persuasion – so-called 'moral force' Chartism – rather than employing sedition and conspiracy to advance their cause.

The Chartists ultimately failed, their campaigns fizzling out everywhere by the early 1850s as the lack of progress undermined their credibility. It took until the Second and Third Reform Acts, passed in 1867–8 by Benjamin Disraeli's Conservatives and 1884 by Gladstone's Liberal government, for some of the Chartists' main aspirations finally to be fulfilled.

The Second Reform Act enfranchised all urban householders, effectively benefiting the working class: by the 1868 election, Scotland's electorate had reached 150,000. The Third did the same for rural Britain, giving the vote to all householders in the counties. Added to the 1872 Ballot Act, which introduced secret voting (stopping the political preferences of employees and tenants being monitored by their supposed superiors), these changes further advanced the politics of mass democracy in Victorian Britain.

The Liberals were the chief beneficiaries in Scotland. The 1886 general election, for example, which saw a Conservative government sweep to power at Westminster, nevertheless yielded 39 Scottish MPs for the Liberals and 16 more for the new Liberal Unionists (dissidents who opposed Gladstone on Irish Home Rule). Just 12 Scottish Tories were returned even in a year of victory UK-wide.

The same skew was seen in the Liberals' famous 1906 landslide victory. This made the Glaswegian businessman Henry Campbell-Bannerman, representing the Stirling Burghs, the new prime minister succeeding his fellow Scot Arthur Balfour, a Manchester Conservative MP from an old Fife landed dynasty. On this occasion the official Liberals secured 58 Scottish seats, the Tories limping home with a mere 8.

In truth, the Conservatives remained hampered in Scotland by being the party of the established churches and the landed class. Accordingly they struggled to attract the working-class vote that they acquired more easily in parts of England. The Liberal Party, by contrast, was high-minded and moderately progressive not just on constitutional matters but on education and welfare issues too – passing, for example, the Factory Acts that stopped children being sent up chimneys and women down mine shafts.

Liberalism thus appealed intuitively to the morally upright evangelicals and Presbyterians who were so numerous in Victorian Scotland. More widely, it attracted a powerful (though inherently unstable) coalition of urban voters: both businessmen and unionized workers, who were becoming more important as the economy industrialized, were bastions of Scottish Liberal support.

Scotland, in short, remained a discernibly different society with a different political culture from England. To understand why, we need to consider the further progress of Scottish industrialization since the 1820s.

The workshop of the world

By the 1820s a new phase in Scotland's economic history was dawning.

At its heart lay the rapid growth of the coal, iron and steel industries, and soon also of their related manufactures, such as railway engines, girders, boilers, large-scale machinery and, above all, ships. As a result, the shape and overall performance of the Scottish economy by the turn of the 20th century would be dominated by what we would now describe collectively as 'heavy industry'.

The triggers for this new transformation lay in the decades before 1830, when two innovations greatly increased the productive capacity of the iron industry. It was the Glasgow engineer James Neilson who invented a new furnace that injected heated air into the smelting process (at a time when received wisdom insisted that the best results occurred at the lowest possible temperature). Patented in 1828, the 'hot blast' technique consumed far less coal while delivering more and better-quality pig-iron. This in turn allowed the full exploitation of a superior new ore, the much richer 'blackband' or carboniferous ironstone (50–70 per cent of which could be turned into metal), which had been found in Lanarkshire and Ayrshire by the metallurgist David Mushet in 1801.

The combined effects of these two discoveries were spectacular. In the year of Neilson's patent Scotland produced just 36,000 tons of pig-iron. By 1840 output had already passed 300,000 tons and by the 1880s it exceeded 1.2 million. Since most Scottish iron masters considered the subsequent stages of metal production unprofitable, pig-iron itself soon became an important export as well as supplying the many other local businesses for which it became the key raw material.

Coal output, partly to feed the rising demand from Scotland's metal industries but also to power steam engines, to warm homes, and for sale to England and overseas, charted a broadly similar course. From just 1 million tons in 1775 and 3 million in 1830, Scottish miners, of whom there were by then well over 100,000, were excavating 42 million tons annually by 1914.

Other local factors also helped propel these industries forward. In particular, 19th-century Scottish workers, many newly arrived from Ireland, earned significantly less than their English counterparts (perhaps only 75 per cent as much in the 1860s). Labour-intensive processes such as coal extraction and iron-smelting thus enjoyed peculiar advantages in Scotland, the main production cost being minimized.

The same was true for the new group of firms that, using the Siemens technique for converting pig-iron into steel, sprung up after the 1870s. Steelmakers like Colville of Dalzell near Motherwell and Beardmore at Parkhead in Glasgow exploited the same plentiful supply of comparatively cheap labour as well as the lower-cost coal and pig-iron available from other local firms.

The large and well-established metal industry that resulted, densely concentrated to the south and east of Glasgow, where adjacent coal and ironstone reserves existed and 18th-century infrastructure like the Monklands Canal linked sites together, allowed other specialist businesses to take on the design and manufacture of derivative products like locomotives, rail tracks and their associated machinery and structures.

Trains quickly became a key Scottish export. Firms such as Neilson and Company of Springburn and Dübs of Polmadie sent tens of thousands of locomotives to India, South Africa, Australasia and South America over several decades. By 1870 as much as one-quarter of all of the world's trains were being fashioned in and around Glasgow. The Scots' contribution to the railway age was, however, most famously embodied in the majestic Forth Bridge: 55,000 tons of carefully assembled steel built by Sir William Arrol & Company of Glasgow, when finally opened in 1890 it was, as it remains today, an exuberant monument to Victorian heavy engineering at its most confident and bombastic.

Temples of industry

Vast, complex railway manufacturing facilities emerged in Scotland in the mid-19th century. The Cowlairs factory at Springburn in Glasgow, was, when it was opened by the North British Railway Company in 1841, the first plant in Britain to integrate locomotive, carriage and wagon construction on one site. The nearby St Rollox works was where the engines of the Caledonian Railway were fabricated from 1856. These were among the greatest industrial workshops of the Victorian age.

Early competitive advantages in producing lower-cost iron and steel in quantity also explain the rise, from virtually nowhere, of what was Scotland's most important industry by the late 19th century. Shipbuilding was transformed in character as Scottish companies swiftly adapted new technologies from elsewhere. Beginning with paddle steamers, they readily embraced the mass production first of iron plating and reciprocating steam engines and then from the 1880s of steel hulls and from the early 1900s of steam turbines too. Ships of all descriptions thus became the specialist Scottish industrial product par excellence. Leading firms like J. & G. Thomson (from 1899, John Brown & Company) at Clydebank, Denny of Dumbarton, Beardmore of Dalmuir and Fairfields of Govan soon acquired worldwide reputations.

> 'The steamer left the black and oozy wharves,
> And floated down between dark ranks of masts.
> We heard the swarming streets, the noisy mills;
> Saw sooty foundries full of glare and gloom,
> Great bellied chimneys tipped by tongues of flame,
> Quiver in smoky heat. We slowly passed
> Loud ship-building yards, where every slip contained
> A mighty vessel with a hundred men
> Battering its iron sides.'
>
> Alexander Smith, *City Poems* (1857)

The results were utterly extraordinary. Glasgow and its satellite riverside towns were alone building more iron ships by the 1870s than the rest of the world put together. A generation later, in 1913–14, no less than 20 per cent of the world's newly launched tonnage – more than either Germany or the United States were then producing – bore the prestigious branding 'Clydebuilt'.

Cheap, reliable and prolific, by the turn of the 20th century Scotland's shipbuilders supplied warships for the world's most powerful navy as well as a vast range of vessels for Britain's merchant fleet. They were also securely established as the country's most successful exporters.

The triumph of Scottish heavy industry brought wider gains too. Everything from banking, accountancy and insurance to technical education, joinery and all the electrical and mechanical trades benefited. As importantly, in making possible regular train services and steamship routes, these products also created a truly British economy, better integrated than ever before.

Local specialist production flourished once modern transportation linked it to much bigger and further-flung markets: granite-quarrying and beef cattle in Aberdeenshire, coal-mining in Fife, trawling for herring (the 'silver darlin's') along the entire east coast and for haddock off Arbroath, milk and cheese in Ayrshire, fruit in Angus, jute production in Dundee (where the necessary raw material actually came all the way from Bengal) and woollen manufacturing in the various Border towns (which exported tweed garments worldwide) all expanded profitably as trains and ships, designed and built in Scotland, made the world a smaller place.

Yet not all the consequences of heavy engineering's central position in Scottish life, nor all the connections that now tied the country into an international economy, were benevolent. For it had spawned a network of separate, mutually dependent, family-owned companies, in most cases highly specialized and also unusually reliant on exports to foreign and colonial markets.

This made it acutely vulnerable to new overseas competition exploiting higher levels of integration, more extensive natural resources or far greater economies of scale. The lower wages paid to Scottish workers also suppressed domestic economic consumption. This in turn discouraged diversification into consumer items and so further reinforced the focus on an industrial monoculture manufacturing a limited range of high-value capital goods: by 1914, for example, over half a million Scottish workers depended directly on making iron and steel products.

For related reasons, those fashionable new consumer goods that were being produced in Scotland by 1914 were often made by foreign-owned companies. Singer, whose Clydebank sewing machine factory opened in 1884, soon employed 7,000 on that site alone. They were among the first of a succession of American firms over the coming decades who, outside the realm of heavy engineering, would gradually make Scottish manufacturing dependent upon overseas firms and their 'branch plant' networks.

The Scots' conspicuous success in labour-intensive forms of work had another looming dark side. Especially in native-owned heavy engineering it encouraged and rewarded a business strategy that prioritized containing wages and hiring and firing to cope with fluctuating demand. Simultaneously it undervalued risk-taking and investment, which in the long term would threaten the country's early technological leadership in capital goods.

Worst of all, this entire model of industrialization hid a dirty secret. For it had helped generate a series of intractable social problems and worsening class tensions that bubbled away just beneath the apparently serene surface of Victorian Scottish society.

Labouring and living

Large scale and rapid urbanization was certainly the most important factor in transforming Victorian social experiences. Indeed, Scotland was quickly becoming second only to England in the extent to which its people had abandoned their traditional rural way of life.

At the 1801 census barely one in five Scots resided in a town or city with at least 5,000 inhabitants. By 1901, however, after a century of industrialization and further agricultural modernization, the proportion already stood at 58 per cent. Urban life, in short, had suddenly become the norm.

Glasgow, the focus of commerce, textile manufacturing and heavy engineering, as well as of immigration (44,000 Irish-born residents were recorded in the 1841 census), had overtaken Edinburgh and was now the country's largest city. From just 77,000 inhabitants in 1801, by the First World War its expanded boundaries encompassed over a million souls – more than one-fifth of all the people in Scotland, making Glasgow a proportionately larger contributor to total national population than other great world cities like London, Paris, Rome or New York. Indeed, if we include its many satellite towns, west-central Scotland, the conurbation later dubbed 'greater Glasgow', was actually home to the clear majority of Scottish residents by the early 20th century.

Key idea: Conurbation

Given the rapid Victorian expansion of metropolitan Glasgow to dominate Scotland's human geography, it is appropriate that the term 'conurbation', describing a dense concentration of urban settlement involving one or more major city centres and a range of satellite towns, was first coined by a Scot. It appeared in *Cities in Evolution* (1915) by Sir Patrick Geddes, a pioneering Aberdeenshire-born town planner, scientist, ecologist and social visionary.

The pace and scale of Scottish urbanization created a whole new set of social problems. Spatial segregation, a classic feature of modern cities, was one of them.

The well-to-do naturally lived in increasing comfort and style. Housing for the masses, however, was both cramped and insanitary. Mainly comprising unregulated rented accommodation in tall, densely packed tenements, large numbers of new blocks were built cheaply – though this was convenient for workers whose own wages remained low – and with few if any domestic amenities.

The result on the ground was some chilling contrasts. Dundee's Broughty Ferry and Glasgow's West End, for example, became much sought-after for their fashionable townhouses and gracious living. Yet neighbourhoods only a couple of miles away, like Lochee, the haunt of Irish immigrants in Dundee, and the Gorbals (often described as Europe's worst slum) and the East End in Glasgow, became notorious for their appalling housing and blighted lives.

The data on working-class accommodation never fail to shock. In 1861 a third of all Scots lived in one-roomed homes ('single ends' in Glaswegian slang). Another third had just two rooms. In such conditions, especially before mains sewerage, clean drinking water and inoculation were widely available, disease was a regular visitor. Cholera epidemics cut a swathe through Glasgow in the 1830s, 1840s and 1850s. Typhus and typhoid were ever-present for most of the century.

As in England's cities, mortality was consistently higher than in the countryside. On average, 28 people per 1,000 were dying each year in urban Scotland in the early 1860s against just 18 in rural areas. In the Gorbals in the 1890s the annual child mortality rate was still running at an astonishing 200 per 1,000.

Most Victorian Scots were, of course, substantially better off than their predecessors. And there can be no doubt that things broadly continued to improve between the 1830s and 1914. Death rates, notwithstanding some appalling black-spots and significant setbacks, declined: 21 Scots in every 1,000 died each year between 1855 and 1860 but only 17 by 1900. Life expectancy also increased, from around 40 years for Scottish men in 1850 to 50 by the First World War. These benign averages undeniably reflect steady improvements in living standards and living conditions for the large majority.

Yet people did not seem any happier or more contented. Partly this was because Scottish society was increasingly unequal and divided. Some were very wealthy indeed. Just 7 per cent of Scots collected 46 per cent of the national income in the 1860s, with a quarter pocketed by just 5,000 individuals. On the other hand, the bottom 70 per cent of earners took home just one-third of the total. At the very top, the richest 1 per cent – including industrialists like David Colville and William Beardmore – enjoyed incomes at least 200 times greater than anyone in the poorest 30 per cent.

The sense of grievance that these contrasts generated was compounded by the fluctuating wage levels and periodic unemployment to which Scotland's export-led industrial economy was particularly exposed.

The official system for coping with destitution, the New Poor Law introduced in 1845 (finally replacing the charitable parish hand-outs of the old Reformation-era regime), was wholly inadequate. Workhouses, meagre payments and a deep reluctance to give anything at all to the able-bodied – based on moral assumptions about the 'undeserving poor' – maintained rather than alleviated poverty.

Mutual support was the natural response of many of the vulnerable. For welfare purposes this meant forming 'friendly societies', as in England, whose members subscribed to a fund that would support the needy. But to manage relations with employers a rather different kind of collective organization was required.

Following the Trade Union Act of 1871, which legalized them for the first time, Scotland's workplaces began to see concerted union activity. This was partly inspired by socialist ideas. But more commonly it was motivated by employees' desire to strengthen their own hand in bargaining over wages, conditions and redundancies. Organizations like the Ayrshire Miners Union, established in 1886, and the National Union of Dock Labourers, founded in Glasgow in 1889, eventually became a significant presence in many working communities.

Yet another logical response was long familiar in Scotland: emigration. Huge numbers, perhaps approaching 2 million between the 1820s and 1914 – disproportionately the young, the skilled and the ambitious – left for the United States, Canada and Australasia. Some who departed applied their talents overseas with startling results. The vast majority of those who emigrated, however, merely lived decent, blameless lives in their new countries. In practice, railways, engineering, government, the military, education and banking – the stereotypical national strengths – invariably gained disproportionately wherever the Scots ended up.

Success stories

Andrew Carnegie, Dunfermline weaver's son turned Pittsburgh steel magnate and philanthropist, was dubbed 'the richest man in the world' by the 1890s and was one of the most famous Scots alive. Allan Pinkerton, too, became a legendary American detective and spy, having started out a mere Gorbals cooper and Chartist activist. The dramatic upwards mobility of some emigrants became a source of much national pride and reinforced the myth of the humble Scot prospering by dint of natural talent and sheer determination.

Even those Victorian Scots least affected by industrialization and urbanization, because they still lived in the most remote rural districts, suffered growing distress and experienced deepening social divisions. In particular, relations between Highland crofters and their landlords, already poisoned by the recent Clearances, were worsened still further by two unforeseen developments.

First, the danger of over-dependence on the potato to feed the newly established crofting communities was brutally demonstrated by *Phytophthora infestans* – the blight fungus that also lay behind the great Irish potato famine of the period. Thriving in the relentless damp of the north and west of Scotland in 1846–7 and successfully destroying the harvest ahead of what turned out to be an unusually harsh winter, it caused severe deprivation.

Suffering crofters, unable to pay rent, were treated in different ways. Certain landlords helped tenants leave for Canada or

Australia. Others organized paid work such as building the 'destitution roads' in remote parts of the Highlands. Some, however, like John Gordon of Cluny, were lambasted in the newspapers for evicting their stricken tenants, while the government made ineffectual attempts to distribute sufficient additional food by ship. In the event large numbers, above all the young, left permanently in the aftermath, reckoning Highland life perhaps unsustainable and certainly unpalatable. The region's total population peaked in mid-century and then declined relentlessly.

The second problem peculiar to the Highlands was that the unusual land economy underpinning crofting also proved untenable. The inadequacy of the agricultural resources available to local communities had again been highlighted by the famine. This was especially contentious when so much acreage was given over to the landlords' sheep farms and to sporting estates catering to the growing enthusiasm of wealthy non-Highlanders for the region's picturesque mountains, woods and wildlife. The ease with which crofters could be evicted also rankled, as did rising rents.

These grievances caused the Highland Land War of the early 1880s. There were rent strikes, occupations and attacks on owners' properties as the Highland Land League, the crofters' collective campaigning vehicle, attempted to secure additional land and enhanced rights for tenants. Eye-catching incidents, like the Battle of the Braes in 1882, in which 50 Glasgow policemen were drafted in to confront crofters resisting an eviction on Skye, secured them sympathetic media attention. No one was killed or badly injured – unlike in Ireland, whose own struggles over land provided general inspiration but no precise model for Scottish activists.

The government, however, was forced to sit up and take notice. The Napier Commission duly investigated and made its recommendations. And Gladstone's Liberal government passed the Crofters' Holdings Act in 1886, giving existing tenants security of tenure and establishing the Crofters' Commission with powers to manage rents.

The political consequences of these specifically Highland troubles were distinctive and yet illustrative of broader Scottish patterns.

A Crofters' Party actually returned four MPs in the 1885 election. But as in Ireland, it was the Liberals who derived most electoral benefit, and the Conservatives who suffered most, from widespread anti-landlord sentiment.

The same was true of growing tensions in Lowland society. Collective workplace organization, facilitated by Liberal legislation, broadly aligned industrial workforces, once they secured the vote, with the party of Gladstone. Yet this was by no means a straightforward political alliance. After all, the Liberals also represented many middle-class Scottish employers. Suspicious of intrusive state intervention in the free market, they were typically hostile to trade unionism, sometimes actually banning it from their workplaces. Many workers, by contrast, were increasingly class-conscious. Growing numbers were also attracted to socialism, with its robustly collectivist prescriptions for the economy.

Increasingly, this basic ideological contradiction led some Scottish workers off in a new direction. A Scottish Labour Party, whose secretary was James Keir Hardie, a Lanarkshire miners' union organizer, was formed in 1888 to field socialist candidates in parliamentary elections. In 1893 its first British-wide successor was established, the Independent Labour Party (ILP), again led by Keir Hardie, by now an MP for a poor London constituency.

With its idealistic worker-friendly manifesto committed to the common ownership of industry and the pursuit of social and economic equality, by the turn of the new century the ILP was becoming the more obvious party for a significant number of unionized working-class Scots to support. No one could yet have known it – especially with Arthur Primrose, 5th Earl of Rosebery, an Eton-educated Scottish aristocrat and racehorse owner, as Liberal prime minister in the mid-1890s – but this shift would soon help bring about the strange death of Liberal Scotland.

Revivalism

Industrialization was so profoundly transformational that its effects reached far beyond the workplace, into the nooks and crannies of everyday life. It altered not just economic structures and political affiliations but also the ways in which people looked at the world around them. It even had the capacity to change how they thought about their own place within it.

This was emphatically so in the religious sphere. Indeed, no mental revolution in Victorian Scotland was more dramatic than the one that began on 18 May 1843. On that day more than a third of the Church of Scotland's clergy, attending that year's General Assembly in St Andrew's Church in Edinburgh, walked out to form a separate Presbyterian church, the Free Church (or Free Kirk) of Scotland.

The immediate cause was, as ever, patronage. Ostensibly this 'Disruption' was the culmination of what was referred to as the Ten Years' War, between a Moderate leadership who still endorsed the Patronage Act and an increasingly vociferous Popular party. The latter, evangelical in inspiration and temperament, flatly rejected the state's interference in clerical appointments, arguing instead for a re-born national church whose only legitimate authority would be Jesus Christ.

> '... it is the duty of civil rulers to recognize the truth of God according to His word, and to promote and support the Kingdom of Christ without assuming any jurisdiction in it, or any power over it.'
> Act and Declaration of the General Assembly of the Free Kirk (1851)

At a deeper level, however, the Disruption reflected contrasting responses to the new Scotland. The Moderates represented the secularizing tendencies of the Scottish Enlightenment nurtured in a genteel 18th-century world of landowners and polite clergymen in prosperous parishes. The evangelicals, led by charismatic figures like Thomas Chalmers and David Welsh, were closely engaged with the challenges of urban, industrial and Highland society – poverty, unemployment, illegitimacy, immorality and a lack of access to churches. Intriguingly, they were also convinced that the solution lay in reviving the spiritual certainties and moral fervour of the Reformation era.

Chalmers and his Free Church colleagues aimed to create nothing less than an alternative national church uncorrupted by political interference. This is why they took 474 of the Church of Scotland's 1,203 ministers with them, constructing 500 new churches in the first two years, often adjacent to the existing parish buildings. They also founded schools, training institutions, charities, publications and overseas missions. All were financed by their own congregations and other well-wishers.

The Free Church quickly attracted most leading Presbyterian theologians, preachers and social activists. And it won particularly strong support in the Highlands, from the urban working classes and among Liberal voters. All in all, the Disruption was a quiet but stunningly effective domestic rebellion – the only really successful one of its kind in the Victorian period – against the British state and the failings of its established institutions.

Even so, the unyielding spirit that had made it possible in the first place, and the habitual preference of strict Presbyterians for a 'stooshie' (Scots for a row) instead of a compromise, came back to haunt the Free Church in due course. It did itself few favours, for instance, by upholding a heresy charge in the late 1870s against one of its own ministers, William Robertson Smith. A brilliant professor at the Aberdeen Free Church College, his articles for the *Encyclopaedia Britannica* failed to uphold the literal truth of scripture: the convicted author consoled himself with a position at Cambridge.

Further splits were always likely given the doctrinal strictness that had originally facilitated the Disruption. After the government abolished patronage in 1874, the Free Church did move closer to the United Presbyterian Church, formed earlier by combining the 18th-century Secession and Relief churches. The negotiated outcome, in 1900, was the United Free Church of Scotland. But one group, later mocked as the 'Wee Frees' (properly it still called itself the Free Church), rejected the deal and continued as before. There had already been another embarrassing rupture in 1893 over the Free Church's gradual dilution of Covenant theology. The opponents of this particular error had also departed to become the Free Presbyterian Church (colloquially the 'Wee Wee Frees').

These two breakaway institutions, again drawing particular support from the Highlands and becoming the dominant force on isolated islands like Raasay, would long maintain their stricter Calvinist views. Coming on top of the old divisions between Episcopalians and Presbyterians and then between the established Church of Scotland and the Free Church, they ensured that 20th-century Scotland's high streets would contain a confusing succession of rival Protestant places of worship, each claiming uniquely to continue the godly mission of the Scottish Reformation.

Religious revival in response to disorienting and destabilizing social change was not confined to the Presbyterian churches. The Episcopalian church itself, for example, blossomed once the restrictions on this formerly Jacobite institution were relaxed in 1792. At Perth in 1851 it opened the first post-Reformation cathedral in Britain. Gradually it restored some of its long-lost respectability and influence. With more than 300 parishes and clergy by 1900, Episcopalianism proved especially good at attracting the landed classes and urban professionals.

The re-birth of Scottish Catholicism, once even more under suspicion, was more spectacular still. It was helped, of course, by the mass influx of Irish adherents and by the government's removal of the remaining legal prohibitions in 1829. Parishes were re-founded, particularly in the industrial towns of the Lowlands on which working-class Irish families converged. Proper dioceses were restored by Rome in 1878. And a full-scale seminary was even instituted at Blairs in Aberdeenshire. From just 30,000 mainly native believers in 1800, Catholicism grew to become once more a major national force by 1901, with 244,100 communicants, overwhelmingly of Irish descent.

Community tensions, however, were the worrying legacy, especially in Scotland's towns and cities. Traditional anti-Catholic sectarianism was given greater force by new concerns over the effects of cheap immigrant labour on prevailing wage rates and by the divisive culmination of the Irish struggle for independence.

The experiences of all of Scotland's main Christian groups in this period had certain features in common, generally traceable to the industrial and urban setting in which they increasingly operated. Determined to recover ground among the 'godless poor' who had moved to new locations to lead new kinds of lives exposed to new threats, every church understandably became noticeably more energetic and more creative.

The urgency of the challenge meant that spiritual zeal and theological precision seemed to matter more than in the 18th century. Committed pastoral outreach also became a top priority. So did charitable efforts to help the needy poor as well as vociferous moral campaigns to hector them into improved behaviour.

Sin and Sundays

Drunkenness was an obsession for most of the Victorian churches. Because alcohol abuse was a personal moral failing with disastrous wider consequences, 'temperance' and 'teetotalism' became cardinal virtues among the respectable church-going working classes as well as among austere Scottish socialists like Keir Hardie (even giving rise in 1901 to its own separate political vehicle, the Scottish Prohibition Party). Sabbatarianism, or observance of Sunday as a day of rest, was another interesting point of overlap between Scottish Presbyterianism in particular and the trade unions who sought to protect hard-pressed workers. Widespread public disapproval prevented shops opening and even train and ferry services operating on Sundays in some places deep into the next century.

Widely perceived too was the churches' obligation to conduct missions overseas. The latter extended the views and values of 19th-century Scotland across a much broader canvas. They were exemplified by the endlessly idolized Dr David Livingstone, the explorer and Congregationalist preacher who traversed southern and central Africa in mid-century, and later by Mary Slessor of the United Presbyterian Church who worked in Nigeria. Each of the competing Scottish churches naturally maintained an institutional campaign of its own. In some parts of Britain's African empire, like Nyasaland (now Malawi) and British East Africa (Kenya), Presbyterianism became the dominant form of Christianity, its imprint detectable even today.

Recreation, culture, nationhood

By the late 19th century the different churches' many-faceted campaign to win converts and retain believers had spread across much of Scottish life.

The 1872 Education Act formally handed control of school education to the civil authorities and made attendance compulsory up to the age of 13. But the Presbyterian churches retained a dominant influence over the ethos and the strong religious content, while Catholic schools remained unchanged and outside the system.

The Sunday Schools movement, which had rather earlier beginnings, was another staple feature of many people's lives by this time, inculcating Christian teachings among the masses. So too were more recent innovations, like the Boys' Brigade, founded by the Free Church in Glasgow in 1883, and the Salvation Army, which arrived from England in 1879. The latter in particular quickly won over many additional Scottish recruits to the trademark cause of temperance.

Yet the churches, desperate to attract support and deflect their members from potentially sinful alternatives, also increasingly exploited essentially secular pastimes. Football had the greatest pulling power. Many parish churches formed amateur teams, taking advantage of what was fast emerging as a ragingly popular working-class pursuit, for spectators as well as for participants.

'Fitba'

Football was a popular pastime in Scotland by 1500 and well-attended matches between professional teams had emerged by 1880. A reputation soon grew for exporting great players to England – Hughie Gallacher in the 1920s, Denis Law in the 1950s, Kenny Dalglish in the 1970s – and formidable managers like Bill Shankly to Liverpool and Sir Matt Busby and Sir Alex Ferguson to Manchester United. But football has deeper significance. Glasgow's 'Old Firm' clubs Celtic and Rangers, dominant on the field, have sectarian associations off it (Irish tricolours and republican songs like 'We are the IRA' versus Union flags and anti-Catholic lyrics like 'The Sash'). The humiliation of Ally MacLeod's much-hyped Scotland team at the 1978 World Cup traumatized people already fretting over the country's constitutional arrangements. And that many Scots clearly enjoy England's losses more than Scotland's victories speaks volumes about the game's palpable political undertones.

By 1900 bicycling clubs (the contraption itself was pioneered by Scottish engineers), choirs and artistic groups were proliferating too. Healthy communal activities always promised much to the churches and their leaders in search of new ways to capture the loyalties of the population.

Yet not all diversions that interested the Victorian public were as easily co-opted in the cause of religion. The theatre, for example, was a common diversion with which religion struggled to compete, a fashion made possible by the growing surplus incomes of workers and by the gradually reducing hours worked. Venues such as the Britannia Music Hall and the Whitebait Music Hall, both opened in Glasgow in 1857, played an increasingly important part in the lives of industrial workers. Such places also provided a venue in which performers like Arthur Lloyd and Harry Lauder could popularize distinctively Scottish songs and cultural symbolism – kilts, bonnets and endless references to the Highlands – that reflected and accentuated the emphatically Scottish identities of their audiences.

Lauder and his maudlin signature love song 'Roamin' in the Gloamin'', hugely popular in England and North America before and after the First World War (Winston Churchill even hailed Lauder somewhat implausibly as 'Scotland's greatest ever ambassador'), were among the most accessible manifestations of a broader trend in which Scottishness of a particularly sentimental and stereotypical kind became a lucrative and influential cultural product. In a slightly more challenging form this same development was represented by what have become known (often sarcastically) as 'Balmorality' and the 'Kailyard'.

Both phenomena can be seen as yet another response to industrialization and urbanization. For they clearly represented a retreat from the mid-Victorian period onwards into a psychological comfort zone, safely away from the increasingly troubling social and political realities of the age. They indicate a deep cultural yearning in many quarters for a Scotland that was stable, contented and unthreatening – for a country that, in truth, had never existed historically, but which was nonetheless far removed from the bleak industrial towns of Lanarkshire and Clydeside, the poverty of the Gorbals and the conflicts over the ownership and use of land in the Highlands.

In another way, too, the attention garnered at the time and ever since by the increasing sentimentalization of Scottish culture does a real disservice to Victorian Scotland. For the period actually saw a fruitful and engaged intellectual life evolve that was no less distinguished and no less widely influential than that produced by the Scottish Enlightenment. The universities, particularly Edinburgh and Glasgow, remained internationally important: Sir James Simpson's discovery of chloroform anaesthetics in 1847, transforming the experience of surgery, took place at the first institution, while Lord Kelvin's work on electricity and on the two laws of thermodynamics, one of the foundations of modern physics, occurred at the second.

The physics of everything

James Clerk Maxwell was one of two great scientific geniuses to pass through Edinburgh University in the early 19th century (Darwin being the other). Born in Edinburgh and a professor at Aberdeen and Cambridge, Maxwell developed the mathematical equations that explain the behaviour of electricity, magnetism, light and gases. His work laid the theoretical foundations for modern physics, made possible colour photography and encouraged many new electrical and electronic technologies: Einstein, who revered him, kept a photograph of Maxwell on his office wall.

In Robert Louis Stevenson and J. M. Barrie, meanwhile, the country produced two of the century's best-loved literary figures – both of them proud Scots though again their most enduring works, *Treasure Island* (1883) and *Peter Pan* (1902), timeless escapist fantasies for children, studiously avoided direct engagement with contemporary Scottish society.

'And though I would rather die elsewhere, yet in my heart of hearts I long to be buried among good Scots clods. I will say it fairly, it grows on me with every year: there are no stars as lovely as Edinburgh street-lamps.'
Robert Louis Stevenson, *The Silverado Squatters* (1883)

More intriguingly, the period from 1850 onwards saw the first dim stirrings of reviving collective concern for national interests and national identity. It was almost as if accelerating industrialization and urbanization, together with the British state's wide-ranging attempts at progressive reform in response, were now being interpreted by some Scots as threatening not just their pre-existing institutions but also traditional Scottish ways of life.

A National Association for the Vindication of Scottish Rights, for example, existed briefly between 1853 and 1856, inspired by a sense among conservative-minded Scots that the Liberal Party had become obsessed with Irish issues. Interest in securing the same form of self-government that Ireland was likely to be offered continued to increase and in time even bore some modest fruit. In 1885 a separate Scottish Office and a Secretary of State for Scotland emerged. A Scottish Home Rule Association started up the next year, seeking devolution within the Union.

Increasingly, the symbolism of Scottish identity also seemed to require vigorous defending. The totemic monument to Sir William Wallace, funded by public subscription, was completed near Stirling in 1869. This was no anti-Unionist statement but rather about reversing a general neglect of Scotland's national heroes. Reflecting a somewhat different standpoint about how to preserve the country's threatened identity, An Comunn Gàidhealach, the organization committed to protecting and promoting Gaelic language and Gaelic culture in Scotland, also came into being at Oban in 1891.

These were small but vital signs, probably more significant in retrospect than they seemed at the time. For they indicated that at least some people recognized that Scotland remained a strongly distinctive country and that this might justify positive action in order to preserve it.

Fact check

1 Which UK prime minister was not Scottish?
- **a** Benjamin Disraeli
- **b** Henry Campbell-Bannerman
- **c** Arthur Balfour
- **d** the Earl of Rosebery

2 Who discovered 'blackband' ironstone in Scotland?
- **a** James Watt
- **b** David Mushet
- **c** James Neilson
- **d** Richard Arkwright

3 What did Dübs of Polmadie manufacture?
- **a** girders
- **b** ships
- **c** cotton
- **d** locomotives

4 In which city was Lochee?
- **a** Glasgow
- **b** Aberdeen
- **c** Dundee
- **d** Edinburgh

5 Which Scottish emigrant became an American steel magnate and philanthropist?
- **a** Allan Pinkerton
- **b** John Witherspoon
- **c** Andrew Carnegie
- **d** James Wilson

6 Which minister led the Disruption of 1843?
- **a** Thomas Chalmers
- **b** Hugh Blair
- **c** Andrew Melville
- **d** Keir Hardie

7 Who took Presbyterianism to Nigeria?
- **a** David Livingstone
- **b** David Welsh
- **c** Mary Slessor
- **d** Annie Besant

8 Who was Sir Harry Lauder?
- **a** a Victorian politician
- **b** a music-hall star
- **c** a footballer
- **d** a Free Church minister

Dig Deeper

John F. McCaffrey, *Scotland in the 19th Century* (Basingstoke, 1998).

W. H. Fraser and R. J. Morris, (ed.) *People and Society in Scotland: Vol. 2—1830–1914* (Edinburgh, 1990).

Sydney Checkland, *Industry and Ethos: Scotland, 1832–1914* (London, 1984).

S. J. Brown and M. Fry, (ed.) *Scotland in the Age of the Disruption* (Edinburgh, 1993).

17

Triumph and disaster

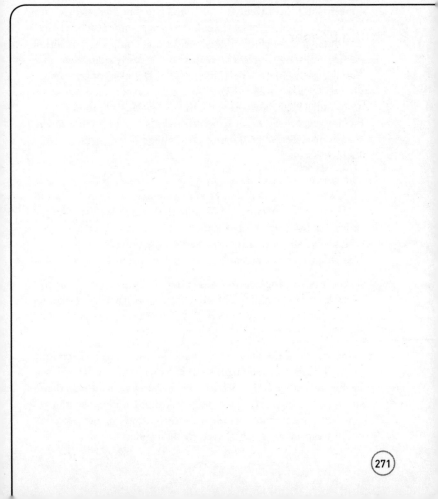

The Scottish empire

Scotland in the years before the First World War remained, as it had been for two centuries, an imperial country.

Its dominant conurbation called itself 'Second City of the Empire' (though Dublin and Liverpool both demurred) and its inhabitants trumpeted their commercial and industrial ties to India, Australasia and the Americas. Heavy engineering was particularly oriented towards the ships, locomotives and other machinery required by the world's principal colonial power as well as by the even larger markets it commanded beyond the British Empire's bounds.

In retrospect, however, we can appreciate that increasing orders for the Royal Navy as war against Germany approached were camouflaging the shipbuilders' weakening competitive position. Their local steel supplies were now more costly than those in English, German or American yards. At Dennys, for example, an average loss of 28 per cent was made on contracts between 1909 and 1913. As worryingly, the technology offered to civilian customers, because Scottish yards had become wedded to labour-intensive production, had already lost its mid-Victorian lead.

The dependence of this lynchpin industry on the vagaries of the global trade cycle had also been highlighted between 1903 and 1905 and again between 1907 and 1910 when Scottish shipyard orders fell by as much as 40 per cent. This inevitably caused serious commercial stresses and consequent restructuring in the sector. Redundancies, hardship and accompanying labour disputes resulted.

Other industrial specializations suffered almost as badly as the economy coughed and spluttered. Urgent workplace reorganizations were often imposed by owners. One lay behind a famous strike at the Singer factory in 1911.

Concern about the fitful performance of the industrial economy allowed a rapidly changing Liberal Party to secure 58 Scottish seats in the December 1910 election. Pushed towards unprecedented social welfarism, and led by Herbert Asquith, an Englishman who was MP for East Fife, the Liberals introduced old age pensions and unemployment benefits for the first time.

The same anxieties boosted union membership, which, strikingly, doubled on Clydeside between 1909 and 1914. They also gave impetus to the ILP: affiliated to the newly founded Labour Party from 1906, it returned three MPs from Scotland in 1910. Some involved were among the tiny band of committed Scottish anti-imperialists whose internationalist socialism would soon lead them also to oppose Britain's war effort.

Scotland's population as a whole also had close living ties to the wider world. But again in 1914 this was still within a firmly British imperial framework. Millions of people with obvious Scottish roots lived overseas under the Union flag. And the map of the earth, colouring the empire's one-fifth of the world's land area in pink, only encouraged pride in the central role of Scots in its exploration, conquest and settlement.

The spying game

The best-known story to come out of early 20th-century Scotland is John Buchan's *The Thirty-Nine Steps* (1915). This much-filmed novel relates the dramatic adventures of Richard Hannay, a Scottish agent pursued by German operatives back to his native country before successfully unravelling a plot to steal Britain's vital military secrets. More widely, it evokes the crisis summer of 1914 and the tense political climate just before the First World War. Buchan was himself politically active as a markedly liberal Conservative MP and, as Lord Tweedsmuir, a popular Governor-General of Canada from 1935.

It was simply no accident that the longest rivers in both Australia and Canada bore Scottish names – Murray and Mackenzie. British territories, meanwhile, were often governed from towns like Dunedin, Blantyre and Perth, which purposely echoed the familiar geography of Scotland or had dynamic young universities (McMaster, McGill, Dalhousie) memorializing philanthropists from Scottish backgrounds. The elected leaders of these vast dominions, including Australian prime ministers like Stanley Bruce and Sir Robert Menzies and their Canadian counterparts Sir John Macdonald and Alexander Mackenzie, also frequently had surnames indicating Scottish birth or descent.

St Andrew's Societies, Burns Suppers, Highland Games, Presbyterian churches, even local regiments that bore Scottish titles and adopted distinctively Scottish dress, all helped further reinforce both blood ties and cultural connections between people in the far-flung British territories and the land that many recent emigrants still thought of as home. Yet even in an empire on which the sun proverbially never set, change was in the air. The Indian middle classes had already formed a National Congress in 1885, helped by Allan Octavian Hume, reforming British civil servant and son of a politically minded Scottish doctor. By 1914 South Africa had followed Canada, Australia and New Zealand to self-governing dominion status.

Scotland's military contribution to the empire was also easily recognizable and a source of much admiration. Forming 11 separate infantry regiments by the 1890s, each with their unique tartan accoutrements and several also sporting kilts and sporrans, Scottish soldiers' striking visibility brought them disproportionate prominence in the small-scale and generally successful warfare waged by Britain across the world between Waterloo and the First World War.

Key idea: Tartan

Scotland's characteristic multi-coloured criss-cross clothing design has antecedents in various countries but it had become particularly common, especially for Highlanders, by the 16th century. The linking of individual tartans with particular wearers was happening by 1700, with local makers developing their own distinctive patterns. It was the aggressive mythologizing of Highland clanship, heritage and military prowess in the 19th century, coinciding with the commercial opportunities brought by industrialized mass production and modern marketing techniques, which finally created the notion of a specific ancient tartan existing for every Scottish name.

Instant identification and conspicuous derring-do combined to make the fighting Scot a figure of soft-focus legend as much as of hard news. The unbreakable 'thin red line' of the 93rd (Sutherland) Highlanders at Balaclava in 1854 and the Gordon Highlanders storming the heights of Dargai on India's North-West Frontier in 1897 to the unbroken playing of the wounded piper Findlater were episodes that entered and shaped the collective memory. Such victories, increasingly presented to the public in breathless journalism and illustrated copiously in paintings or early photographs, only further embellished the traditional reputation of the Scots as fearless and naturally formidable warriors.

Yet in truth the Scottish soldier actually suffered at least as many setbacks as any of his British comrades, especially in the sobering Boer War in South Africa. The four battalions of the Highland Brigade incurred heavy casualties at Magersfontein in 1899. The Cameronians were badly mauled at Spion Kop the following January. These experiences in fact whispered – almost no one was listening – that the world's pre-eminent naval and colonial power, and its most glamorous troops, might struggle against a technologically advanced European army using unfamiliar tactics.

Not that Scotland's soldiers were just convenient working-class cannon-fodder led by braying English aristocrats – though this is what many in the early 21st century, uncomfortable with the Scots' enthusiastic contributions to militarism and imperialism, often prefer to think. On the contrary, several of the greatest military leaders of the Victorian period, the decisive figures who made and maintained the empire and who captured the contemporary public's imagination, were Scottish.

As governor-general of India, the 1st Marquess of Dalhousie oversaw the conquest of the Punjab in the 1840s and Burma in the 1850s. Sir Colin Campbell, a Glasgow carpenter's son, led the Highland Brigade in the Crimea before quelling the Indian Mutiny. General Andrew Wauchope, a Black Watch officer with a distinguished record in colonial warfare, fell leading the Highland Brigade at Magersfontein.

The tragic hero

Wauchope's successor Sir Hector MacDonald rose from crofter's son to dashing major-general in the final defeat of the Boers in 1902: sensationally, 'Fighting Mac', a darling of the Victorian media, shot himself the next year in a Paris hotel room when facing a court-martial over alleged liaisons with schoolboys. Even so, 30,000 people showed their undiminished affection for a Scottish hero by filing past his Edinburgh grave.

Few Edwardian Scots actually shared Rudyard Kipling's sense of foreboding about the future of Britain and its empire at the end of Victoria's reign. Fewer still felt anything but pride at the out sized Scottish contribution. Yet there were already enough warning signs to have justified legitimate concerns about what lay ahead.

Armageddon

The epochal events of the summer of 1914 took place far away from Scotland. But on 4 August war was declared between Britain and Germany. What would soon become the First World War – the Great War – had begun. And Scotland was fully involved from the outset.

As conflict loomed the Grand Fleet, the Royal Navy's key strategic asset, was moved to Scapa Flow in Orkney, to keep the German fleet penned in the North Sea and Germany itself blockaded. It was from there and from Rosyth on the Forth that 37 British battleships and battle-cruisers sailed to the Battle of Jutland in 1916.

Yet it was in the British army, where the Scottish regiments each raised dozens of extra wartime battalions, that Scotland's contribution was most obviously seen. In the final reckoning, 150,000 of Britain's 880,000 war dead were Scots – nearly one-fifth of the total from a country with less than one-tenth of the population. Twenty-six per cent of Scottish combatants (more than one in ten of all young males in Scotland) were killed, as against twelve per cent of British servicemen as a whole.

This tragic imbalance arose because the 'poor bloody infantry', where the Scots were traditionally over-represented, bore the brunt of the slaughter in a conflict that, to everyone's surprise, including that of the generals, turned out largely to revolve around interminable trench warfare on an industrial scale. Scots were also chief among the senior commanders who later took the blame – Sir Douglas Haig, the Edinburgh-born son of a whisky distiller, on the Western Front; Sir Ian Hamilton, a Gordon Highlander, at Gallipoli.

There were other important consequences of the war that meant life would never be the same again. Above all, the government, to win the war, took unprecedented control of Scotland's heavy industrial economy. After victory it was therefore harder to defend a return to *laissez faire* and correspondingly easier to demand detailed state direction of manufacturing.

The diversion of manpower into the armed services also required the mass recruitment of new employees into industries previously dominated by unionized workers. Many were female, and often married – an unheard-of development. After 1918 this quickly helped women win the long-running argument over the right to vote. Female activists like Helen Crawfurd of the ILP and Govan housewife Mary Barbour led a series of strikes against wartime rent rises, making housing a key post-war electoral issue, especially in Scotland.

In many workplaces, wartime conditions bred a new militancy. Attempts to contain wages, tie employees to their employers and impose 'dilution' of skilled workforces with new hands led to the emergence of the Clyde Workers Committee to confront the policies of both management and government.

Many union officials involved were also anti-war ILP activists. The result was a series of strikes in the Clydeside factories, notably in 1915 (when Lloyd George, minister for munitions, was shouted down at a Glasgow public meeting) and again in the winter of 1917–18. Hinting at a broader political agenda informed by socialist ideas, an anti-war demonstration even saw 100,000 Glaswegians stop work in protest on May Day 1918.

A flawed peace

To say that the early post-war years were a disappointment, particularly in Scotland, would be an understatement.

The shipyards experienced a brief revival as lost merchant vessels were replaced: 650,000 tons were launched in 1919. But the collapse of naval ordering, the return of the old problem of increasing technological obsolescence and the existence of steadily improving larger-scale foreign competition boded ill. The resulting over-capacity, especially when placed in the context of a global downturn that became a slump after 1929, left the sector teetering on the brink: in 1933 the total launched Scottish tonnage collapsed to just 74,000.

A vision of depression

The iconic image of the downturn in industrial fortunes by the early 1930s is a photograph of Hull 534 at John Brown's yard. A massive steel silhouette, half-complete and rusting with all work suspended, it stood starkly against a cloudy Clydebank sky. It was later completed with government subsidy and became the famous Cunard liner *Queen Mary*.

But shipbuilding was no isolated victim. Similar problems of shrinking markets and stiffer competition beset the locomotive manufacturers and the rest of the heavy industrial economy. Coal exports, for example, were 20 per cent lower by the mid-1930s than in 1914.

The raw data on output, however, tell only half the story. The human costs were immense. More than 40,000 Scottish shipyard workers lost their jobs in just 18 months in 1919 and 1920. At no time in the 1920s did Scottish unemployment drop below 14 per cent. By 1932, as the Great Depression bottomed out, it approached 30 per cent – and a scarcely believable 50 per cent in some mining and shipbuilding communities.

Some local specializations were as badly hit as heavy engineering. Contraction and competition in the jute market, for example, brought misery to Dundee. Here the industry had long sustained an unusually large and economically significant female workforce, leading some to describe it as 'a woman's town'. Jute's waning imposed a crushing 50 per cent unemployment rate on Dundee by the early 1930s.

As before, people's responses varied. Emigration remained a favourite Scottish strategy: 400,000 people left in the 1920s alone – roughly 8 per cent of the population (when in England the proportion departing was just 0.5 per cent). A less common but far more visible reaction, attracting much press comment at the time and still exercising historians, was the series of more or less political activities that earned the label 'Red Clydeside'.

Red Clydeside

On 31 January 1919 a red flag flew over George Square in central Glasgow at a rally called to demand rent control and a 40-hour working week. This was a worrying portent in the aftermath of the Bolshevik Revolution and it encouraged a nervous government to deploy tanks and soldiers onto the streets. Yet a sober view suggests that this greatly over stated the danger in the west of Scotland. The evidence implies that the movement's wider public appeal rested not on the revolutionary socialism of some leaders like Willie Gallacher and John Maclean ('the Scottish Lenin', jailed in 1918 for fomenting mutiny and sedition) but on the specific employment and welfare concerns of working people.

This leftwards drift had practical political consequences. In the 1922 general election the Conservatives won power under another Scottish prime minister, Andrew Bonar Law, MP for Glasgow Central, born in Canada into an emigrant Free Church preacher's family. Critically, however, the Liberals were replaced as the main opposition at Westminster by Labour. The latter's numbers were swelled by Scottish ILP MPs like James Maxton and David Kirkwood, propelled to fame by events on Clydeside.

> 'I am not here as the accused; I am here as the accuser of capitalism dripping with blood from head to foot.'
> John MacLean on trial (1918)

Overall, 29 Labour candidates won in Scotland in 1922, against 27 Liberals and just 13 Conservatives – strong evidence once more that Scottish voting patterns were distinctive. That a new Scottish and British politics had emerged was confirmed in 1924 when the first Labour government – the largest party in the Commons but without an absolute majority – won power under yet another Scottish premier, Ramsay MacDonald, the illegitimate son of a Moray farm labourer.

Other responses to the post-war challenges had equally significant long-term implications. Large-scale slum clearance began. Many people moved out from over-crowded Victorian inner-city private tenements to the first of the council estates ('schemes', in Scottish parlance) in newly constructed suburbs like Mosspark and Riddrie on the edge of Glasgow, soon bulwarks of Labour's emerging electoral power in Scotland.

Health improved too. By the 1930s maternity and child health provision was available, while better accommodation, advances in public medical programmes and higher standards of living all worked their magic effects. As a result, infant mortality fell despite the economic crisis. Life expectancy also continued to increase: from the low 50s in 1918 to around 60 by 1939.

Yet not all inter-war social trends were benign. Life in working-class homes and on Scottish streets could be extremely tough. Indeed in certain respects things appeared to be getting worse.

Violence pays

The most flavoursome Scottish novel of the Depression era is Alexander McArthur's *No Mean City* (1935). No literary masterpiece, it is nonetheless an utterly compelling insight into vicious gang warfare and casual thuggery among Glasgow's poorest communities in harsh conditions. Its frankness provoked much controversy at the time and it still shocks readers today.

One dimension to the social tensions of the inter-war years proved especially problematic. For animosity seemed to grow between Protestant and Catholic Scots. Sectarianism was often sharpened by concern that Irish 'immigrants' threatened 'native' jobs and wage rates at a time of cripplingly high unemployment. But the decision in 1918 to grant state funding to Catholic schools ('Rome on the rates' to critics) hardly helped allay suspicions among poor Protestants.

Even literary figures were not immune to this nagging sense that immigration in particular threatened the very nature of Scotland. The critic George Malcolm Thomson claimed in *Caledonia* (1927) that the Scots were a 'dying people being replaced in their own country by a people alien in race, temperament and religion, at a speed which is without parallel outside the era of the barbarian invasions.'

The thistle blooms

The feeling that it was Scotland itself that was in terminal decline, not merely capitalism and the industrial economy, was increasingly widely shared by authors and intellectuals as the inter-war crisis deepened.

> 'Scotland is gradually being emptied of its population, its spirit, its wealth, industry, art, intellect and innate character.'
> Edwin Muir, *Scottish Journey* (1935)

What has come to be known as the 'Scottish Renaissance' was a cultural response that tried to address these inter-connected anxieties. Hugh MacDiarmid (Christopher Murray Grieve's pen-name, helping him sound more Scottish) was the movement's visionary prophet and leader. In many poems, composed in a peculiarly rich form of so-called 'synthetic Scots' or 'Lallans' he had devised as a radical alternative to conventional literary English (he famously described 'anglophobia' as one of his hobbies in his *Who's Who* entry), MacDiarmid tried to show that defining and defending Scotland's distinctive culture was an essential precondition of its much-needed political re-birth.

Lewis Grassic Gibbon (another pseudonym: actually James Leslie Mitchell) was the movement's other literary giant. He, too, offered passionate polemic in *A Scots Quair* (1932–4), a narrative trilogy deeply moving about traditional communities and the powerful forces tearing them apart. Written in a broad but accessible Scots, these novels, reflecting the author's fervent Marxism, were everything that Balmorality was not. Unsparing in their gritty depiction of harrowing human experience, they condemned what Grassic Gibbon believed were its underlying social and economic causes.

A slightly more practical response to the feeling that Scotland and Scottishness were in jeopardy, though closely linked to this cultural phenomenon and involving some of the same people, was the emergence of organized political Nationalism – the first in 200 years, although still very much a fringe interest.

A National Party of Scotland was duly established in 1928, and its successor the Scottish National Party (SNP), under Sir Alexander MacEwen, six years later. This motley assortment of disparate and in many ways irreconcilable opinions did not initially have independence as its goal. MacDiarmid, who certainly did advocate secession, was subsequently expelled for being a Communist (as well as from the Communist Party on account of his Nationalism). He had also flirted with Mussolini's fascism and in 1941 even claimed that a Nazi conquest of England was desirable for Scotland, alleging that Hitler's regime was 'less dangerous than our own government in the long run and indistinguishable in purpose'. MacEwen, an Inverness town councillor of otherwise impeccably respectable views, could not have been more different: basically a right-wing imperialist, he envisaged Scotland imitating Canada and Australia as an internally self-governing crown dominion, sharing its external policies with Westminster.

> *'Scotland shall share with England the rights and responsibilities they, as mother nations, have jointly created and incurred within the British Empire.'*
> Sir Alexander MacEwen, *Aberdeen Journal* (1934)

It was only after predictable internal strife that Douglas Young, a St Andrews professor and poet whose sense of his own Scottishness was so intense he was imprisoned for obstructing wartime conscription under what he thought illegitimate Westminster laws, won control in 1942. And thereafter the SNP's official line was unambiguous, demanding dissolution of the Union and sovereign independence for Scotland. In April 1945 it won its first seat, in the Motherwell by-election (though promptly lost it again in July's general election).

What all this said about Scotland's future direction was, however, far from certain at the time. After all, it was not immediately obvious that a war that had united the British people under Churchill in a desperate but ultimately victorious struggle for survival would necessarily assist a party seeking the voluntary dismemberment of Britain itself.

Fact check

1 Who wrote *The Thirty-Nine Steps*?
- **a** John Buchan
- **b** Robert Louis Stevenson
- **c** J. M. Barrie
- **d** Hugh MacDiarmid

2 Which Scot commanded the British army on the Western Front?
- **a** Sir Ian Hamilton
- **b** Sir Hector MacDonald
- **c** Andrew Wauchope
- **d** Sir Douglas Haig

3 Who led the Glasgow rent strikes?
- **a** John Maclean
- **b** David Kirkwood
- **c** Mary Barbour
- **d** Lewis Grassic Gibbon

4 Which staple industry collapsed in inter-war Dundee?
- **a** jute
- **b** coal
- **c** shipbuilding
- **d** cotton

5 Who first led the SNP?
- **a** Edwin Muir
- **b** Allan Octavian Hume
- **c** the Earl of Rosebery
- **d** Sir Alexander MacEwen

6 Who led the SNP from 1942?
- **a** Hugh MacDiarmid
- **b** Douglas Young
- **c** Andrew Dewar Gibb
- **d** David Kirkwood

Dig Deeper

Christopher Harvie, *No Gods and Precious Few Heroes* (London, 1981).
T. M. Devine and Richard Finlay, (ed.) *Scotland in the 20th Century* (Edinburgh, 1996).
Richard Finlay, *Modern Scotland, 1914–2000* (London, 2004).
Catriona Macdonald and E. W. McFarland (ed.) *Scotland and the Great War* (East Linton, 1999).

Retreat and resurgence

Finest hour

Scotland's direct military contribution to the Second World War was broadly similar to that made in the First.

Scottish regiments again served in all theatres and experienced both defeat and victory along with the rest of Britain's forces. Scotland was also crucial once more to the war at sea. Scapa renewed its acquaintance with the Home Fleet, the Royal Navy's two finest wartime admirals, Sir Bruce Fraser and Sir Andrew Cunningham, were from emigrant Scottish backgrounds, and the many ports and protected coastal waters of the Clyde were the last parts of Britain seen by many servicemen headed for Africa or the Far East and the first parts encountered by arriving American personnel.

Approximately 50,000 Scottish combatants died. Civilian casualties were not insignificant but, resulting from targeted air raids, were unevenly distributed. Clydebank, the jewel in the crown of strategic shipbuilding, was blitzed in March 1941, killing 528 people in just two nights and rendering 35,000 homeless. The city of Dundee, by contrast, suffered just a single death by bombing.

Dundee is different

A bizarrely improbable local legend maintains that Dundee was spared aerial bombardment on Hitler's express instructions in gratitude for the city's humiliating ejection of Winston Churchill, its Liberal MP since 1908, at the 1922 general election and his replacement by Edwin Scrymgeour, the only Scottish Prohibition Party candidate ever returned to Westminster. What is true is that Churchill was sufficiently bruised that during the Second World War, as prime minister and symbol of defiance against Nazi Germany, he declined the offer of freedom of the city.

The second war's wider effects were similar to those of the first. Women again proved crucial in the heavy engineering sector, and direct state invention in the labour market, in industrial decision-making and in the allocation of resources (everything from food to fuel was rationed) increased dramatically. Victory also appeared to vindicate such approaches, suggesting that governments could and should play the dominant role in directing productive activity. In particular, it was believed that this would avoid a repetition of the 1920s and 1930s and prevent the return of depression and mass unemployment.

As a result, when Clement Attlee's Labour government was elected on a landslide in 1945 – scooping 37 Scottish seats against the Conservatives' 24 – there was much optimism that a new age was dawning in which economic efficiency, equality and social justice would go hand in hand. It remained to be seen whether the aftermath of another global war in which Britain had emerged on the winning side would be a happier affair second time around.

Building Jerusalem

The most influential and enduring achievement of the Attlee government was the foundation of the National Health Service in 1948 as part of a wider programme aimed at building a comprehensive welfare state. This created a government-run health care system funded out of general taxation and largely free at the point of use. The 64,000 hospital beds and 900 senior clinical staff in Scotland were brought under a single authority for the first time.

Yet despite these UK-wide improvements, Scotland's health remained stubbornly worse than England's over the succeeding decades. By 1961, for instance, the average male Scot died at 66 while his English counterpart lived to 69, despite NHS spending in Scotland being 20 per cent higher per head. Damaging lifestyle choices embedded in Scottish culture were increasingly being blamed for the contrasts. For example, in Scotland 34 per cent of men and 32 per cent of women smoked in 1998 as against 32 per cent and 29 per cent in England: this meant that however much free health care was provided, Scots would remain higher up the grim international league tables for deaths from lung cancer and heart disease.

A commitment to providing other forms of assistance for the population 'from the cradle to the grave' ensured that a wide range of financial benefits also now became available. Payments were offered in all cases of unemployment but they were also progressively made available for sickness, maternity, retirement, widowhood and disability. Almost at a stroke Scotland's traditional poor law system, long enshrining an ethical vision rooted in Calvinist values, disappeared, replaced by a modern UK-wide benefits regime devised by London-based liberals.

Other social provision also proliferated under Attlee, as it did under Harold Wilson who led the next Labour government from 1964 to 1970. Social services departments emerged, run by local councils, providing social work and residential homes for children and the elderly. Wilson's government also commissioned the *Wheatley Report*, which recommended the abolition of the traditional Scottish councils, some of which had governed small burghs like Cupar and rural counties like Kinross-shire since the 12th century. This came in 1975, with larger administrative units called 'regions' appearing – Highland, Grampian, Tayside and others – to carry the increasingly complex and costly burdens comprehensive welfare provision required.

Simultaneously the school system, previously local government's principal responsibility, was further expanded and refined. Legislation in 1945 extended free compulsory education up to the age of 15 and compelled councils to create the first nursery schools. By the early 1960s local authorities were also being required to provide maintenance grants and fees to those qualified to enter higher education. Student numbers in Scotland were enhanced in part by the foundation of new universities.

University challenge

In 1951 there had been just 15,000 university students in Scotland but by 1981 there were 100,000 and by 2011 around 215,000. From the 1960s onwards higher education, long important to Scotland's identity and often a potent source of national pride, sprouted additional institutions to facilitate this expansion. New universities

If a panoply of welfare provision and new social institutions
were Labour's noblest legacy from the post-war years, another
set of policies, equally determined by ideology, had a less
happy effect. Sworn to socialism interpreted in a peculiarly
British fashion, Attlee's ministers began a programme of
nationalization, taking many businesses into government
ownership. This, however, was an unforced error with damaging
long-term consequences, especially in Scotland.

One problem was that nationalization strengthened Scottish
industries' habitual disinclination to change. Partly this was
because ministers and civil servants lacked entrepreneurial
instincts: the former, to whom key business decisions now fell,
oscillated unhelpfully between trying to buy votes and pursuing
ideological objectives. But innovation also costs money. It
would therefore have required the long-term commitment of
government funds that promised more immediate electoral
payback if directed into pensions, schools or hospitals. British
Rail, nationalized in 1948, was a classic victim. Under-
investment limited electrification across Scotland and delayed
high-speed services between London and Edinburgh for decades,
while all the time the inherited Victorian infrastructure eroded.

Another difficulty soon obvious was that powerful trade
unions, controlling Labour ministers and cowing Tory ones,
had much more leverage once politicians were calling the
shots. Union protection for out-dated and inefficient working
methods (mystifyingly known as 'Spanish practices') predictably
characterized those industries that advanced from heavy-handed
government intervention to outright state ownership under the
two subsequent Labour administrations, like car manufacturing
and the airlines (in the merged monoliths British Leyland and
British Airways), as well as those fully nationalized straightaway
by Attlee, such as road haulage, the docks and electricity.

No less damaging was the fact that the old Scottish predilection for labour-intensiveness was set in stone by the government's pursuit of full employment. Creating and preserving jobs rather than pleasing customers, let alone making profits, became the raison d'être of over-manned state-owned businesses like British Telecom and British Steel. Moreover, because nationalization also often involved consolidation to create monopolistic 'national champions' like British Aerospace and British Shipbuilders – on the socialist doctrine that competition wastes resources rather than improving performance – the resulting organizations became even less responsive to new technologies and changing market conditions.

Sadly this aversion to commercial realities, just when post-war international competition was intensifying and the pace of technological and organizational change worldwide was accelerating dramatically, eventually proved not the salvation but the undoing of many of Scotland's major industries.

Another peculiar consequence of these attempts to build Jerusalem across Britain was the further erosion of Scottish distinctiveness. Centralization, the guiding principle of the age, promised consistency and economies of scale. It also, however, imposed uniformity and erased historic differences.

The nationalization of industries like shipbuilding and steelmaking, for instance, completed the transfer of power from Scottish family owners on Clydeside to mandarins and ministers in London. This reinforced the existing tendency for the Scottish economy, as a result of mergers, takeovers and inward investment, to be controlled increasingly from outside Scotland – the dubious phenomenon of the 'branch plant', often focused on lower-status work, with research and development and decision-making authority located elsewhere, and usually easier to run down or shut completely.

Convergence between Scottish and English social experiences also accelerated as the welfare state expanded relentlessly. For example, as grants were introduced to help young people leave home to attend university, institutions like Edinburgh and St Andrews acquired growing English intakes and became less obviously Scottish in flavour. More young Scots, meanwhile, also took advantage and studied away from home, weakening the age-old Scottish tradition of attending the local university. Indeed almost every new benefit or service introduced after 1945 was standardized UK-wide: there was no fundamental difference between what the NHS offered in Dundee and what it provided in Doncaster, between the welfare payments received in Bognor and in Benbecula.

Winds of change?

Scotland in the 1950s and early 1960s appears in retrospect a country poised on the brink of radical change.

One area in which substantial transformation was certainly underway was the liquidation of the empire. Between Indian independence in 1947 and the decision of the Wilson government to pull British forces out from east of Suez, just 20 years elapsed. 'The winds of change' famously detected in 1960 by Conservative prime minister Harold Macmillan (the Scottish surname came from a crofting great-grandfather), frequently attained gale force.

The velocity and direction of those winds actually caused unexpected structural damage in Scotland. Obviously the steady stream of jobs in colonial administration from which generations of middle-class Scots had benefited slowed to a trickle and then stopped completely. The armed forces, especially the infantry with its disproportionate Scottish affiliations, also shrank, with far fewer outposts to garrison.

At a deeper level, and in ways that no one could have foreseen, the loss of empire also uprooted one of the key foundations on which many Scots' relationship with Britain itself had rested. It was, after all, the common experience of imperialism and the shared spoils of empire (of which the Scots had always taken more than their due) that had made the Union so strong. Britain's stature on the world stage – its wealth, power and prestige – was what more than anything else had justified its continuation. But by 1970 it suddenly seemed legitimate to ask whether Scottish interests were still best served by political arrangements with England that had been entered into in circumstances that no longer applied.

Another important change was the political eclipse of Scottish Conservatism. Under Churchill's successor Sir Anthony Eden in 1955 they had secured 50.1 per cent of the Scottish vote, and they still collected 41 per cent in 1964 under their Scottish leader, and Macmillan's successor as prime minister, Alec Douglas-Home. By October 1974, however, under Edward Heath, they were winning just 25 per cent.

Some of this slow subsidence was an unavoidable side-effect of Britain's shrunken post-imperial role. The most strongly British of parties simply appeared less relevant in the new conditions. But also loosening a traditional identification with the Conservatives was the gradual erosion of Protestantism as an electoral factor after the 1960s. Slowly it lost its power to galvanize Scottish voters. So too did Ulster, once critical for many Scots, especially those of Loyalist heritage whose families had arrived from Northern Ireland. All of these factors steadily ate away at the Conservatives' voter base long before the Thatcher governments of the 1980s applied the final nails to the coffin.

It is tempting also to point to popular fashions in Scotland and Britain from the mid-1950s onwards as evidence of wider changes underway. Certainly the arrival of new forms of youth culture, closely associated with the contemporary music scene, brought unmistakable novelty. Even tin ears could tell that Buddy Holly, Elvis Presley and The Beatles were worlds apart from the bland, Brylcreemed crooners of the 1940s. And many Scottish parents could hardly fail to notice the steady lengthening of their son's hair or his self-conscious identification in dress and demeanour with the Teddy Boys, Mods or Rockers or even, by the late 1960s, the hippies.

Rather more obscure but no less striking in its own way was another new trend – the growth, or rather revival, of Gaelic literature. Leading lights like the Raasay poet Sorley Maclean and the Lewis writer Iain Crichton Smith mingled left-wing politics and Nationalism with imaginative re-working of traditional themes and forms. Aficionados of this movement could have been in no doubt that, in Scottish culture, the times were indeed a-changing.

Yet this is still to see only part of the picture. The mid-20th century was also marked by a broadly based and deeply conventional mass culture in Scotland, with which an older generation remained entirely comfortable. And this was still firmly located within a piper's lament or a tossed caber of the Kailyard. The increasingly universal television, dominated by a British-wide BBC and ITV but with a local Scottish inflection, faithfully reflected and reinforced this common, unifying experience. Favourites from the era included *Dr Finlay's Casebook* (1962-71), which followed a Scottish country doctor in the heart-warmingly timeless fictional village of Tannochbrae. *The White Heather Club* (1958–68), a medley of singing, tartan-clad dancing and humour that was later derided for its unintentional parody of Scottish folk culture, also did not seem much like a spoof at the time.

But if one cultural artefact epitomizes the safe conformism of much of Scottish society through these decades it is surely a newspaper, *The Sunday Post*, published by D. C. Thomson of Dundee. This unthreatening cocktail of local comment, sentimental fiction, practical advice, quaint fashion, inoffensive cartoons and conservative Protestant morality was reportedly read in the late 1950s by as many as 60 per cent of Scottish adults. *The Guinness Book of Records* solemnly pronounced this the highest per capita market penetration achieved by any newspaper anywhere in the world.

The wee man

'Oor Wullie' (i.e. 'Our Willie') is a long-running cartoon strip in *The Sunday Post* with a cult status that may well baffle non-Scots. This hyperactive nine-year-old and his gang of friends have entertained readers since 1936 with their scrapes and misdemeanours. The characters deliver a rich dialogue in Scots and are widely seen as embodying cheeky but basically decent Scottish children everywhere. Oddly this national institution was invented and long drawn by Dudley Watkins, an Englishman.

If this seems surprising half a century later, with *The Sunday Post* a shadow of its former self, it is necessary to recall that the decline of Scottish conservatism, like the decline of

Scottish Conservatism, was intimately connected with the declining reach and impact of Scottish religion, and especially of Presbyterianism. As late as the 1950s, however, the churches retained a firm grip. In 1961 the Church of Scotland alone had 1.3 million names on its congregational registers, an all-time high. Other Presbyterians, the Episcopalians and the Catholics accounted for many more. The cultural and moral influence of Christianity remained substantial. Not just Sunday Schools but also dances, sports clubs, brass bands, walking holidays and cycling clubs all remained popular ways of tying people, especially the next generation, into church life in the 1950s and 1960s.

In this culture sabbatarianism too proved notably resilient. Visitors hoping to shop on the Scottish high street on a Sunday afternoon even in the early 1980s would have been sorely disappointed. Sunday ferry sailings to islands where the 'Wee Frees' or 'Wee Wee Frees' held sway remained contentious for even longer. More widely the licensing laws were far less forgiving than in England until 1976, when the wartime rules were finally relaxed. Alcohol could be served on Sundays only by hotels and even then only to those described in law as 'bona fide travellers'. For the rest of the week pubs shut after lunch and then for good at 10 p.m. Many parishes, exploiting Edwardian legislation making it a matter for local referenda, were still legally dry.

If the English poet Philip Larkin was correct that the permissive society began in precisely 1963, someone had presumably forgotten to tell great swathes of Scottish society about it.

Devaluation and devolution

Clearly some aspects of life in mid-20th-century Scotland exuded a reassuring calm and stability. Yet the tectonic plates of the country's economy, underlying everything else, were generating unnerving levels of seismic activity, with consequent threats to the comfort and wellbeing of the population.

Between nationalization and 1979 the number of working Scottish mines shrank drastically from 187 to just 18. Coal's fate was symptomatic of a wider malaise in industries that had been world-beating in the late 19th century but which were now in real trouble. Just between 1962 and 1977, for example, Glasgow alone shed 85,000 manufacturing jobs. Scotland as a whole lost 40,000 textile workers in the same period. That the economy was in very serious difficulty was increasingly hard to deny.

Ministers' well-meaning attempts to address the problem frequently had unintended consequences that in retrospect seem almost comically self-deluding. At Linwood near Glasgow, for example, the Rootes car company built a new plant in 1961 at the behest of Macmillan's government, which was concerned about local joblessness and desperate to boost a forward-looking industry in which Scotland was little involved. By 1973 this facility supported 8,000 employees directly and thousands more indirectly. Yet it was always distant from its English component suppliers, as Rootes itself had originally complained. Worse, it soon became known for its dowdy models, shoddy build-quality and worker militancy. Chrysler eventually took over both Linwood and the company but the problems proved as persistent as the demands for taxpayer bail-outs.

Politically directed investment was also responsible for flagship projects in the far north and west, an approach to dealing with disadvantaged parts of Scotland confirmed by Wilson's government in 1965 with the formation of the Highlands and Island Development Board to disburse public funds.

At Corpach, near Fort William, an unemployment black spot was presented in 1964 with a pulp paper mill, run by Wiggins Teape but again under government sponsorship. It eventually devoured 10,000 trees daily, offering 900 jobs directly and sustaining many more in local commercial forestry. But high transport costs soon saw the losses racking up and the business in severe commercial difficulty, with taxpayer hand-outs essential to its survival. Similarly at Invergordon on the Cromarty Firth a smelter opened in 1971 on the back of lavish HIDB subsidies for the owners, British Aluminium. Soon it employed upwards of 1,000 people. Once again, however, the cost of importing bauxite from the Caribbean to northern Scotland and then bringing electricity to an isolated location before transporting the product out again made the facility unavoidably loss-making.

It turned out that there were in fact very good economic reasons why large and profitable industrial employers had not spontaneously emerged in certain parts of Scotland. Colossal sums of taxpayers' money were spent in the 1960s and 1970s, however, just to prove that no amount of wishful-thinking by politicians in London could alter them.

One feature of the growing economic troubles of the period, which may have been encouraged by this evidence that politicians could be persuaded to intervene directly in troubled businesses either by nationalizing them or by offering open-ended subsidies, was a deterioration in industrial relations. Articulate but abrasive Scottish trade union leaders – often Communists like Jimmy Airlie of the shipyard engineers and Mick McGahey of the Scottish miners – played a disproportionate part in the strikes and other disruptive activities which from the mid-1960s onwards were mocked across Europe as 'the British disease'.

The Clydeside Cicero

Jimmy Reid, Communist electrician and union leader at Upper Clyde Shipbuilders, a troubled entity created by a government-directed merger, was propelled to wider fame when captured on film instructing a packed meeting during a strike in 1971 that, in order to maintain discipline and the moral high ground during a workers' occupation, there should be 'nae bevvying' (i.e. no drinking). Natural charisma and remarkable eloquence ensured him a subsequent media career as an authentic 'working-class hero' commenting on Scottish affairs. One later speech, advising Glasgow students that 'A rat race is for rats', was placed by the *New York Times* second only to Lincoln's Gettysburg Address.

Throughout the same period, a quite different response to the parlous economic situation was the steady rise of the SNP. From 0.8 per cent of the Scottish vote and no MPs in 1959, the party improved steadily. Winnie Ewing sensationally won the Hamilton by-election from Labour in 1967 on a staggering

38 per cent swing. Seven MPs were returned in February 1974 and an unprecedented 11 in October of the same year (on 30 per cent of the Scottish vote).

> 'Stop the World, Scotland wants to get on!'
> Winnie Ewing (1967)

Much of the dramatic increase in the SNP's popularity reflected public anger at the inability of the two dominant British parties to heal Scotland's ailing industrial economy. The discovery of North Sea oil also influenced some, adding ballast to the claim that Scotland would be not merely economically viable but actually richer once independent.

The black gold

The slogan 'It's Scotland's oil!' gave the SNP a powerful electoral boost in the early 1970s. It suggested that an independent Scotland would be enriched by bountiful natural resources while also implying (without tactlessly stating) that the country's wealth was currently being plundered by the English. The government's use of the tax revenues in the 1980s and 1990s to fund Britain's economic restructuring and welfare payments remained contentious in Scotland.

But there are longer-term factors, too. In particular, the places where the SNP was now winning seats, especially the north-east, indicated that many adherents were people who either had or would have voted Conservative two decades earlier. Hence the rise of the SNP was not unconnected with the demise of Scottish Conservatism – which explains the potent Labour jibe in the 1960s, coined by Harold Wilson's formidable Scottish secretary Willie Ross, that they were simply 'tartan Tories'. All in all, when the radical Scottish academic Tom Nairn published *The Break-Up of Britain* (1977), the momentum built up by the SNP (though Nairn was no admirer) seemed to lend his title real descriptive accuracy.

Interestingly, however, the long march of Nationalism then came to a juddering halt. The SNP lost 9 of its existing 11 MPs in 1979 on a Scottish vote-share down to 17 per cent. To some degree this was a classic 'third-party squeeze': voters correctly identified this epoch-defining election as a straight fight over Britain's future between two diametrically opposed governing parties – socialist Labour or free-market Conservative. The SNP did even worse in 1983 (two MPs and just 12 per cent) and things improved only marginally (three MPs and 14 per cent, including the humiliating loss of their leader Gordon Wilson) in 1987. This suggested that the problems perhaps ran deeper.

One response after 1979 was to shift leftwards in order to shake off the 'tartan Tory' tag and seduce traditional Labour supporters. As the poor performance during the 1980s reveals, however, this strategy, with ex-Labour MP Jim Sillars and future leader Alex Salmond prominent, was slow to pay dividends. It was also likely that the 'third-party squeeze' was still hurting a Scotland-only party that could never hope to seize the levers of power in London. An even more alarming interpretation, though, was that Nationalism had somehow become collateral damage in the self-inflicted embarrassment of Labour's devolution scheme.

'Devolution' was the term adopted in the late 1970s to describe a peculiar form of self-government offered to certain parts of the UK. In essence the Labour administration led by James Callaghan proposed creating elected parliaments or assemblies in Labour-inclining Scotland and Wales (though not, many noted, in more Tory-friendly England) with significant decision-making powers. The calculation was that this would simultaneously blunt the demands of Scottish and Welsh Nationalists for independence, permanently entrench reliable Labour administrations in Edinburgh and Cardiff and yet still allow Labour MPs from Scottish and Welsh constituencies to sit at Westminster where they would help Labour govern England.

The scheme, however, was not even universally popular in Labour's own Scottish ranks. Some, like Ross, were anxious lest limited self-government fan rather than douse the unpredictable flames of Nationalism. Others argued that the proposal was unfair because it would leave the English people subject to a Westminster

Parliament in which Scotland's MPs, whose own voters would now mostly be governed by an exclusively Scottish parliament in Edinburgh, would continue to pass laws binding England alone. This asymmetry became known as the 'West Lothian Question', after the constituency near Edinburgh represented by Tam Dalyell, Labour's leading anti-devolutionist (and descendant and namesake of the scourge of the Covenanters), who first posed it.

> 'How can it be that I can vote on education in Accrington, Lancashire, but not on education in Armadale, West Lothian?'
> Tam Dalyell, MP (1978)

Fully aware that many Scots were unenthusiastic, hostile Labour MPs therefore amended the rules for the referendum to ensure that not just a majority of votes cast but also 40 per cent of the total electorate needed to endorse the proposals. The SNP officially supported the scheme, too, though many Nationalists loathed this watered-down version of self-government and worried that it might reduce public support for outright independence. In the event the 'Yes' campaign achieved a slim majority with 51.6 per cent. On a turnout of just 63.8 per cent, however, this represented only 33 per cent of the electorate (in Wales there was a comprehensive 4:1 defeat). Labour's plans for devolution lay in tatters – and what the episode said about the SNP's demands for independence was also unclear (as the party's electoral disappointments during the 1980s showed).

There was, however, a more immediate result of the devolution debacle. An SNP motion of no confidence in the Labour government actually triggered the general election of 1979. Though jeering Labour MPs would never let them forget it, the Nationalists had unwittingly played the initial walk-on part in what would prove to be a drama based on a new and deeply unsettling script.

The empire strikes back

On 4 May 1979, Margaret Thatcher, Britain's first female prime minister took office, with a strong (though largely non-specific) commitment to confront the grave economic crisis facing the UK.

Thatcher, the self-conscious embodiment of small-town provincial England, never connected with Scotland. The misunderstanding was mutual, even if the loathing from the Scottish side only produced wounded puzzlement in a prime minister who was prone to quoting Adam Smith in a cut-glass English accent and then wondering aloud why his modern compatriots seemed so hostile to his economic liberalism.

The truth was that the Scottish dominance of Labour and the unions – institutionally, culturally and ideologically – meant that her views were never going to strike a chord with most Scots. Increasingly suspicious of commercial values and inclined to welcome collectivist approaches to life's challenges, they instinctively recoiled from Thatcher's aspirational individualism and no-nonsense homilies on thrift, enterprise and self-reliance. Many thought her moralizing at best archaic, at worst heartless and divisive.

The Sermon on the Mound

On 21 May 1988 the prime minister addressed the General Assembly of the Church of Scotland on The Mound in Edinburgh. Thatcher argued that capitalism found justification in the Gospels and that hard work and personal responsibility were the keys to spiritual redemption for individuals and so for communities. Her Presbyterian audience, largely convinced that the pursuit of wealth was morally harmful and socially divisive if not actively un-Christian, profoundly disagreed. Decorum was preserved but 'the Sermon on the Mound' epitomized the non-meeting of minds between Thatcherite Conservatism and Left-inclined mainstream opinion in late 20th-century Scotland.

It has to be said, too, that hard statistics counted against her being greeted with open arms. For Scotland had more people in state housing and in state employment than England and had a greater reliance on state-owned industries and state subsidies. As a result, most Scots and much of the Scottish establishment ranged themselves against Thatcher once the 'Iron Lady' began her revolutionary campaign to reverse the state's post-war expansion across Britain's social and economic life.

'Selling off the family silver'

The nationalized industries, which since 1945 had absorbed £40bn in taxpayer write-offs and returned an abysmal minus 1 per cent on the public's £100bn investment, bore the brunt of Thatcher's frontal assault on the post-war consensus.

British Steel alone, for example, with its immense complex at Ravenscraig in Lanarkshire (yet another Scottish industrial monolith sited in the wrong place for political rather than commercial reasons), contrived to lose £1.8bn on a mere £3bn turnover in 1980. This earned it an exquisitely badly timed place in *The Guinness Book of Records* for the largest corporate loss in British history. By the mid-1980s, despite a long and bitter strike, the Thatcher government had obliged the organization to shed 90,000 jobs UK-wide and halve its total workforce. Yet revealingly, it was still producing just as much steel.

In the event the UK's nationalized sector, which delivered an aggregate £3bn loss in the year of Thatcher's election, would be contributing an annual £9bn in corporate taxation to the public purse by 1996, once comprehensively restructured and back in shareholder ownership. Privatization, however, as this transformational process became known, was profoundly controversial.

Above all this was because, especially in Scotland and in the Labour movement (though also to old-school Tories like Macmillan who sniffed at Thatcher 'selling off the family silver'), it was never accepted that commercial judgements based on losses, debts, shrinking markets and the ballooning cost of bailouts were remotely appropriate. Instead, despite the dubious quality of their goods and services and the sometimes grotesque inefficiencies, catastrophic industrial relations and disastrous loss-making for which they were proverbial, these organizations were still seen as necessary providers of decent employment as well as totemic national representatives in important global industries. Accordingly their continued public ownership at virtually any cost was considered by most on the Left to be by definition in the public interest.

Still-rising unemployment, soon at levels not seen since the war, was a curse even before privatization began in earnest. By a bitter irony, this was in some respects the downside of Scotland's oil bonanza. For it was this that stimulated a steep increase in the value of sterling and hence a drop in the international competitiveness of British exports. High interest rates, imposed to suppress runaway inflation which early in 1980 peaked at 22 per cent, did the rest, further powering the pound's appreciation and punishing both exporters and those seeking business finance.

What resulted was the worst recession since 1945. Around 20 per cent of all remaining Scottish manufacturing jobs were lost in just two years. High-profile casualties included Singer at Clydebank in 1980 and then the plants at Linwood, Corpach and Invergordon, all closed in the *annus horribilis* of 1981 once taxpayer support ceased. Ravenscraig actually lingered on, protected by its symbolic status and a huge anti-closure campaign, until 1992.

It is in this context that the social impact of privatization needs to be understood. Coming on top of the partly unavoidable industrial disaster of 1979–81, this massive restructuring across large parts of the economy ensured that Scottish unemployment quickly reached crippling levels. Five years later the City of London was partying into the night, with a new boom, fuelled by financial services and consumer spending, letting rip across middle England. In Scotland's 'rustbelt' communities, however, formerly reliant on traditional manual jobs and increasingly also on government intervention and subsidy, the recession just ran and ran.

By the mid-1980s 15 per cent of the Scottish workforce was unemployed. But more than a decade later, in 1997, with far more now working in tourism and in call centres than in shipbuilding or mining and with whisky a more valuable Scottish export than cotton goods and locomotives put together, the figure remained a depressing 9 per cent.

Marvellous malts

An industry now worth £4bn annually, whisky gets its familiar name from the Gaelic *uisge beatha* ('water of life'). Distilled from a mixture of fermented malt and local fresh water aged and coloured in oak casks, the earliest documentary reference to production comes from the reign of James IV in 1495, who reputedly enjoyed a 'wee dram' (small measure) himself. Many regional types exist – the smoky Islays and the diverse Speysides are the best-known – and the 'single malt' versions, associated with specific producers, have a large and devoted overseas following.

In certain areas, such as former pit villages and factory towns, joblessness often became a permanent way of life. It also combined with other factors to make urban Scotland from the early 1980s onwards a by-word for the ills of post-industrial society. Registered disability reached sky-high levels and stayed there. Drug addiction, particularly on the publicly owned housing schemes, was another new problem that intermingled with the familiar old ones of ill-health, criminality and gang activity.

Even more destructive of the Conservatives' reputation was the introduction of a new system of local government finance. It was known as the 'Poll Tax' because, in an attempt to deal with the fact that many households (as much as 40 per cent in Scotland) contributed nothing to their councils, all adults would pay the same amount for the services provided. In 1989 Scotland became the first part of the UK to implement it – by explicit request from the Scottish Conservatives, who foolishly imagined its simplicity would be popular, rather than through Thatcher's sadistic determination to subject the Scots to a cruel experiment, a myth which, typically, would later be almost universally believed.

The Poll Tax provoked rioting in London and spawned a non-payment campaign across Scotland (with the slogan 'Can't Pay, Won't Pay') where it further accelerated the collapse of the Tory vote at all levels. By 1995 in Fife, for example, with its not-untypical mixture of ex-mining communities, run-down ports, commuter belt, small market towns and prosperous farms, the councillors, 78 all told, included more elected Communists (two) – this several years after the Berlin Wall had fallen – than Conservatives (precisely none).

Another visceral reaction to Thatcher was the urgent attempts to keep alive the flickering embers of devolution. For in uniting disparate Scots in hatred, she had re-energized those who, after the events of 1979, had had most reason to be disheartened. The fact that the Tories by 1987 held just ten of the 72 Scottish seats at Westminster (Labour had 50) further sharpened the point: by what mandate did this prime minister govern Scotland?

In effect devolution (and, for the SNP, independence) was increasingly understood to be about preventing a British government like Thatcher's ever again ruling Scotland. The Claim of Right, signed by campaigners in 1989 on the tri-centenary of the identically named Williamite declaration, proclaimed the Scottish people's unqualified right to self-determination. A melancholy vigil was even maintained from the fourth consecutive Tory victory in 1992 (taking just 11 Scottish seats) at the old Royal High School buildings in Edinburgh, which, had the referendum gone the other way, would have housed Scotland's devolved Parliament.

Few were surprised, then, when Tony Blair, educated at Fettes College, one of Edinburgh's top private schools but obviously an English politician effortlessly attuned to the outlook and values of middle England, swept Labour, or 'New Labour' as he had re-branded it, back to power at Westminster in May 1997 in a landslide of historic proportions, leaving the Tories without a single MP in Scotland.

Not-so-New Labour

Blair in truth won few new converts for Labour in Scotland, despite his three crushing electoral victories south of the border. After all, 'Old Labour' had never suffered the drubbings from Scottish voters that the party had experienced in England in the 1980s.

One result of this was that an unusually high proportion of the party's senior figures by 1997 were Scots.

Above all there was Gordon Brown, a Presbyterian minister's son from Kirkcaldy, originally Blair's friend but thereafter a uniquely dominant Chancellor for a decade as well as brooding heir-apparent and constant thorn in the prime minister's side. Robin Cook ran foreign affairs and then led the Commons. Donald Dewar, Scottish Secretary, delivered the long-delayed devolution scheme in which Blair (unhelpfully heard likening a Scottish Parliament to a mere 'parish council') had little interest.

George Robertson, remembered ever after for the daring prediction that devolution would 'kill Nationalism stone dead', became Britain's Defence Secretary and later headed NATO. John Reid, a pugnacious political heavyweight, successively ran the English NHS, English home affairs and defence. Alistair Darling held a number of briefs before becoming Chancellor after Brown.

Scotland also provided Labour with some of its highest-profile back-benchers, troublesome and quotable in equal measure, like Dalyell (now in his mid-60s but still doggedly asking the West Lothian Question), Dennis Canavan and George Galloway.

Paradise postponed?

Devolution, the cherished ambition of Blair's more left-wing predecessor John Smith, a Lanarkshire MP who had died suddenly in 1994, was delivered quickly and smoothly by Smith's old friend Dewar.

The necessary referendum was held in the first flush of Labour's triumph late in 1997. With everyone but the still-traumatized Tories supportive, approval was inevitable. A 60 per cent turnout, intriguingly down on 1979, delivered a thumping 74 per cent endorsement. The Scotland Act 1998 duly progressed into law at Westminster. Wales had also backed an assembly for Cardiff, though with just 50 per cent support, so both devolution packages sailed through in tandem.

The greatest complication when a Scottish Parliament met at Holyrood in Edinburgh for the first time in 292 years was caused by the chosen electoral system. Dewar and his allies had devised a complex mixture of 73 Westminster-style constituency representatives and 56 additional members. This made the final allocation of seats proportional to each party's share of the vote. But it was also meant to encourage a 'new politics' where alliances and agreements were likely.

Accordingly, no single party obtained a majority of Members of the Scottish Parliament (MSPs) in the first election on 6 May 1999. With 56 Labour MSPs, Dewar as First Minister therefore led a coalition Executive (as the devolved administration was called) with the Liberal Democrats who had won 17. Alex Salmond's SNP, with 35, became the main opposition.

> 'The Scottish Parliament, adjourned on the 25th day of March in the year 1707, is hereby reconvened'
> Winnie Ewing, MSP (1999)

The 'new politics' – a term repeatedly heard amid the orgy of smug self-congratulation when Queen Elizabeth II opened the Parliament in July 1999 – was certainly different in that many unknown ex-councillors suddenly became national figures. Yet in other ways it was strikingly familiar. Despite early talk about a more inclusive and diverse politics, only a handful of the first MSPs were not career politicians from existing parties. Furthermore, the Executive and the Opposition both inclined leftwards.

To some extent this reflected Scotland's known preferences. But it was accentuated by the Parliament's spending being funded by direct grant from Westminster – MSPs' function being merely to decide how to distribute large sums of public money among their own constituents. This further exaggerated the advantage for politicians promising to deliver their voters ever greater spending without having to worry about also handing them the bill.

The Parliament's early years also revealed an assumption that the state's hand should continually reach into new areas. Legislative attacks on activities that offended MSPs' sensibilities (though not necessarily those of their voters) soon accumulated, seemingly motivated by a determination to show that Holyrood could be even stricter and more censorious than Westminster. Everything from pub strippers and horse-branding to air guns, cheap alcohol promotions, fox-hunting, private landlords, smoking in public places, drinking caffeinated tonic wines and the parental smacking of children – not forgetting mink farms, eagerly outlawed in 2002 despite there being not a single example in the country – were soon on an impressively miscellaneous list for further restriction or prohibition.

More constructively but also much more expensively, Holyrood promised free care for Scotland's elderly and spared Scottish students up-front university fees – though English taxpayers, footing most of the bill but not getting the benefits, were often less thrilled. There were also notable achievements in land reform and in extending the rights afforded to homosexuals.

Labour nevertheless had growing problems, mostly caused, strangely, by being unable to shake off the association with Blair, whose credibility was fatally damaged by the Iraq war, even less popular in Scotland than elsewhere. Following Dewar's untimely death, Jack McConnell's Labour-led coalition had continued after the 2003 election, but May 2007 brought a photo-finish: 46 MSPs for Labour and 47 for the SNP. The implications were initially uncertain, since Labour and the Liberal Democrats together no longer commanded a majority. Salmond then announced that, as leader of the largest party, he would be First Minister of a minority Executive (or 'Government', as, to Labour's annoyance, the Nationalists predictably now called it).

This brought a whole new dimension to devolution into play – the one that Dewar and Robertson had discounted and Dalyell had foreseen. With a Nationalist administration manipulating the levers of power and managing Scotland's relationship with London, would it be possible to use Holyrood to unravel the very fibres of the Union?

> 'Devolution is a motorway without exit to an independent state.'
> Tam Dalyell, MP (1998)

Actually, the reality of the first SNP government proved less traumatic than the expectations. The First Minister's own MSPs were heavily outnumbered by the Unionist parties and he was unable to do much more than regularly generate opportunistic friction with Westminster. In particular, the SNP on its own could not pursue its long-standing objective: a referendum to approve independence. Hence the First Minister himself soon announced that none would be held before the next Scottish election in 2011.

The son of the manse

After many years of trying unsuccessfully to force the issue, Gordon Brown finally managed to become Britain's prime minister following Blair's resignation in June 2007.

His short administration enjoyed some brief moments of optimism and managed a couple of genuine achievements. He persuaded other Western governments to write off developing world debt. He played a leading role in co-ordinating international actions to stabilize the global financial system in the crisis of 2008. As a tribal loyalist steeped in Labour politics, he also attracted much more genuine loyalty and affection inside his party than Blair – who relished challenging its socialist assumptions – had ever done.

Yet Brown always faced an uphill struggle in winning over the wider electorate. And frequently there was little that he himself could have done about it.

His Scottishness, for example, hardly his fault, was increasingly highlighted by opponents. Being governed by a Scottish MP for a Scottish seat was simply more of an issue for some English voters, thanks to devolved self-government for Scotland, than it had been in the days of Campbell-Bannerman and Bonar Law: Brown was, it appeared, the West Lothian Question made flesh.

His transition from number-crunching back-room wizard to media-savvy leader of the nation was also hindered by appearing ill-at-ease in public. Attempts to coach a winning smile only made things worse. The new prime minister found himself exactly the wrong sort of YouTube sensation.

Yet it was the onset of a deep recession in 2008, with accompanying stock market crash and plunging house prices, that did more than anything else to damage the reputation of someone whose most memorable catch-phrase as Chancellor had been 'no more boom and bust'. Starting with the implosion of a financial sector whose biggest offender, Royal Bank of Scotland, he, like Salmond, had openly courted, the crisis reminded voters that Brown had invented an entirely new system of banking regulation for the UK that failed its first serious test and that he had also pushed public spending to unsustainable levels far in excess of normal tax receipts.

In the event, Brown's defeat in the May 2010 general election was narrower than some had feared, given the dire unpopularity which at times in 2008 plumbed new post-war polling depths. And the fact that the Tories, on just 36 per cent, failed to secure a majority was especially gratifying. But with Labour on 29 per cent (its second-worst finish ever) and largely wiped out across much of England outside the inner cities, the result was hardly worthy of celebration.

Unfinished business

As a coalition between David Cameron's Conservatives and the Liberal Democrats got underway in London and Labour pondered how best to combat it, Scotland's own future was about to become even more uncertain.

Cameron, very much part of the English elite but with an evocative Highland surname and distinguished Scottish ancestors (including, extraordinarily, Isabella MacDuff), found himself with just a single Scottish Tory MP. He therefore prudently inserted a Liberal Democrat as his Scottish Secretary and signalled a willingness to work constructively with Scotland's minority SNP administration, including by devolving more powers to Holyrood.

This situation, however, was transformed by the explosive outcome of May 2011's Scottish election, which, at least on Dewar's original calculations, should have been impossible.

Losing seats in its Glasgow heartland as well as several big names, Labour was humiliated as the SNP returned 69 MSPs. Suddenly Salmond had a majority and free rein to pursue the Nationalists' agenda.

This presented the First Minister with both an opportunity and a problem. His party dominated Scottish politics and could hold a referendum on independence. Yet opinion polls continued to show that not much more than one-third of Scots favoured secession. Voting for the SNP to fight Scotland's corner inside Britain was one thing. Voting to leave remained quite another.

Salmond therefore deferred the referendum until 2014 – much to London's irritation – in the hope of turning public opinion around not least by exploiting the nationalistic high of that summer's Commonwealth Games in Glasgow and the 700th anniversary of victory at Bannockburn. At one stage it seemed Cameron might agree to the vote including the more popular option of 'devo-max', the vague buzzword for further power-transfers from Westminster, especially for taxation. But Cameron, risking the Union in the expectation but not the certainty of defeating Nationalism, insisted that the referendum, when it finally happened, should only propose independence.

Once the battle started in earnest, both sides had problems consistently striking the right notes. For the 'Yes' side Salmond insisted the monarchy was safe and Scottish business would boom even as his radical socialist and Green bedfellows waxed lyrical about a republic with potent anti-capitalist and environmental credentials. The 'No' side, called 'Better Together' and fronted by Labour's Alistair Darling, struggled to sound positive about the Union, just attacking 'Yes' relentlessly.

The final months of the campaign were dominated by two questions about the practical consequences of independence which the 'Yes' campaign, despite the Nationalists having had years to think about it, never answered convincingly.

One asked whether Scotland, which wanted to continue using sterling, would have an official currency union with London and thus its independent government and financial institutions underwritten by the Bank of England and non-Scottish taxpayers. Salmond repeatedly asserted that this would happen. But he was ridiculed by senior figures in England who, with one eye on the crisis-hit Eurozone from which Britain had abstained (but which Salmond had forecast would be a great success and long envisaged Scotland joining), ruled out replicating Europe's unhappy experiment in operating a currency union outside a political union.

Better Together also questioned the Nationalists' insistence that Scotland would retain both European Union membership and the UK's controversial opt-outs, including from the euro. This issue was particularly fraught because Salmond initially claimed to have confidential legal advice to this effect but then had to confess that it did not exist. Leading Continental politicians, some with their own separatists eagerly watching to discover if a seceding part of an EU member state would really be given automatic entry on attractive terms, stated categorically that the Scots would face a complex application process, potentially requiring painful concessions in return for admission.

Some imagined the 'Yes' side's credibility would be destroyed by having had Salmond's sweeping assurances comprehensively demolished by outsiders who were clearly also in a position to veto them. Nor was it helpful that several financial services giants, including Royal Bank of Scotland and the insurer Standard Life, disclosed contingency plans to transfer core functions to England in the event of independence – nor indeed that Jim Sillars, still a totemic Nationalist figure, reacted by threatening 'a day of reckoning' and punitive nationalization against firms like BP, which increasingly voiced grave reservations.

With the referendum approaching, however, the opinion polls steadily narrowed. 'Yes' regularly breached 45 per cent by early September. Some surveys in the final fortnight even put it ahead.

Salmond's reliance on the retort that the innumerable politicians, financial institutions, companies, economists and lawyers across Britain, Europe and America whose statements flatly contradicted his own promises were all just 'scaremongering' or bluffing, and the accompanying insinuation by his supporters that this was part of a systematic Westminster-orchestrated conspiracy to intimidate the Scots and thwart their democratic will, actually seemed to boost the popularity of the 'Yes' campaign. Detailed technical points about EU treaties, central bank facilities and credit ratings, it appeared, often got lost in the furious noise. Many voters seemingly heard only the sound of a populist patriotic underdog gamely fending off attacks from the rich and powerful.

Evidence of this apparent late 'Yes' surge forced the main Westminster parties behind Better Together into hurriedly re-emphasizing their own commitment to still more devolution within Britain. All three UK party leaders as well as Gordon Brown – centre stage again and suddenly speaking with unprecedented emotional conviction – toured the country in the days before polling, arguing strenuously for the Union.

The result on 18 September was clearer than expected, whether owing to late mind-changing caused by the acute economic uncertainties or merely voters not having been entirely frank with pollsters in a thoroughly poisonous atmosphere in which Unionists often found themselves being demonized as 'anti-Scottish'. Better Together actually won by 55 per cent to 45 per cent on an astonishingly high 84.6 per cent turnout.

Combining the detailed results with key findings from the prior polling, it was plain that the Scots were hopelessly divided, with political aspirations every bit as divergent as those between Scotland and England – which had first helped drive Nationalism's rise. The over-55s, Orkney, Shetland and the Borders were two-to-one for 'No'. Aberdeen and Edinburgh and those with degrees and professional careers were also preponderantly Unionist. Conversely Dundee, Glasgow, the poorest and the young voted 'Yes'. Most strikingly, women decisively preferred the status quo, some polls showing twice as many distrusted as believed Salmond's various promises. Men, however, perhaps more taken with the irrepressible bluster, marginally favoured independence.

For Scotland itself therefore the future was not much clearer in the immediate aftermath on 19 September 2014. And two questions in particular hung uncomfortably in the air as the smoke of battle cleared. First, how long would it be before the

Nationalists, who seemed unlikely to take 'No' for an answer and who heard that very day that Salmond would be resigning as their leader and as First Minister, would want the referendum repeating? Second, what exactly would further devolution from Westminster look like – and what would be its implications not just for Scotland but also for the rest of Britain, where both the West Lothian Question and traditional London-centric politics were under greater-than-ever scrutiny?

One thing, however, was obvious. Ahead lay another fascinating but thoroughly unpredictable phase in the long history of the Scottish people.

Fact check

1 Who beat Winston Churchill in Dundee in the 1922 election?
   a Clement Attlee
   b David Lloyd George
   c Edwin Scrymgeour
   d Arthur Balfour

2 Which party won over 50 per cent of the Scottish vote in 1955?
   a Labour
   b the Liberals
   c the SNP
   d the Conservatives

3 Who was Sorley Maclean?
   a a Gaelic poet
   b a Labour politician
   c the SNP's first MP
   d a Free Church clergyman

4 What did Rootes make at their Linwood factory?
   a trains
   b sewing machines
   c watches
   d cars

5 Who said 'A rat race is for rats'?
   a Jimmy Reid
   b Jimmy Airlie
   c Winnie Ewing
   d Mick McGahey

6 Who first asked the West Lothian Question?
   a James Callaghan
   b Tam Dalyell
   c Tony Blair
   d Donald Dewar

7 When did the new Scots Parliament open?
   a 1978
   b 1997
   c 1999
   d 2007

8 Who led the 'Better Together' campaign for the 2014 independence referendum?
   a Tony Blair
   b Gordon Brown
   c Alex Salmond
   d Alistair Darling

Dig Deeper

Trevor Royle, *Time of Tyrants: Scotland and the Second World War* (Edinburgh, 2011).

A. Dickson and J. Treble, (ed.) *People and Society in Scotland: Vol. 3—1914–1990* (Edinburgh, 1992).

Jack Brand, *The National Movement in Scotland* (London, 1978).

Christopher Harvie and Peter Jones, *The Road to Home Rule* (Edinburgh, 2000).

Christopher Harvie, 'Scotland after 1978' in R. A. Houston and W. W. J. Knox, (ed.) *The New Penguin History of Scotland* (London, 2001).

Fact-check answers

CHAPTER 1
1 d
2 c
3 b
4 a

CHAPTER 2
1 c
2 b
3 a
4 c
5 d
6 c
7 b

CHAPTER 3
1 d
2 a
3 c
4 a
5 c
6 b

CHAPTER 4
1 a
2 d
3 d
4 c
5 d
6 c
7 a

CHAPTER 5
1 b
2 a
3 d
4 c
5 d
6 a

CHAPTER 6
1 b
2 d
3 a
4 b
5 c
6 d
7 a

CHAPTER 7
1 d
2 b
3 a
4 c
5 d
6 b
7 b
8 a

CHAPTER 8
1 d
2 a
3 b
4 c
5 a
6 b
7 c
8 b

CHAPTER 9	CHAPTER 12	CHAPTER 15	CHAPTER 18
1 a	1 a	1 a	1 c
2 a	2 d	2 c	2 d
3 d	3 b	3 d	3 a
4 a	4 a	4 c	4 d
5 c	5 c	5 a	5 a
6 b	6 d	6 c	6 b
7 a	7 a	7 c	7 c
8 d	8 d	8 d	8 d
9 b			

CHAPTER 10	CHAPTER 13	CHAPTER 16
1 a	1 a	1 a
2 d	2 d	2 b
3 c	3 b	3 d
4 b	4 a	4 c
5 a	5 c	5 c
6 c	6 c	6 a
7 a	7 a	7 c
	8 d	8 b

CHAPTER 11	CHAPTER 14	CHAPTER 17
1 c	1 c	1 a
2 c	2 a	2 d
3 a	3 d	3 c
4 d	4 c	4 a
5 d	5 d	5 d
6 c	6 d	6 b
	7 c	
	8 a	

Index

Aberdeen, 5, 85, 97, 106, 124, 147, 208

Act Anent Peace and War (1703), 198

Act of Proscription (1746), 209

Act of Revocation (1625), 162

Act of Security (1704), 199

Act of Settlement (1690), 191

Act of Settlement (1701), 198

Act Rescissory (1661), 178

Adam, Robert, 242

Aethelfrith of Northumbria, 27

agriculture, 5, 11, 17, 224–6, 227, 229, 234, see also crofting

Aikenhead, Thomas, 192

Alba, Kingdom of, 28, 29, 35, 40–8, 56

Albany, Murdoch Stewart, 2nd Duke of, see Stewart, Murdoch, 2nd Duke of Albany

Albany, Robert Stewart, 1st Duke of, see Stewart, Robert, 1st Duke of Albany

Alexander I (1107–24), 54, 56–8

Alexander II (1214–49), 66, 69–71

Alexander III (1249–86), 66, 71–3, 78, 113

Alien Act (1705), 199

Alt Clut, Kingdom of, 19–20, 22, 28, 34

An Comunn Gàidhealach, 268

Angles, 18

anglicization, 55, 56, 62

Angus, George Douglas, 1st Earl of see Douglas, George, 1st Earl of Angus (Red Douglas)

Antonine dynasty, 15

Antonine Wall, 15

Arbroath, Declaration of (1320), 101–2

Arbroath Abbey, 68, 101

Argyll, Archibald Campbell, 3rd Duke of, see Campbell, Archibald, 3rd Duke of Argyll

Argyll, Archibald Campbell, 1st Marquess and 8th Earl of, see Campbell, Archibald, 1st Marquess and 8th Earl of Argyll

Argyll, Archibald Campbell, 9th Earl of, see Campbell, Archibald, 9th Earl of Argyll

Argyll, John Campbell, 2nd Duke of, see Campbell, John, 2nd Duke of Argyll

Arminianism, 163

Arran, James Hamilton, 2nd Earl of, see Hamilton, James, 2nd Earl of Arran

Arthur, King, 20, 93

Articles of Grievances, 188

Athelstan, 43–4

Atholl, Earl of, see Stewart, Walter, Earl of Atholl

Auld Alliance, 81, 128, 135

Avondale, James Douglas, 1st Earl of (and 7th Earl of Douglas), see Douglas, James, 1st Earl of Avondale and 7th Earl of Douglas

Avondale, William Douglas, 2nd Earl of (and 8th Earl of Douglas), see Douglas, William, 2nd Earl of Avondale and 8th Earl of Douglas

Babington plot, 140–1

Badenoch, Wolf of, see Stewart, Alexander, Earl of Buchan

Baird, John, 218

Balliol, Edward (1332–6), 103–6
Balliol, John (1292–6), 80–3, 93, 94
Ballot Act (1872), 248
Balmorality, 266
banking, 193, 214, 228–9, 311, 312–13
Bannockburn, Battle of (1314), 98–100
Barrie, J. M., 267
Battles:
  Bannockburn (1314), 98–100
  Bonnymuir (1820), 218
  Bothwell Brig (1679), 182, 189
  of the Braes (1882), 258
  Brunanburh (937), 43–4, 45
  Carberry Hill (1567), 139
  Corbridge (918), 42, 45
  Cromdale (1690), 189
  Culloden Moor (1746), 208, 209
  Dalrigh (1306), 96
  Degsastan (603), 27
  Drumclog (1679), 181
  Dunbar (1650), 171
  Dunkeld (1689), 189
  Dunnottar (900), 41
  Dupplin Moor (1332), 103–4, 105
  Falkirk (First) (1298), 87
  Falkirk (Second) (1746), 208
  Faughart (1318), 101
  Flodden Field (1513), 125
  Gallipoli (1915), 277
  Halidon Hill (1333), 104
  Killiecrankie (1689), 189
  Largs (1263), 71
  Mag Rath (637), 27
  Marston Moor (1644), 168
  Mons Graupius (AD 83 or 84), 13, 14
  Nechtansmere (685), 19, 28
  North Inch (1396), 115
  Otterburn (1388), 113–14
  Pinkie Cleugh (1547), 133
  Pitgaveny (1040), 47

  Prestonpans (1745), 207
  Rullion Green (1666), 180
  Sauchieburn (1488), 122, 123
  of the Standard (1138), 59
  Stirling Bridge (1297), 86, 87
  Stracathro (1130), 59
  Tippermuir (1644), 168
Beaton, Cardinal David, 132
Beaton, James, Archbishop of St Andrews, 126, 128
Bede, 17, 19, 22, 26
Bernicia, 18, 19, 34
Berwick, sacking of, 82
Berwick, Treaty of (1357), 107
'Better Together' referendum campaign, 312–14
Birgham, Treaty of (1290), 79, 81
Bishops' Wars, 165–6
Black Acts (1584), 146, 147
Black Death, 104
Black Dinner, 119
'Black Saturday', see Pinkie Cleugh, Battle of
Blair, Tony, 306–10
'Bluidy Tam', see Dalyell of the Binns, General Sir Thomas
Bonar Law, Andrew, 279
'Bonnie Dundee', see Graham, John, of Claverhouse, 1st Viscount Dundee
Bonnie Prince Charlie, see Stuart, Charles Edward
Bonnymuir, Battle of (1820), 218
Bothwell, James Hepburn, 4th Earl of, see Hepburn, James, 4th Earl of Bothwell
Bothwell Brig, Battle of (1679), 182, 189
Braes, Battle of the (1882), 258
brochs, 12
Bronze Age, 11, 32
Brown, Gordon, 307, 310–11, 314
Bruce dynasty, see Robert I; David II

Bruide of the Picts, 19, 28

Brunanburh, Battle of (937), 43–4, 45

Buchan, Alexander Stewart, Earl of, *see* Stewart, Alexander, Earl of Buchan

Buchan, John, 273

Burns, Robert, 238–9

'Butcher Cumberland', *see* Cumberland, Prince William, Duke of

Bute, John Stuart, 3rd Earl of, *see* Stuart, John, 3rd Earl of Bute

Caledonii, 13, 14, 16

Calvinism, 134, 137, 145, 146–7, 163, 169–70, 190–1, 290

Cameron, David, 311, 312, 314

Cameron, Donald, 206

Cameron, Richard, 182

Campbell, Archibald, 3rd Duke of Argyll, 209, 213

Campbell, Archibald, 1st Marquess and 8th Earl of Argyll, 165, 166, 167, 170, 171

Campbell, Archibald, 9th Earl of Argyll, 185

Campbell, John, 2nd Duke of Argyll, 204, 213, 236

Campbell of Glenure, Colin, 209

Canute, *see* Cnut

capitulation of Irvine, 84–5

Carberry Hill, Battle of (1567), 139

Carnegie, Andrew, 257

Carrick, John Stewart, Earl of, *see* Robert III

Carrick, Robert de Brus, Earl of, 78

Casket Letters, 139, 140

Catholicism, 61, 128, 132, 136–41, 185–90

Cellach, 45–6

Charles I (1625–49) (King of England, Scotland and Ireland), 155–7, 162–71, 172, 187

Charles II (1660–85) (King of England, Scotland and Ireland), 171–4, 178, 181–4

Chartism, 247–8

Christianity, 21, 32, 42, 45, 53–4, 56

Church, the, 42, 45, 53–4, 57, 60–2, 69, 134, 136, 146, 154–7, 181, 238, 261

Churchill, Sir Winston, 288

Civil War, 167–71

Claim of Right, 188

Claverhouse, John Graham of, 1st Viscount Dundee, *see* Graham, John, of Claverhouse, 1st Viscount Dundee

clans, 34

Cleland, William, 183, 184

climate, 6–7, 10, 30, 104

Clydeside, 273, 277, 279, 298

Cnut (1016–35), 34

coal mining, 5, 232, 250, 252, 278, 296–7

coalition government, 308, 309, 311

Committee of Estates, 167, 168

Comyn, John (Black Comyn), 80

Comyn, John (Red Comyn), 87, 92–4, 95

Confession of Faith, 137, 146

Constantín I (AD 862–77), 34, 41

Constantín II (AD 900–43), 41–4, 53, 57

conurbation, 254, *see also* urbanization

conventicles, 179, 180–1, 183, 185

Cope, General Sir John, 207

Corbridge, Battle of (918), 42, 45

Covenanters, 165–71, 179–83, 185–6, 191, 237–8, 261

crofting, 227–8, 257–9

Cromdale, Battle of (1690), 189

Cromwell, Oliver, 167, 169–74, 180

Culdees, 42, 44, 45, 54

Culloden Moor, Battle of (1746), 208, 209
Cumberland, Prince William, Duke of, 208–9
Cunningham, William, 9th Earl of Glencairn, 173, 178

Dálriata, Kingdom of, 27, 28–9, 33, 45
Dalrigh, Battle of (1306), 96
Dalyell of the Binns, General Sir Thomas, 180, 183
Dalyell, Tam (Sir Thomas Dalyell of the Binns), 301, 309
Darien scheme, 193, 200, 201, 230
Darling, Alistair, 307, 312
Darnley, Lord Henry Stewart, see Stewart, Henry, Lord Darnley
David I (1124–53), 58–62
David II (1329–71), 103–8
Declaration of Arbroath, see Arbroath, Declaration of
Degsastan, Battle of (603), 27
demography, 104, 225, 226, 233–5, 254–6, 276, 279
devolution, 268, 296–301, 306, 307–15
'devo-max', 312
Dewar, Donald, 307–8, 309
Disarming Act (1716), 205
'Disruption', the, 260–1
Domnall Brec, 27
Donald II (889–900), 41
Donald III (1093–7), 55–6
Douglas, Archibald, 104
Douglas, Archibald, 5th Earl of Douglas, 118
Douglas, George, 1st Earl of Angus (Red Douglas), 85
Douglas, James, 2nd Duke of Queensberry, 200
Douglas, James, 1st Earl of Avondale and 7th Earl of Douglas, 118–19

Douglas, William, 4th Duke of Queensberry, 186
Douglas, William, 1st Earl of Douglas, 112
Douglas, William, 2nd Earl of Avondale and 8th Earl of Douglas, 119
Drumclog, Battle of (1679), 181
Drummond, James, 4th Earl of Perth, 186
Drummond, William, 152, 157
Dunbar, Battle of (1650), 171
Duncan I (1034–40), 46–7
Duncan II (1094), 55–6
Dundas, Henry, 213–14, 215, 217
Dundee, 5, 85, 86, 172, 228, 252, 255, 278–9, 288, 291, 295
Dundee, 1st Viscount, see Graham, John, of Claverhouse, 1st Viscount Dundee
Dunkeld, Battle of (1689), 189
Dunkeld dynasty, see Duncan I; Mac Bethad; Lulach; Malcolm III; Donald III; Duncan II; Edgar; Alexander I; David I; Malcolm IV; William I (The Lion); Alexander II; Alexander III
Dunnottar, Battle of (900), 41
Dunnottar Castle, 172
Dupplin cross, 17
Dupplin Moor, Battle of (1332), 103–4, 105
Durham, Treaty of (1136), 59

Edgar (1097–1107), 54, 55, 56
Edinburgh, 5, 18, 20, 71, 98, 123, 124, 133, 135, 139, 164, 166, 171, 172, 178–9, 182–4, 188, 201, 216, 242, 254, 260, 301, 302, 306, 307
Edinburgh Castle, 54, 56, 60, 69, 108, 119, 121, 128, 140, 144, 172, 217
Edinburgh University, 147, 215, 238, 267

Edinburgh, Treaty of (1560), 135,
138
Edinburgh–Northampton, Treaty of
(1328), 102–3
Edith, 53
education, 123, 137, 142–3,
147, 193, 264, 290, see also
universities
Edward I (1272–1307) (King of
England), 79, 80–8, 92–7
Edward II (1307–27) (King of
England), 93, 97–100, 102
Edward III (1327–77) (King of
England), 102–3, 105–6
Edward VI (1547–53) (King of
England), 132, 133
Elgin, sacking of, 113
Elizabeth I (1558–1603) (Queen of
England), 134, 137–8, 140, 141,
147–8
enfranchisement, 246–9, 259, 277
engineering, 5, 231, 251, 253, 254,
257, 272, 278, 288
Enlightenment, see Scottish
Enlightenment
Episcopalianism, 146, 154, 163,
165, 173, 178–81, 188–9,
190–1, 203, 210, 214, 238, 262
Erskine, John, 6th Earl of Mar,
203–4
Erskine, John, 17th Earl of Mar,
144
Ewing, Winnie, 298–9, 308

Falaise, Treaty of (1174), 69
Falkirk, Battle of (1298), 87
Falkirk, 2nd Battle of (1746), 208
famine, 7, 100, 192–3, 225, 227,
233, 257–8
farming, see agriculture
Faughart, Battle of (1318), 101
feudalism, 52, 55, 58, 60, 61, 80, 82,
102, 122, 126, 209, 213

'Fifteen', the, 203–4
First World War (1914–18), 273,
276–7
fishing industry, 228, 252
Five Articles of Perth, 155
Fletcher, Andrew, 200
Flodden Field, Battle of (1513), 125
football, 264–5
forestry, 226, 297
Fortriu, 17, 28, 47
'Forty-five', the, 206–8
Fraser Highlanders, 210
friendly societies, 256

Gabrán mac Domangairt, 28
Gaelic language, 22, 27, 28, 29, 34,
44, 45, 46, 54, 59, 112, 123,
154, 235, 242, 268, 294, see
also Gaelicization
Gaelicization, 42, 44, 52
Gallacher, Willie, 279
Gallipoli, Battle of (1915), 277
Geddes. Sir Patrick, 254
geology, 2–5, 240
Giric mac Dúngail, 41
Gladstone, William Ewart, MP, 247
Glasgow, 5, 60, 106, 123, 165, 209,
214, 226, 230, 234, 250–2,
254–5, 264–6, 273, 277–80,
297, 298, 312
Glasgow, University of, 123, 147,
215, 216, 231, 241, 266, 298
Glencairn, William Cunningham,
9th Earl of, see Cunningham,
William, 9th Earl of Glencairn
Glencoe massacre (1692), 192
Glorious Revolution, 186–90
Gododdin, The, 18, 20
Golden Act (1592), 147
golf, 136
Gorbals, 255, 257, 259
Graham, James, 1st Marquess of
Montrose, 164, 165, 167–9, 171

Graham, John, of Claverhouse,
    1st Viscount Dundee ('Bonnie
    Dundee'), 181–3, 189
Grassic Gibbon, Lewis, 282
Great Cause, 79–82
Great Depression, 278–9
Greenwich, Treaty of (1543), 132
Guardians, 78, 80, 81, 86, 87, 92, 93,
    94, 98, 103–4, 106, 118, 120, 126

Hadrian's Wall, 15, 42
haggis, 234
Haig, Sir Douglas, 277
Halidon Hill, Battle of (1333), 104
Hamilton, Sir Ian, 277
Hamilton, James, 2nd Earl of
    Arran, 132
Hardie, Andrew, 218
Hardie, James Keir, 259, 263
Hawley, General Henry, 208
Henry II (1154–89) (King of
    England), 67, 69
Henry III (1216–72) (King of
    England), 70, 71
Henry VIII (1509–47) (King of
    England), 128, 132
Hepburn, James, 4th Earl of
    Bothwell, 139–40
Heritable Jurisdictions Act (1747),
    209
Highland Clearances, 227–8
Highland Host, 181
Highland Land League, 258
Highland Land War, 258
Highlands, 2–4, 6, 112, 127, 153–4,
    205, 227, 228, 234, 258, 261
hoards, 11, 12, 15, 32
Home Rule Association, 268
House of Bruce, see Bruce dynasty
House of Dunkeld, see Dunkeld
    dynasty
House of Mac Alpin, see Mac Alpin
    dynasty

House of Stewart, see Stewart
    dynasty
House of Stuart, see Stuart dynasty
housing, 234, 255, 277, 302
Hume, David, 224, 239, 240
Hutton, James, 4, 5, 240

ILP, see Independent Labour Party
imperialism, 275, 293
Independent Labour Party (ILP),
    259, 273, 277, 279
industrial revolution, 229–33,
    249–53
industrial strike, see strike action
Iona, 21, 30, 35
Ireland, 21, 26–7, 34, 96, 100, 167,
    198, 203, 247, 250, 259, 294
Irish rebellion (1641), 167
Iron Age, 12–13
iron industry, 5, 232–3, 249–52, 253

Jacobitism, 189, 191–211
James Francis Edward Stuart,
    Prince of Wales, 142, 150, 155,
    161
James I (1406–37), 116–18, 123
James II (1427–60), 118–20, 123
James III (1460–88), 120–22, 127
James IV (1488–1513), 123–6
James V (1513–42), 126–8, 132
James VI (1567–1625) (as James
    I of England and Ireland
    1603–25), 141–8, 152–5, 198
James VII (1685–88) (James II of
    England and Ireland), 184–90,
    198
Jarlsof, 32–3
John of Fordun, 57, 61, 68, 70, 87

Kailyard, 265, 266, 295
Kenneth I (843–58), see Mac Alpin,
    Kenneth
Killiecrankie, Battle of (1689), 189

'Killing Time', 180–4, 192, 238
King James Bible, 143
kingship, 40–1, 42, 48, 52–3, 79–80, 102, 116, 124
Knox, John, 134, 136, 137, 143–4, 146

language, 16, 18, 20, 22, 27, 44, 46, 112, 154, 237, 268, see also Gaelic
Largs, Battle of (1263), 71
Lauderdale, John Maitland, 2nd Earl of, see Maitland, John, 2nd Earl of Lauderdale
Lennox, Esmé Stewart, 1st Duke of, see Stewart, Esmé, 1st Duke of Lennox
Lennox, Matthew Stewart, 4th Earl of, see Stewart, Matthew, 4th Earl of Lennox
Lewis chessmen, 32
Lockhart, Sir George, 200
Lords of the Congregation, 134–6
Lordship of the Isles, 72, 124
Lowland Clearances, 226
Lowlands, 2, 4–6, 225, 229, 230, 236, 262
Lulach (1057–8), 48

Macadam, John Loudon, 229
Mac Alpin dynasty, see Mac Alpin, Kenneth; Constantín I; Giric mac Dúngail; Donald II; Constantín II; Malcolm I; Malcolm II.
Mac Alpin, Kenneth, 29, 34, 42
Macbeth, see Mac Bethad
Macbeth, 48
Mac Bethad, 46, 47–8, 52
Mac Gabráin, Áedán, 27
McArthur, Alexander, 280
MacColla, Alasdair, 167–8
MacDiarmid, Hugh, 281–2

MacDonald, Sir Hector, 276
MacDonald, Ramsay, 280
MacDuff, Isabella, 95–6, 311
Mackay, Hugh, 189
Maeshowe, 11
Mag Rath, Battle of (637), 27
Maitland, John, 2nd Earl and 1st Duke of Lauderdale, 180–1, 183
Malcolm I (943–54), 45–6
Malcolm II (1005–34), 46, 47
Malcolm III (1058–93) (Canmore), 48, 52–3
Malcolm IV (1153–65), 66–8, 69, 70
Mar, John Erskine, 6th Earl of, see Erskine, John, 6th Earl of Mar
Mar, John Erskine, 17th Earl of, see Erskine, John, 17th Earl of Mar
Margaret of Norway, 72, 78–9
Marston Moor, Battle of (1644), 168
Mary of Guise, 128, 132, 133, 134, 135
Mary I, Queen of Scots (1542–67), 128, 132–41, 143, 144, 145, 146
Mary II (1689–94) (Queen of England, Scotland and Ireland), 187–90, 198
Maxwell, James Clerk, 267
Mealmaker, George, 217
Mearns, 55, 57
Melville, Andrew, 147
mercenaries, 165–6
Mesolithic Age, 10
metal industry, 11–12, 249–51
Middleton, John, 1st Earl of Middleton, 173, 178, 180
Midlothian Campaign, 247
Migdale Hoard, 11
migration, 3, 26–7, 30, 71, 193, 226–7, 235–6, 254, 256–7, 274, 279, 281, 288
Moderates, the, 238–9
monasticism, 54, 55–6, 60, 61, 66, 71

Monmouth, James Scott, 1st Duke of, *see* Scott, James, 1st Duke of Monmouth

Monmouth rebellion, 185–6

Mons Graupius, Battle of (AD 83 or 84), 13, 14

Montrose, James Graham, 1st Marquess of, *see* Graham, James, 1st Marquess of Montrose

Moray, Andrew, 83–6

Moray, James Stewart, 1st Earl of *see* Stewart, James, 1st Earl of Moray, Regent of Scotland

Moray, Sir Andrew, 104, 106

mormaers, 57, 58, 70

mortality rates, 233–4, 255, 280

Muir, Thomas, 216–17

Mure, Elizabeth, 117

Murray, Lord George, 206, 207, 208

Napier Commission, 258

Napoleonic Wars, 218

National Association for the Vindication of Scottish Rights, 267

National Health Service, 289–90, 293

Nationalism, 194, 300, 307, 312, 314

Nationalization, 291–2, 296, 313

Nechtansmere, Battle of (685), 19, 28

neeps and tatties, 234

Neolithic Age, 10–11

New Model Army, 169–71

New Poor Law, 256

Normans, the, 52–62, 67, 70, 71, 82

Norrie's Law, 17

North Inch, Battle of (1396), 115

North Sea Oil, 299, 304

Norway, 4, 30, 31, 32, 33, 71, 72, 79, 169, 229, *see also* Vikings

Óengus (732–61), King of Fortriu, 28

oil, 5, 6, 299, 394

Old Pretender, *see* Stuart, James Francis Edward (Prince of Wales)

'Oor Wullie', 295

Orkney, 11, 13, 30–1, 32, 33, 46, 47, 48, 60, 79, 120, 171, 276, 314

Otterburn, Battle of (1388), 113–14

overlordship, 13, 43, 69, 80, 87, 94

Owen, King of Alt Clut, 43

patronage, 191, 260

Patronage Act (1711), 214, 238

Perpetual Peace, Treaty of (1502), 124

Perth, 68, 82, 98, 115, 118, 134, 135, 172, 204, 206–7, 216, 229, 262

Perth, James Drummond, 4th Earl of, *see* Drummond, James, 4th Earl of Perth

Perth, Treaty of (1266), 71–2

Philip IV (1285–1314), King of France, 81, 88, 93

Philip VI (1328–50), King of France, 106

Picts, 16–17, 19, 21, 22, 26, 28–9, 32, 33, 34–5, 42, 44, 45, 46

Pike plot, 217

Pinkerton, Allan, 257

Pinkie Cleugh, Battle of (1547), 133

Pitgaveny, Battle of (1040), 47

Poll Tax, 305

Poor Law (Scotland) Act (1845), 256

Presbyterianism, 146–7, 154–5, 156, 163, 164–5, 167, 169–71, 179, 181–4, 186, 188–93, 200, 214, 234–5, 238, 248–9, 260–4, 296, 307

Prestonpans, Battle of (1745), 207

privatization, 303–4

Protestantism, 127, 135–8, 155, 167, 173, 185, 190, 294

public health, 280, 289–90, 305
Queensberry, James Douglas, 2nd
    Duke of, see Douglas, James,
    2nd Duke of Queensberry
Queensberry, William Douglas, 1st
    Duke of, see Douglas, William,
    4th Duke of Queensberry
Quitclaim of Canterbury (1189), 69

radicalism, 215–19
Radical War (1820), 218, 235
Raeburn, Sir Henry, 242
rail industry, 250–1, 291
Ramsay, Allan (elder), 237
Ramsay, Allan (younger), 242
recession, 304–5, 311
Red Clydeside, 279
Red Douglas see Douglas, George,
    1st Earl of Angus
Reform Acts, 246–7, 248
Reformation, 126, 127, 128, 132–8,
    142, 145
Reid, Jimmy, 298
Reivers, 127
Relief Church, 238, 247–8, 261
Restoration, 174, 178–9
retail industry, 229–30
Rizzio, David, 138–9, 144
Robert I (1306–29), 85, 87, 92,
    95–102
Robert II (1371–90), 108, 112–14, 117
Robert III (1390–1406), 114–15, 117
Robert the Bruce, see Robert I
Romans, 13–16, 18, 20, 26, 27
Ross, Euphemia, 118
Rothesay, David Stewart, 1st Duke
    of, see Stewart, David, 1st
    Duke of Rothesay
'Rough Wooing', 132
royal regalia, 172
Rullion Green, Battle of (1666), 180
runrig system, 225
Ruthven Raid, 145

Sabbatarianism, 263, 296
Saint Columba, 21, 45
Saint Margaret, 52–5
Saint Ninian, 21, 22, 45
Salmond, Alex, 300, 308, 309, 311–15
Sanquhar Declaration (1680), 182
Sauchieburn, Battle of (1488), 122,
    123
Scone, 29, 56, 58, 66, 80, 83, 84, 95,
    104, 114, 116, 171, 172
Scotch, see whisky
Scotland Act (1998), 307
Scott, James, 1st Duke of
    Monmouth, 182, 185
Scott, Sir Walter, 172, 214, 224,
    237, 241–2
Scottish Association of the Friends
    of the People, 216
Scottish Enlightenment, 237–42,
    260, 266
Scottish Executive, 308, 309
Scottish National Party (SNP),
    282–3, 298–301, 306, 308–10,
    311–12
Scottish Prohibition Party, 263, 288
Scottish Referendum, 312–15
Scottish Renaissance, 281–2
Scrymgeour, Edwin, 288
Secession Church, 238, 247–8
Second World War (1939–45), 288–9
Selgovae, 13, 16, 20
Septimus Severus, 15, 16
Sermon on the Mound, 302
Seton, Sir William, 200
'seven ill years', 192–3
Seven Men of Moidart, 206
Sharp, James, 179, 181
Shetland, 12, 29–31, 32, 33, 120,
    314
shipbuilding, 251–2, 272, 276, 278,
    288, 292, 298, 304
Sigurdsson, Thorfinn, 46, 47
Sillars. Jim, 300, 313

Skaill, 32
Skara Brae, 11
Smith, Adam, 241
SNP, *see* Scottish National Party
social services, 290
socialism, 259, 273, 279, 291
Solemn League and Covenant
	(1643), 167
Somerled, 33, 67
Sophia of Hanover, 198, 199, 203
steam power, 231, 232, 251, 252
Stephen (1135–54), 59
Stevenson, Robert Louis, 267
Stewart, Alexander, Earl of Buchan,
	113–14
Stewart, Allan, 209
Stewart, David, 1st Duke of
	Rothesay, 114–15
Stewart, Esmé, 1st Duke of Lennox,
	144, 145
Stewart, Henry, Lord Darnley,
	138–40, 144
Stewart, James, 209
Stewart, James, 1st Earl of Moray,
	Regent of Scotland, 136, 138,
	140, 143
Stewart, John, Earl of Carrick, *see*
	Robert III
Stewart, Matthew, 4th Earl of
	Lennox, 144
Stewart, Murdoch, 2nd Duke of
	Albany, 116–17
Stewart, Robert, 1st Duke of
	Albany, 114–15, 116–17
Stewart, Walter, Earl of Atholl, 118
Stewart dynasty, 112–13, 117–18,
	121, *see also* Stuart dynasty
Stirling, 81, 82, 117, 124, 135, 143,
	144, 172, 291
Stirling Bridge, Battle of (1297),
	86, 87
Stirling Castle, 5, 69, 98, 100,
	118–19

Stone Age, *see* Mesolithic Age;
	Neolithic Age
Stone of Destiny, 83
Stone of Scone, *see* Stone of Destiny
Stracathro, Battle of (1130), 59
Standard, Battle of the (1138), 59
Strathclyde, 19, 46, 47, 53, 58, *see
	also* Alt Clut, Kingdom of
Strathclyde, Owen of, *see* Owen,
	King of Alt Clut
strike action, 218, 272, 277, 298,
	303
Stuart, Charles Edward ('Bonnie
	Prince Charlie', the Young
	Pretender), 132, 202–3, 206,
	211, *see also* Jacobitism
Stuart, James Francis Edward (the
	Old Pretender), 198, 203–4,
	205–6, 211, *see also* Jacobitism
Stuart, John, 3rd Earl of Bute,
	211–12
Stuart dynasty, 171, 174, 184,
	202–3, 21, *see also* Stewart
	dynasty
Sunday Post, The, 295

Tables, the, 164–5
tartan, 209, 274
Telford, Thomas, 229
Ten Years' War, 260
textile industry, 227, 230–2, 297
Thatcher, Margaret, 294, 301–6
Thomas of Ercildoune, 72–3
Tippermuir, Battle of (1644), 168
Toleration Act (1712), 214
Toom Tabard, 81, *see also* Balliol,
	John
tower houses, 122
trade, 199, 201, 228–30
trade unions, 256, 259, 263, 273,
	277, 291, 293, 298
Traprain Law, 12
Treatise of Human Nature, A, 240

Treaties:
  Berwick (1357), 107
  Birgham (1290), 79, 81
  Durham (1136), 59
  Edinburgh (1560), 135, 138
  Edinburgh–Northampton (1328), 102–3
  Falaise (1174), 69
  Greenwich (1543), 132
  Perpetual Peace (1502), 124
  Perth (1266), 71–2
  Union (1707), 199–202, 209, 214
  York (1237), 70

unemployment, 218, 256, 272, 278–9, 289–90
Ungus, see Óengus
union, constitutional, 199–203
Union, Treaty of (1707), 199–202, 209, 214
Union of the Crowns, 141, 151, 152, 155
United Scotsmen, the, 217
universities, 116, 123, 147, 209, 215–16, 238, 267, 290–1, 292–3, 309
urbanization, 5, 225, 233, 234, 248, 249, 254–5, 266, 267, 305

Vikings, 4, 7, 29–35, 41, 42, 43
Votadini 12, 13, 16, 18, 20

Wallace, Sir William, 84–8, 92, 94, 268
Warriston, Lord Archibald Johnston of, 164

Wars of Independence, 83–8, 92–108
water power, 231
Watson, James, 237
Watt, James, 231
Watt, Robert, 217
welfare state, 290, 291, 292–3
Wessex dynasty, 42
West Lothian question, 300–1, 307, 310, 315
whisky, 214, 304–5
Wilkes, John, 211–12
William I (1066–87) (the Conqueror), King of England, 53
William I (1165–1214) (The Lion), King of the Scots, 66, 68–9
William II (1087–1100) (Rufus), King of England, 55
William II (1689–1702), King of Scotland, and England & Ireland (as William III), 187–94, 198
Williamites, 189, 191, 192, 200, 206
William of Orange, see William II (1689–1702)
Wilson, James, 218
Wolfe, General James, 210
workhouses, 256
World War One, see First World War
World War Two, see Second World War

York, Treaty of (1237), 70
Young Pretender, see Stuart, Charles Edward